# Private Power, Public Law

Susan K. Sell's book shows how power in international politics is increasingly exercised by private interests rather than governments. In 1994 the WTO adopted the Agreement on Trade-Related Aspects of Intellectual Property Rights (TRIPS), which dictated to states how they should regulate the protection of intellectual property. This book argues that TRIPS resulted from lobbying by twelve powerful CEOs of multinational corporations who wished to mould international law to protect their markets. This book examines the politics leading up to TRIPS, the first seven years of its implementation, and the political backlash against TRIPS in the face of the HIV/AIDS crisis. Focusing on global capitalism, ideas, and economic coercion, this work explains the politics behind TRIPS and the controversies created in its wake. It is a fascinating study of the influence of private interests in government decision-making, and in the shaping of the global economy.

SUSAN K. SELL is Associate Professor of Political Science and International Affairs at The George Washington University. She is the author of *Power and Ideas: North–South Politics of Intellectual Property and Antitrust* (1998).

CAMBRIDGE STUDIES IN INTERNATIONAL RELATIONS: 88

# Private Power, Public Law

CAMBRIDGE STUDIES IN INTERNATIONAL RELATIONS

*Series list continues after index*

# Private Power, Public Law
## The Globalization of Intellectual Property Rights

Susan K. Sell

*The George Washington University*

CAMBRIDGE
UNIVERSITY PRESS

PUBLISHED BY THE PRESS SYNDICATE OF THE UNIVERSITY OF CAMBRIDGE
The Pitt Building, Trumpington Street, Cambridge CB2 1RP, United Kingdom

CAMBRIDGE UNIVERSITY PRESS
The Edinburgh Building, Cambridge, CB2 2RU, UK
40 West 20th Street, New York, NY 10011-4211, USA
477 Williamstown Road, Port Melbourne, VIC 3207, Australia
Ruiz de Alarcón 13, 28014 Madrid, Spain
Dock House, The Waterfront, Cape Town 8001, South Africa

http://www.cambridge.org

First published 2003

*Typeface* Palatino 10/12.5 pt      *System* LATEX 2$_\varepsilon$   [TB]

*A catalogue record for this book is available from the British Library*

*Library of Congress cataloguing in publication data*

Sell, Susan K.
Private power, public law: the globalization of intellectual property
rights / Susan K. Sell.
    p.   cm. – (Cambridge studies in international relations; 88)
Includes bibiographical references and index.
ISBN 0 521 81914 8 – ISBN 0 521 52539 X (pbk.)
1. Intellectual property. 2. Foreign trade regulation. 3. Lobbying.
4. International business enterprises – Political activity. I. Title. II. Series.
K1401. S4553 2003
346.04'8 – dc21 2002035020

ISBN  0 521 81914 8 hardback
ISBN  0 521 52539 X paperback

Transferred to digital printing 2004

In loving memory of Donald Miller Sell, father, teacher, and wonderful friend

# Contents

# Figures and tables

## Figures

## Tables

# Acknowledgments

This book is the result of a long process. The thoughtful and constructive comments of a number of colleagues, students, and friends have been enormously helpful. I wish to thank the following people who read and commented upon various chapters at various stages of the project: Jonathan Aronson, Deborah Avant, Alasdair Bowie, Gregg Bucken-Knapp, R. Kurt Burch, A. Claire Cutler, Dalia Dassa Kaye, Peter Drahos, Graham Dutfield, Harvey Feigenbaum, Lee Ann Fujii, Jeffrey Hart, Virginia Haufler, Richard Higgott, David Johnson, Scott Kennedy, James Lebovic, David Levy, Renee Marlin-Bennett, Duncan Matthews, Chris May, Craig Murphy, Chuck Myers, Henry Nau, Tony Porter, Brian Portnoy, Aseem Prakash, Anitha Ramanna, Jerome Reichman, Wayne Sandholtz, Timothy Sinclair, Jay Smith, Roger Tooze, Jenab Tutunji, Geoffrey Underhill, Stacey Vandeveer, Andrew Walter, and Stephen Wilks. I thank Geoffrey Underhill for urging me to extend my work on intellectual property to the new issues in the WTO. Lee Ann Fujii's insightful comments on the final draft led to significant improvements in several chapters. Aseem Prakash has been wonderfully supportive throughout this process. Christopher May went above and beyond the call of duty, collegiality, and friendship, and provided constructive comments on every chapter. I have learned a lot from Chris by working together on a project exploring the history of intellectual property.

I would like to thank the University of Chicago's Program on International Politics, Economics, and Security for giving me the opportunity to present aspects of the argument, and particularly Joel Westra, who provided excellent constructive criticism. I thank the Washington International Theory Seminar for the helpful comments on presentations that I gave early on in the project. The International Studies Association provided support for a workshop on private authority, led by A. Claire

Cutler, Virginia Haufler, and Tony Porter. This workshop and the project that developed out of it brought together a number of scholars grappling with similar analytic issues, with fruitful results. I am very grateful to Peter Yu of the Benjamin N. Cardozo School of Law at Yeshiva University, Thomas Cotter of the University of Florida Law School, and Heinz Klug and Geoffrey Shaffer of the University of Wisconsin at Madison Law School. They invited me to present my work at their law schools' conferences; these proved to be richly rewarding venues for my research and further stimulated my thinking about the politics of intellectual property.

Financial support for this research was provided by the George Washington University's University Facilitating Fund, and the George Washington University Center for the Study of Globalization. Debbie Botteri cheerfully assisted me with the diagrams.

Several people deserve special mention for their generosity in sharing materials and insights: Jonathan Band, Peter Choy, Graham Dutfield, Eric Smith, and Stephen Woolcock.

I could not have written this book without Jacques Gorlin, James Love, and Ellen 't Hoen, whose work has given me an important story to tell. But beyond that, I thank Jacques Gorlin and James Love for their incomparable generosity in sharing their stories, materials, insights, and perspectives.

Ernst Haas helped to keep my spirits up through the years in which no one in political science seemed to think that intellectual property was an appropriate topic. I am grateful for his mentoring and friendship over the years.

I thank John Haslam of Cambridge University Press for his good work in guiding this project from manuscript to publication, and two anonymous reviewers for Cambridge, for incisive and constructive comments. I am grateful for the intellectual journey that they inspired me to take. I am grateful to Sheila Kane for her excellent copyediting, and to Alison Powell for managing the production process.

Finally, thanks are due to my family for their unfailing love and support – my father, to whom this book is dedicated; my mother, Estelle Quinn Sell; and my sister Ellen Sell. Doug Abrahms, Nicholas Quinn Abrahms, and Timothy Michael Abrahms have kept me grounded by sharing their love and laughter throughout the process.

An earlier version of Chapter 4 was published as "The origins of a trade-based approach to intellectual property protection," *Science Communication* 17, 2: 163–185. © Reprinted by permission of Sage

Publications, Inc. Sage Periodicals Press, 1995. Parts of Chapter 5 were published as "Multinational corporations as agents of change: the globalization of intellectual property rights in Private Authority and International Affairs," A. Claire Cutler, Virginia Haufler, and Tony Porter (eds.), the State University of New York Press. © 1999 State University of New York. Reprinted by permission of the State University of New York Press. All Rights Reserved. An earlier version of parts of Chapters 2 and 5 was published as "Agents, structures, and institutions: private corporate power and the globalisation of intellectual property rights," in *Non-State Actors and Authority in the Global System*, Richard Higgott, Geoffrey Underhill and Andreas Bieler (eds.), reprinted by permission of Routledge, © 2000. An earlier version of pages 164–172 of Chapter 7 was published as "Big business and the new trade agreements: the future of the WTO?" in Richard Stubbs and Geoffrey Underhill, *Political Economy and the Changing Global Order* (Don Mills, Ont.: Oxford University Press, 2000). Reprinted by permission of Oxford University Press, Canada.

# Abbreviations

AAP        American Association of Publishers
ACTN       Advisory Committee for Trade Negotiations
ACTPN      Advisory Committee on Trade Policy and Negotiation
ASEAN      Association of Southeast Asian Nations
BAM        Business for Affordable Medicines
BDI        Bundesverband der Deutschen Industrie
BIOTHAI    Thai Network on Community Rights and Biodiversity
BSA        Business Software Alliance
CAFC       Court of Appeals for the Federal Circuit
CBD        Convention on Biological Diversity
CBERA      Caribbean Basin Economic Recovery Act
CBI        Caribbean Basin Initiative
CEO        chief executive officer
CMA        Chemical Manufacturers Association
CPT        Consumer Project on Technology
DSB        Dispute Settlement Body
DSM        Dispute Settlement Mechanism
DSU        Dispute Settlement Understanding
ECAT       Emergency Committee for American Trade
EC         European Community
EU         European Union
FDI        foreign direct investment
FLG        Financial Leaders Group
FTAA       Free Trade Area of the Americas
G7         Group of Seven
GATS       General Agreement on Trade in Services
GATT       General Agreement on Tariffs and Trade
GRAIN      Genetic Resources Action International

| | |
|---|---|
| GSP | Generalized System of Preferences |
| HAI | Health Action International |
| HHS | Health and Human Services |
| IIPA | International Intellectual Property Alliance |
| IP | intellectual property |
| IPC | Intellectual Property Committee |
| IPR | Intellectual Property Rights |
| ITC | International Trade Commission |
| LDC | less developed country |
| MAI | Multilateral Agreement on Investment |
| MFA | Multi-Fibre Arrangement |
| MFN | Most Favored Nation |
| MNC | multinational corporation |
| MNE | multinational enterprise |
| MPAA | Motion Picture Association of America |
| MSF | Médecins Sans Frontières |
| NAFTA | North American Free Trade Agreement |
| NGO | non-governmental organization |
| NICs | Newly Industrializing Countries |
| OECD | Organization for Economic Cooperation and Development |
| PCT | Patent Cooperation Treaty |
| PhRMA | Pharmaceutical Research and Manufacturers of America |
| PMA | Pharmaceutical Manufacturers of America |
| PTO | US Patent and Trademark Office |
| RAFI | Rural Advancement Foundation International |
| TNC | Trade Negotiations Committee |
| TRIMS | Agreement on Trade-Related Investment Measures |
| TRIPS | Agreement on Trade-Related Aspects of Intellectual Property Rights |
| UNAIDS | Joint United Nations Program on HIV/AIDS |
| UNDP | United Nations Development Program |
| UNICE | Union of Industrial and Employers' Confederations of Europe |
| UPOV | Union for the Protection of New Varieties of Plants |
| URAA | Uruguay Round Agreements Act |
| USTR | United States Trade Representative |
| WHO | World Health Organization |
| WIPO | World Intellectual Property Organization |
| WTO | World Trade Organization |

# 1 Introduction

In 1990 an American-based private business association used its power not only to reject, but to actively shape, the legislation of a foreign, sovereign government. Up until 1991 Chile, like many developing countries, refused to grant patent protection for pharmaceutical products. This refusal was an effort to keep the prices of necessary medicines affordable by placing public health considerations above property rights concerns. In the late 1980s Chile faced increasing pressure from the US-based Pharmaceutical Manufacturers of America (PMA) to revise its laws to extend patent protection to pharmaceutical products. The PMA sought a law providing for monopoly pricing protection for twenty-five years, potentially placing necessary medicines out of reach for the average Chilean. In 1990 the Chilean government proposed a revised patent law, which the PMA rejected as inadequate. In response, the Chileans went back to the drawing board. Chile finally came up with a law providing patent protection for pharmaceutical products for a fifteen-year period. The PMA declared that it was satisfied. The PMA's role in this matter was intriguing. Where did this power come from? How had this situation come to pass?

The Chilean incident foreshadowed a related and even more dramatic event – the adoption of the 1994 Agreement on Trade-Related Aspects of Intellectual Property Rights (TRIPS) administered by the World Trade Organization (WTO). TRIPS ushered in a full-blown, enforceable global intellectual property (IP) regime that reaches deep into the domestic regulatory environment of states. The central player in this drama was an even smaller group, the *ad hoc* US-based twelve member Intellectual Property Committee (IPC).

Consisting of twelve chief executive officers (representing pharmaceutical, entertainment, and software industries), the Intellectual

Property Committee[1] successfully developed international support for strengthening the global protection of intellectual property (patents, copyrights, trademarks, and trade secrets). The IPC, joined by its counterparts in Europe and Japan, crafted a proposal based on industrialized countries' existing laws and presented it to the General Agreement on Tariffs and Trade (GATT) Secretariat in 1988 (The Intellectual Property Committee, Keidanren, and UNICE, 1988). By 1994, only a few years later, the IPC achieved its goal in the Agreement on Trade-Related Aspects of Intellectual Property Rights of the Uruguay Round. In doing so, the IPC offered important lessons about the increasing role of private power in international politics. Industry revealed its power to identify and define a trade problem, devise a solution, and reduce it to a concrete proposal that could be sold to governments. These private sector actors succeeded in getting most of what they wanted from a global IP agreement, which now has the status of public international law. How and why did a group of private sector actors succeed in establishing a high-protectionist global IP agreement? And why did these actors fail to achieve the same results in parallel issue areas? How, in other words, do agents and structures interact to produce particular outcomes, what explains variation, and what explains change over time?

## Analytic perspectives

This project has been through many changes over the years. In presenting pieces of it over time in various venues I realized I needed to write a book about it, because the pieces alone were misleading. In this section I discuss some different perspectives that offer insights into the globalization of IP rights. I cannot treat each of the alternative perspectives fully (each would need a chapter-length treatment). The following portrayals are meant only to provide the context for my synthetic approach and highlight why I have developed the perspective I employ in the rest of the book.

On one level, TRIPS is a "can do" story about twelve men (the members of the IPC) who made IP rules that now bind most of the globe. However, the "can do" story with which I began, of twelve incredibly efficacious individuals, was compelling only in the absence of historical context. It begged the larger question of how these particular individuals

---

[1] In 1986 the members of the IPC were: Bristol-Myers; CBS; Du Pont; General Electric; General Motors; Hewlett-Packard; IBM; Johnson & Johnson; Merck; Monsanto; and Pfizer.

became so powerful at this particular point in time. Were there larger forces at play that propelled them toward the forefront of global business regulation? Yes, certainly. Changes in global capitalism and technology facilitated their triumph. Intellectual property had become a highly valued resource and the comparative advantage of technological leaders. On another level, it is a structural story about the inexorable march of globalization and the power of the transnational capitalist class. The story became a kind of ideological and analytic Rorschach test. Free marketeers loved this tale of the triumph of business interests and the "constructive" collaboration between business and government. Gramscians and Marxists also responded positively in so far as it confirmed their world views.

Structural conditions loomed large in establishing the conditions for the IPC's success. To what extent did structural change determine the outcome? Was the IPC's triumph inevitable, or was it historically conditioned? Did everything that preceded its success point to this outcome? No, historical context did not point in only one direction. While structural factors overshadowed the efforts of these individuals, it did not determine them. Entrepreneurship and agency still counted for something in this tale. This was even more clearly the case when contrasted with parallel efforts in other issue areas such as investment and services.

A macro-level structural account of the making of global IP rules could focus on the inexorable march of globalization – either materially or culturally defined (Wallerstein, 1974; Thomas, Meyer, Ramirez, and Boli, 1987). Like a tidal wave, global capitalism/Western culture was reaching into every global nook and cranny eradicating difference, making the world ever safer for global capital/Western culture. In the material account, the process was eliminating obstacles to international commerce under the economic might and ideological orthodoxy of the transnational capitalist class. Global IP rules were just the latest triumph, neither the first nor the last. One hardly needs agency to account for the fact that the economically most powerful transnational actors acted in concert with the economically and politically most powerful states to devise global rules to benefit them all (and at the expense of most others). But this perspective cannot account for variation in outcomes, or the uneven triumph of the transnational capitalist class.[2] Its triumph has in fact, been patchy and uneven (as examined in greater detail in

[2] Neo-Gramscian scholarship has grappled with this problem by providing more nuanced discussions of factions of capital. Bieler distinguishes between "short-term thinking" finance capital versus "long-term thinking" manufacturing interests, and the privileged

Chapter 7) – undeniable in intellectual property and financial services, but questionable in, for example, foreign direct investment. Located in the same changing structure of global capitalism, including many of the same players, and engaged in the very same set of trade negotiations (the Uruguay Round), US-based private sector activists were supremely successful in both intellectual property and financial services. But the General Agreement on Trade in Services (GATS), and the Agreement on Trade-Related Investment Measures (TRIMS) proved to be disappointing for the private sector activists. For example, the fact that the global pharmaceutical firm, Pfizer Inc., was a key player in spearheading both the TRIPS and the TRIMS efforts demonstrates that power and resources alone do not determine outcomes.

One needs an account about agency to capture the politics behind these divergent outcomes. In the successful cases, private sector activists organized themselves into streamlined *ad hoc* lobbying groups – the IPC and the Financial Leaders Group (FLG) – bypassing their traditional industry associations. This organizational form may have contributed to their success. Focusing on agency permits one to analyze the efforts and strategies of those who sought new rules and how, in particular, they were able to exploit the context-dependent preoccupations of their governments. The activities of agents help to explain the timing and the particulars of the desired agreement. I argue that the entrepreneurial way in which agents linked intellectual property and trade fundamentally shaped the substance of the ultimate global property rules. What if the twelve individuals had never mobilized to press for stronger global rules? What kind of IP rights regime would we see today?

While structural explanations alone are found wanting, so too are agent-centric explanations. For example, a micro-level agent-centric account of the making of global IP rules could be rooted in rational choice and liberal pluralism. Such an account takes us a good distance in explaining how these twelve individuals overcame their collective action problems in order to present a united front and collaborate in their quest for global rules that would benefit them. Functional versions of this could emphasize the actors' desire to reduce transactions costs by switching from cumbersome *ad hoc* bilateral negotiations to binding

role of state institutions linked to global markets versus institutions focused on "national" problems (2000: 26, 13). Levy and Egan have highlighted the difference between regulatory and market-enabling institutions and subsequent variability of transnational capital's authority (2000). The initial turn toward Gramsci was in part inspired by scholars' frustration with the limits of Wallerstein's analysis (Murphy, 1998).

global rules. Understanding the micro foundations of state behavior and the domestic sources of state interests is a worthy enterprise. However, ahistorical "strict" rational choice perspectives neglect the broader context and structures within which interaction takes place. This can lead analysts to overemphasize the efficacy of the agents and the voluntarism possible in the situation. Recent advances in liberal theorizing have endeavored to incorporate more contextual variables to correct for some of these shortcomings (Moravcsik, 1997). Unit-level constructivist analyses have explicitly incorporated non-material factors and have situated advocacy in a wider and more contingent context (Klotz, 1995; Litfin, 1999; Price, 1998). Nonetheless, while more sensitive to context, these perspectives tend to underplay power considerations. Preferences and norms are crucial, but are not the whole story.

"Bottom-up" analyses need to be situated in time and space, and to be understood as embedded in deeper structures that determine who gets to play the "game" in the first place. Structure exerts a significant causal force that is ignored or remains outside the purview of these theories. Structure helps to identify the significant agents in any particular context and also shapes preferences. Structural factors also alert us to whose preferences are likely to matter, not just in the domestic context, but in the international arena as well. Focusing on asymmetrical power capabilities of states helps to explain effects abroad as well as negotiated outcomes. Institutional change in the American state had larger effects than similar changes in other states; US institutions became vehicles for economic coercion and the exercise of preponderant power to force changes abroad. Neither the economic power of private actors nor their activities would have made much difference had they been based in Burma. Analyzing either the micro level or macro level alone renders an incomplete picture.

Looking to history, it is important to appreciate that things have not always been as they are today. IP rights used to be considered "grants of privilege" that were explicitly recognized as exceptions to the rules against monopolies (Sell and May, 2001). To consider these to be privileges underscores their temporary and unstable nature. The sovereign may grant privileges but is in no way obligated to do so. Shifting to the term "rights" suggests that it is the sovereign's duty to uphold them. The difference is not merely semantic. The way that issues are framed can make a great deal of difference in terms of what is and is not considered legitimate. For much of the twentieth century patents were perceived as "monopolies" in American jurisprudence. Anti-trust (anti-monopoly) legislation checked the power of patent holders in important ways. The framing of intellectual property as being "pro-free trade" would not have been persuasive during earlier eras in which IP protection was seen, at best, as a necessary evil and at odds with free trade (Machlup and Penrose, 1950). It is only recently that the courts have ceased referring to patents as monopolies, and that anti-trust legislation has been relaxed. Tracking these variable conceptions and corresponding institutional manifestations allows us to examine the relationships between normative and institutional change. When and why did intellectual property catapult to the top tier of the United States' trade agenda? Had the two issues always been linked? Had IP protection always been so revered? How has the United States treated domestic intellectual property rights? Why did "it" decide to globalize its own perspective?

These sets of considerations led me into the tense and central spaces between agents and structures, the micro level and the macro level. Both micro-level (agents) and macro-level (structures) explanations are persuasive. Both capture important aspects of the story. Yet neither ultimately is compelling because each misses something quite important. In this case, institutions are the critical link between the micro level and the macro level. By institutions I mean legal norms, the legislative, executive, and judicial branches of the US government, and international organizations (e.g., the WTO). All these institutions are dynamic. They both act and are acted upon. They both constitute and are constituted by agents. They constitute and are constituted by structures. This dynamic process of mutual constitution is driving global business regulation in intellectual property rights.

It is necessary to examine the links and mechanisms connecting agents and structures. In this respect I examine concrete institutions such as the US judiciary, the legislature, the executive branch (e.g., USTR), and the WTO as targets of human agency, "without at the same time severing these institutions from their wider social context" (Germain, 1997: 176). The way that structural changes acted upon institutions is an important component of the explanation. How were American state institutions changing in response to larger structural forces? American policymakers had not always defined IP protection as being in the national interest. What was different now and why? How, for example, did the American focus on economic competitiveness[3] manifest itself in judicial

[3] The "competition state" is derived from structural explanations of globalization. See, e.g., Philip Cerny, 1994.

interpretations of IP rights and competition? How, in turn, did changing judicial conceptions of property rights facilitate the actions of agents seeking to strengthen global IP protection? How did the institutions of the state come to be persuaded that such global rules were worth pursuing? What access did the state provide for these individuals to press their case? Did it provide equal access for alternative views?

In a nutshell, this book argues that the global regulation of IP rights is a product of structured agency. Agents are embedded in structures that make their actions possible. Institutions mediate between structures and agents in two directions. Structures alter institutions, and create new agents. In turn, agents alter institutions, and create new structures. Different combinations of elements can lead to vastly different outcomes.

The remainder of this chapter provides an overview of TRIPS. It then offers a historical perspective on TRIPS and highlights some of its controversial features. The chapter goes on to indicate how TRIPS is embedded in broader trends in the global political economy. Next, it presents a discussion of structures, agents, and institutions to introduce the analytic framework. Finally, it provides a road map for the rest of the book.

## An introduction to TRIPS

The Uruguay Round of the GATT negotiations ushered in a new era in multilateral trade policy by dramatically expanding the scope of disciplines covered, and strengthening the dispute resolution mechanisms. GATT's success in cutting tariffs and reducing border impediments over successive negotiating rounds has led negotiators to address inside-the-border, or structural, impediments and non-tariff measures that undermine free trade. These new issues, such as investment, trade in services, and the protection of IP rights, implicate domestic regulatory policy, fundamentally challenging states' policymaking discretion. The Uruguay Round was unusual in so far as this agenda of new issues was driven almost entirely by the private sector, particularly by activist elements of the US business community.

TRIPS is a dramatic expansion of the rights of IP owners and a significant instance of the exercise of private power. The approach embodied in the TRIPS Agreement, extending property rights and requiring high levels of protection, represents a significant victory for US private sector activists from knowledge-based industries. In the TRIPS case, private actors worked together, exercised their authority and achieved a result that effectively narrows the options open to sovereign states and firms, and extends the opportunities of those firms that succeeded in gaining multilateral support for a tough global IP instrument. State-centric accounts of the Uruguay Round are at best incomplete, and at worst misleading, as they obscure the driving forces behind the TRIPS Agreement. The TRIPS process was far more complex than a state-centric account would lead us to believe. In the TRIPS case, private actors pursued their interests through multiple channels and struck bargains with multiple actors: domestic interindustry counterparts, domestic governments, foreign governments, foreign private sector counterparts, domestic and foreign industry associations, and international organizations. They vigorously pursued their IP objectives at all possible levels and in multiple venues, successfully redefining intellectual property as a trade issue. However, it was not merely their relative economic power that led to their ultimate success, but their command of IP expertise, their ideas, their information, and their framing skills (translating complex issues into political discourse).

Not all ideas are equally privileged in political life; therefore how one defines "interests" is central to understanding which sets of ideas affect policy. Furthermore, it is important to identify *who* is defining them. By promoting their particular vision as a solution to pressing US trade problems, the IP activists captured the imagination of policymakers and persuaded them to adopt their private interests as US national interests. Additionally, their initiative in producing concrete negotiating proposals significantly strengthened their hand.

TRIPS is part of the multilateral trade agreements that were made binding on members in the Final Act of the Uruguay Round. Adhering to the TRIPS Agreement is obligatory for all states that wish to join the WTO, and is part of the common institutional framework established under the WTO. The Agreement covers all IP rights, patents, trademarks, copyrights, trade secrets, including relatively new rights such as semiconductor chip rights. It incorporates the Berne Convention for copyright norms, and adds additional copyright protection for computer software, databases, and sound recordings. TRIPS adopts a patent law minimum well above the previous standards of the 1883 Paris Convention, extending both subject matter covered and term of protection. Patent rights are extended to virtually all subject matter (with the exception of plants and animals other than micro-organisms), including pharmaceutical products, chemicals, pesticides, and plant varieties, and are to be granted for twenty years from the date the application is filed. Under TRIPS, semiconductor chips and the "mask works" (or the layout designs of integrated circuits) which are "fixed" in the chips are protected under a *sui generis* (special or more specific) system. States are required to provide adequate and effective enforcement mechanisms both internally and at the border. The Agreement makes the WTO's dispute settlement mechanism available to address conflicts arising under TRIPS, and significantly provides for the possibility of cross-sectoral retaliation for states that fail to abide by WTO's Dispute Settlement Body's (DSB) rulings. Infractions in intellectual property can lead to sanctions on goods. The WTO is empowered to monitor compliance to ensure that defendants carry out their obligations within a reasonable time period. If the defendants fail to comply, the WTO will authorize the complainant to impose retaliatory trade sanctions if requested to do so.[4]

This far-reaching agreement has important implications for innovation, research and development, economic development, the future location of industry, and the global division of labor. Indeed, the dramatic expansion of the scope of IP rights embodied in TRIPS reduces the options available to future industrializers by effectively blocking the route that earlier industrializers followed. It raises the price of information and technology by extending the monopoly privileges of rights-holders, and requires states to play a much greater role in defending them. The industrialized countries built much of their economic prowess by appropriating others' intellectual property; with TRIPS, this option is foreclosed for later industrializers. The agreement codifies the increasing commodification of what was once the public domain, "making it unavailable to future creators" (Aoki, 1996: 1336). States and firms whose comparative advantage lies in imitation stand to lose under the new regime.

Since the vast majority of developing countries consume rather than produce intellectual property, and import rather than export intellectual property, one may wonder why they signed on to TRIPS. As will be discussed in more detail in later chapters, they did not fully realize the impact of TRIPS at the time of the negotiations. They were subjected to pronounced economic coercion leading up to and during the negotiations. Furthermore, they assented to an IP agreement in exchange for the Organization of Economic Cooperation and Development (OECD) commitments to expand market access for developing countries' agricultural and textile exports.

[4] For a useful guide to the TRIPS provisions, see M. Blakeney (1996), *Trade-Related Aspects of Intellectual Property Rights: A Concise Guide to the TRIPS Agreement* (London: Sweet and Maxwell).

The long-term redistributive implications of TRIPS are not yet fully understood. The short-term impact of stronger intellectual property protection undoubtedly will be a significant transfer of resources from developing country consumers and firms to industrialized country firms (Rodrik, 1994: 449). While some analysts have concluded that the United States and its firms whose comparative advantage lies in innovation and intellectual property will receive "significant benefits from [the] TRIPS Agreement" (Doane, 1994: 494), others are not so sanguine (Reichman, 1993; Foray, 1995).

TRIPS increases the range of regulatory standards that states are obliged to implement; specifies in greater detail what those standards must be; requires states to implement those standards; mandates and institutionalizes greater substantive convergence of national IP systems; and ties the principle of national treatment to a higher set of standards for intellectual property (Drahos, 1997: 202–203). Overall, TRIPS has "added solidly to the property power around the world of corporations with high technology resources" (Arup, 1998: 376).

## TRIPS in historical perspective

The TRIPS Agreement introduces a new era in the evolution of IP rights by effectively globalizing IP protection. The history of IP protection can be divided into three broad phases: national, international, and global (Drahos, 1997). Until the end of the nineteenth century, IP protection covering patents and copyrights was strictly a national matter. States passed laws of their own design; the protection that these laws provided did not extend beyond national borders. The expansion of international commerce increasingly strained this national patchwork of IP protection, and, by the early 1800s, a number of European governments had negotiated a network of bilateral copyright agreements. In the early nineteenth century British authors and publishers complained of widespread "piracy" of British books abroad. Reprinting books was perfectly legal in many other countries; in fact, the reprinting of texts by popular British authors such as Charles Dickens was a thriving industry in America. The British book trade recognized that this practice was reducing potential profits and eliminating major export markets for legitimate British editions (Feather, 1994: 154). There was a growing demand for codification in an international treaty. States with copyright laws sought international regulation of the book trade to protect copyrighted works beyond their territorial borders.

Similarly, inventors who sought protection of their inventions within foreign countries raised concerns over patents. In the 1870s, the Austro-Hungarian empire sought to host in Vienna international exhibitions of inventions. Foreigners were reluctant to participate because they feared their ideas would be stolen. German and American inventors were particularly concerned, as they were widely recognized to be among the most innovative (Murphy, 1994: 93). Therefore, in 1873 the empire adopted a temporary law providing protection for foreigners in order to encourage foreign inventors' participation in the international exhibitions; this protection was to last through the duration of the exhibition. A number of European countries already had domestic patent systems, and met in Vienna in 1873 to discuss prospects for an international agreement to protect patents. They convened several follow-up Congresses in 1878 and 1880; the latter Congress adopted a draft convention which became the basis for the 1883 Paris Convention (WIPO, 1988: 49–50). As in the case of copyright, the overriding objective was to devise a system in which states would recognize and protect the rights of foreign artists and inventors within states' own domestic borders (Gana, 1995: 137).

States responded to the increasingly strained patchwork of national legislation by adopting two international IP conventions: the Paris Convention for the Protection of Industrial Property (covering patents, trademarks, and industrial designs) in 1883, and the Berne Convention of 1886 (for copyright). The underlying principles of these international agreements were non-discrimination, national treatment, and the right of priority. Non-discrimination provides that there should be no barriers to entry of the foreign author or inventor in a member state's national market. National treatment means that once an inventor or author has entered a member state's market that person should be treated no differently than nationals. The right of priority protects the rights holder from unauthorized use of the copyrighted or patented work. Under this system, states were free to pass legislation of their own design but were obligated to extend their legislative protection to foreigners of member states.

In the international era the territorial basis of IP rights was preserved, albeit extended beyond jurisdictional confines through the "contractual device of treaty-making" (Drahos, 1997: 202). Unlike the TRIPS Agreement, these Conventions neither created new substantive law nor imposed new laws on member states; rather, they reflected a consensus among member states that was legitimated by domestic laws already in place (Gana, 1995: 138).

This system permitted wide variation in the scope and duration of protection. For example, many countries denied patent protection for pharmaceutical products in order to contain the cost of necessary medicines. This was perfectly acceptable under the terms of the Paris Convention. Indeed, before TRIPS, practices that US stakeholders decried as "piracy" were often lawful economic activities under various national legal systems and existing international IP agreements. States had considerable autonomy to craft laws that reflected their levels of economic development and comparative advantages in either innovation or imitation. Thus, the "old system" recognized inherent variations in the development levels of different countries.

By contrast, the global approach ensconced in the TRIPS Agreement is a much less flexible regime for IP protection. It promotes universality in IP rights protection. Behavior that once was legal is now illegal. TRIPS requires states to adopt both civil and *criminal* penalties for IP rights infringement. The Paris Convention made no mention of what items must be protected or the duration of protection to be offered. The TRIPS Agreement specifies obligations regarding the scope, subject matter, and duration of IP protection. Under the new global regime, states are required to extend patentability to "virtually all fields of technology recognized in developed patent systems"; to extend patent protection for a uniform term of twenty years; and to secure "legal recognition of the patentee's exclusive right to import the relevant products" (Reichman, 1993: 182). These new regulations reach "deep into national territories in requiring respect for intellectual property from products destined for domestic markets such as pharmaceuticals, processes internal to production such as chemicals, and practices in local agriculture, medicine and education which were outside of market relations" (Arup, 1998: 374). With respect to copyrights, states are now obligated to comply with the standards embodied in the Berne Convention (as revised in 1971). Additional obligations include extending copyright protection to computer programs and compilations of data, and providing rental rights to holders of copyrighted computer programs (Reichman, 1993: 216). Furthermore, for the first time the multilateral IP regime incorporates enforcement mechanisms. In short, the global era is marked by a sharp reduction in the scope of state autonomy for determining appropriate levels of intellectual property protection at home (Aoki, 1996: 1343).

In light of the historical background of IP protection, TRIPS is striking on many levels. First, the US-based proposal to globalize a commitment to stronger IP protection was surprising, given the fact that domestic US enforcement of IP rights was relatively lax until about 1982 (Whipple, 1987). In a very short time period, the US changed its domestic approach to intellectual property, then sought to globalize this commitment by incorporating intellectual property into 1984 and 1988 amendments to its domestic trade laws. The United States employed a coercive trade-based strategy, threatening trade sanctions and the denial of trade benefits for countries whose IP regimes were deemed unacceptably weak. This redefinition of US interest requires an explanation. Second, TRIPS closely mirrors the expressed wishes of the twelve chief executive officers of US-based multinational corporations who spearheaded the effort. The stated rationale for this IP agreement – that it will promote economic development worldwide – has virtually no empirical support. Third, it is based on a controversial conception of intellectual property that privileges protection over diffusion (i.e., private rights over public goods). Indeed, both economists and legal scholars have argued that this conception could have deleterious effects on global welfare (Ordover, 1991; David, 1993; Deardorff, 1990; Frischtak, 1993; Maskus, 1991; Primo Braga, 1989; Litman, 1989; Boyle, 1992; Silverstein, 1994). Fourth, it largely advances a "one size fits all" approach to intellectual property, which many analysts have roundly condemned (Aoki, 1996; Dhar and Rao, 1995; Thurow, 1997; Oddi, 1987; Scotchmer, 1991; Trebilcock and Howse, 1995). The notion that one set of uniform standards is appropriate for all countries and all industries defies both economic analysis and historical experience (Reichman, 1993: 173–174; Alford, 1994). Fifth, in two departures from GATT precedent, the TRIPS Agreement applies to the rights of *private individuals* rather than to goods (Reiterer, OECD, 1994), and does not merely circumscribe the range of acceptable policies governments may practice, but "obliges governments to take positive action to protect intellectual property rights" (Hoekman and Kostecki, 1995: 156).

In so far as IP rights confer monopoly privileges, there is a natural tension between competition (or anti-trust) policy and IP rights. Intellectual property rights confer exclusive rights. As Cornish suggests, "exclusive rights to prevent other people from doing things are at least monopolistic in a legal sense, if not necessarily in an economic one" (Cornish, 1993: 47). Intellectual property rights *per se* do not constitute monopoly power and ultimately the market determines their value. However, IP rights raise the problem of monopoly power in so far as they constitute "a form of monopoly rent to the innovator" (Trebilcock and Howse, 1995: 249); rights-holders have the opportunity to raise prices and reduce output.

Furthermore, rights-holders have the power to withhold their inventions by refusing to license them. Watt, the British innovator and creator of the steam engine, was awarded a patent for his invention in 1769. In 1775, Parliament renewed his patent for an additional twenty-five years during which time Watt refused to license his invention. According to one observer, by doing so "he held back the development of the metalworking industry for over a generation. Had his monopoly expired in 1783, England would have had railways much sooner" (Renouard, 1987).[5]

The economic rationale for IP rights is that "unless invention or creation is compensated at its full social value there will be sub-optimal incentives to undertake it" (Trebilcock and Howse, 1995: 250). In the language of public goods, without compensation invention and creation will be underprovided and economic development will suffer. The so-called "free rider" problem lies at the heart of this perspective: individuals and firms will be unlikely to make costly investments in innovation or creation if imitators can reproduce these innovations or creations and "capture or appropriate at little or no cost a significant part of the economic returns of the investment in question" (Trebilcock and Howse, 1995: 250).

Much of the demand for first, international, and now global, IP protection arose from the complaints of inventors and creators over widespread free riding. Whether coming from British authors and book-sellers in the nineteenth century, or American software, entertainment, and pharmaceutical concerns in the late twentieth century, the problem lies in the appropriability of the intellectual property. Recent changes in technology have exacerbated this appropriability problem, in so far as new technologies have made it vastly cheaper and easier for imitators to replicate expensively developed products and processes. For example, computer software, compact discs, and pharmaceuticals that are costly to develop are simple and relatively inexpensive to copy.

Yet policy must strike a balance between the private interests of IP owners, who seek adequate returns on their investments in knowledge-based products and processes, and the public interest in having access to the inventions and their benefits (Oddi, 1987: 837). Boyle presents

---

[5] In contrast, Douglass North (1981: 162–166) argues that sustained innovation only began in earnest after the establishment of IP rights to raise the private return for innovation. He attributes the delay in the dissemination and fuller exploitation of Watt's invention to the inadequate development of companion technologies, rather than to the power of withholding property and the social inefficiencies generated by such withholding.

the dilemma as follows: "Intellectual property rights...produce monopolies as well as incentives; they produce incentives because they are monopolies. If we undervalue the public domain, we will tend to give too many intellectual property rights, thus delivering a powerful anticompetitive, oligopolistic chunk of state-backed market power into the hands of the established players" (Boyle, 1996: 179). The merits of granting exclusive rights to IP owners have to be balanced against the economic effects of higher product costs and the potential "exclusion from the market of competitors who may be able to imitate or adapt the invention in such a way that its social value is increased" (Trebilcock and Howse, 1995: 250). Put simply, IP rights reflect an inherent tension between creation and diffusion. This tension poses the question whether intellectual property should be treated as "a public goods problem for which the remedy is commodification, or a monopoly of information problem for which the remedy is unfettered competition" (Boyle, 1992: 1450).

The TRIPS Agreement stands out in the broader context of the Uruguay Round of trade negotiations. One of the primary aims of the Round was to extend and institutionalize the broader global economic trend toward deregulation and trade liberalization. However, IP protection stands apart in so far as it "has become the strongest suit of internationally driven reregulation" (Arup, 1998: 367). By requiring states to regulate to provide a high substantive level of protection,

> the Round was saying that intellectual property was pro-trade rather than a necessary evil which was to be tolerated because it promised its own benefits...Traders expressed their interest in obtaining *security* for their products and processes as much as freedom; they were not going to rely solely on economic advantages such as earlier innovation, superior quality, or cheaper prices.
>
> (Arup, 1998: 374, emphasis added)

As Cornish suggests, "in a competitive market imitation is mostly to be reckoned virtuous, not sinful" (Cornish, 1993: 63). Yet the TRIPS Agreement, with its emphasis on providing security for rights-holders, renders many forms of imitation "sinful" – branding once legitimate entrepreneurs as "knowledge criminals".[6]

Numerous analysts have suggested that this movement is quite at odds with a broad commitment to freeing global trade, and claim that it smacks of residual mercantilism (Reichman, 1993: 175; Porter, 1999).

---

[6] I thank Chris May for this term.

The TRIPS Agreement reflected the assumption that "gains from unlicensed uses of foreign technologies in developing countries represent *illicit* losses to entrepreneurs in developed countries" (Reichman, 1993: 175; emphasis added). This assumption reflects a mercantilist perspective in so far as it undercuts a system based on norms of free competition based on superior product performance, lower prices, or more efficient production processes and represents a trade-off in favor of security for holders of licensing rights. "Weak intellectual property laws ensure access to markets for second comers who provide cheaper and better products through imitation and incremental innovation" (Reichman, 1993: 175); thus strengthening such laws can have anti-competitive effects.

Furthermore, as Borrus points out, "it is not obvious whether an economy derives greater long-term benefits from stricter IPR [intellectual property rights] protection that rewards innovation or from protecting less and choosing to favor the more rapid exploitation and use of technology" (1993: 367). Moreover, even the United States, the most ardent advocate of TRIPS may pay a significant economic price for the agreement. According to Reichman:

> neither the developed countries as a group, nor the United States in particular, should expect to reap a painless bonanza from the TRIPS undertaking. Although some developed countries may benefit more than others, all will feel the social costs of strengthened protection for intellectual property rights pinching some sectors of their respective economies. (1993: 181)

Other analysts have suggested that the current state of IP regulation is woefully out of step with the economics of innovation (Scotchmer, 1991; Foray, 1995). Foray argues that in so far as "innovation is no longer driven by technological breakthroughs but by the routine exploitation of existing technologies" (Foray, 1995: 77, 112) property systems designed to protect and exclude (such as that embodied in TRIPS) have a chilling effect on innovation because they hinder vital diffusion of existing knowledge bases. To the extent that the nature of research and discovery is cumulative, and most innovators "stand on the shoulders of giants" (Scotchmer, 1991: 29), strong patent protection may result in socially inefficient monopoly pricing, and may provide deficient incentives for competitors to develop second-generation products (Scotchmer, 1991: 31, 34).

What is clear is that the balance struck in the TRIPS Agreement is one that redounds to the benefits of rights-holders at the possible expense of the public weal. A former general counsel for the Office of the United States Trade Representative turned executive vice president of the Pharmaceutical Research and Manufacturers of America crisply stated that "in fact, the TRIPS Agreement establishes and protects the rights of innovators; it does not include a bill of rights for users of innovation" (Bello, 1997: 365). May (2000) also sees TRIPS as benefiting those who control intellectual property. Under TRIPS, IP owners have secured stronger and more concentrated rights.

## A structural perspective: TRIPS in the global economy

The TRIPS case is embedded in a broader set of trends within the global political economy. This section discusses two important changes – the increasing mobility of capital and the ideological shift toward a radical free-market agenda. These two factors served to enhance the power of the particular actors and sectors that pushed for TRIPS. Economic and ideational changes also affected international organizations, such as the GATT and WIPO, in directions that favored advocates of TRIPS. In effect, these structural economic and ideational factors *created* new agents and delivered them to the forefront of global business regulation.

Since the early 1970s, the post-World War II commitment to an essentially Keynesian bargain combining social welfare policies and multilateralism has unraveled, and has been replaced by monetarist neoliberalism. Cox calls this "hyperliberalism," which, he argues, is "the ideology of globalisation in its most extreme form" endorsing an almost Darwinian conception of global economic competition (Cox, 1993: 272). Perhaps the most important and emblematic manifestation of this is the globalization of the financial structure, including the international monetary system and the system of credit allocation (Strange, 1988: 88; Germain, 1997). Credit creation and allocation are central to all other economic activities; credit makes production, investment, and trade possible.

Strange locates the origins of the globalization of the financial structure in policies of the American state and its conscious choices (Strange, 2000: 85). The postwar Bretton Woods monetary system included fixed exchange rates and capital controls. The US dollar was fixed to the value of gold, which helped provide stability for postwar economic recovery and international commerce. However, the dollar-based system also included a huge outflow of US dollars via the Marshall Plan ($18 billion), and the US military buildup during the Korean and Vietnam Wars. At the same time, US-based corporations had expanded their direct foreign investment throughout the 1960s, further contributing to the outflow of dollars. Bankers followed corporations abroad and firms began to raise capital (dollars) abroad (Underhill, 2000a: 110). Britain, hoping to rejuvenate the City of London as a world financial center, permitted the growth of offshore banking. American corporations were thus able to expand the supply of dollars through the credit multiplier of bank lending; and these offshore capital markets were unregulated by US monetary or supervisory authorities (Underhill, 2000a: 110). This resulted in an oversupply of dollars. Meanwhile, US spending soared as President Johnson embarked upon his ambitious and expensive anti-poverty "Great Society" program in the late 1960s, as the Vietnam War was escalating. The oversupply of dollars, combined with US spending, sharply eroded confidence in the dollar's value. Between 1968 and 1971 currency speculators bet that the dollar could not be backed by gold. At this point, the United States had several choices. It could rein in its banks and corporations. It could cut military spending. It could cut domestic welfare spending. Or, it could sever the dollar's connection with gold and unilaterally abdicate its role as the pillar of the fixed system. In 1971 Nixon did exactly that and inaugurated a new era of the floating dollar. It was this latter choice, according to Strange, that unleashed an array of structural forces that have rendered the world economy more difficult for states to manage (Underhill, 2000b: 120). Thus international monetary governance shifted from the old system of state intervention to maintain stability toward a market-based system to promote efficiency.

As private firms, which had been borrowing freely in offshore capital markets, began to enjoy the "unrestricted transnational financial game" they increasingly lobbied their governments for financial deregulation (Underhill, 2000a: 111). This has led to the accelerated growth of the capital markets that originally had undercut the fixed rate system. States gradually removed capital controls (Goodman and Pauly, 2000); domestic financial deregulation and the cross-border integration of capital markets proceeded apace. This privatization has created "an explosion in the availability of private liquidity which governments are hard pressed to control" (Germain, 1997: 105).

Private banking and securities firms now enjoy more power relative to the state. But this has not necessarily led to the "retreat of the state" *per se*, but perhaps more accurately a "state-market condominium" defined as "a changing balance of public and private authority within the state, hence a changing *form* of state embedded in structural market transformations" (Underhill, 2000b: 118, italics in original). In other words, "the private interests of the market are integrated into the state, asymmetrically and in accordance with their structural power and organizational capacity, through their close relationship to state institutions in the policy decision-making process and in the ongoing pattern of regulatory governance of market society" (Underhill, 2000b: 129).

Further, it is not *all* "private interests" that have been privileged by this confluence of events. Cox has posited a "hierarchy of capital" consisting of "(1) those who control the big corporations operating on a world scale, (2) those who control big nation-based enterprises and industrial groups, and (3) locally based petty capitalists" (Cox, 1987: 358). The more footloose, transnational capital of group (1) has benefited disproportionately. Germain suggests that transnational firms in knowledge-intensive sectors such as computers, software, and pharmaceuticals "have the resources, motivations and capabilities to roam the world searching for the kind of opportunities that promise lucrative rewards" (2000: 81). These privileged sectors participate in "globalized" markets in so far as "there are a small number of participants who know one another and operate across countries with a common conception of control" (Fligstein, 1996: 663). According to Fligstein, "conceptions of control are shared cognitive structures within and across organizations that have profound effects on organizational design and competition" (1996: 671). Strict IP laws reflect one conception of controlling competition (Fligstein, 1996: 666). The TRIPS advocates represented these privileged sectors and sought to globalize their preferred conception of control.

These changes in the economy have been accompanied by important changes in prominent economic ideas. By the mid-1970s neo-classical economics was resurgent in both academic and policy circles (Eisner, 1991). As Bieler points out, "a neo-liberal, monetarist policy replaced Keynesianism from the mid-1970s onwards, when it had become clear that the latter's expansionary response to the economic crisis of the early 1970s had failed" (Bieler, 2000: 22). The Reagan and Thatcher revolutions in the United States and the United Kingdom embraced an anti-Keynesian approach to economic policy. Both leaders implemented a radical free market agenda that favored finance capital and other mobile factors of production (Baker, 2000: 364). This new approach was "not just a change of policies but a conscious effort to change ideas and expectations about the appropriate role of government, the importance of private enterprise, and the virtues of markets" (Gill and Law, 1993: 101).

The ideology of neo-classical economic liberalism spread throughout the globe in the 1980s and came to predominate in major international organizations (Biersteker, 1992; Gill, 2000: 55).

In the early and mid-1980s the GATT Secretariat in Geneva was preoccupied with becoming relevant to the "North" again. At the outset of the Uruguay Round, GATT civil servants responsible for the negotiations expressed fear that if they could not serve an OECD agenda GATT would be through as an organization.[7] They bemoaned the fact that in the early 1980s North–South issues had dominated GATT's agenda out of all proportion to developing countries' role in world trade. They perceived the Uruguay Round as their last chance; they did not want GATT to suffer the fate of UNCTAD and "wither on the vine" as irrelevant. The Reagan administration's fairly open contempt for the United Nations system as irrelevant and wrong-headed increased pressure on the GATT Secretariat to prove its worthiness (Murphy, 1994: 257–259). Added to this was the fact that OECD governments increasingly bypassed multilateral organizations with Group of Seven (G7) summitry and bilateral negotiations. While the GATT Secretariat was small, and its functions largely administrative, the Secretariat's preoccupation with renewed relevance signaled unqualified endorsement of whatever agenda the OECD favored for the upcoming round. The GATT as an institution thus evolved along neo-liberal lines, changing from "a passive caretaker of a multilateral legal instrument to an international body committed to the promotion of exports" (Stanback, 1989: 921 at note 16).

In the 1970s the World Intellectual Property Organization (WIPO) enjoyed a reputation as a fairly balanced agency that weighed the interests of both OECD and developing countries. These days, many regard it as little more than a tool for promoting the interests of the proponents of the most protectionist IP norms. It has come to reflect the interests of the favored factions of capital highlighted by Cox and Germain, and indeed its biggest source of income is its Patent Cooperation Treaty service (PCT). The PCT "vastly enhances the efficiency of the search and registration aspects of the worldwide patent decision and information process" (Doern, 1999: 44). Businesses have increased their use of WIPO's PCT service dramatically since the late 1980s, and now provide 85 percent of WIPO's operating budget. The "large chemical and pharmaceutical firms (US, European, and Japanese) have by far the biggest stake in an efficient, effective patent system . . . and banks and financial

[7] Author's interview with GATT Secretariat personnel, Geneva, July 21 1986.

institutions...are among the fastest growing users of the IP system" (Doern, 1999: 49). Given that WIPO plays a key role in providing technical assistance to developing countries to help them comply with TRIPS, WIPO's dependence on purveyors of high protectionist norms undoubtedly guides its advocacy.

## Structures, agents, and institutions

One of the more difficult challenges facing social scientists is to provide explanations that acknowledge and encompass both structure and agency. In recent years, a number of scholars have emphasized the notion of "mutual constitution," that agents create structures and structures create agents (Wendt, 1987; Dessler, 1989; Giddens, 1979; Onuf, 1997). Authors have addressed the agency-structure "problem" from a diverse range of perspectives: constructivism (Wendt, 1987); structuration theory (Giddens, 1984); positivist methodological individualism (Friedman and Starr, 1997); neo-Gramscian political economy (Bieler and Morton, 2001); and "historicized" international political economy (Amoore *et al.*, 2000). Despite praise for these various efforts, critics insist that the "problem" of combining structure and agency has yet to be solved and that there are still "two stories to tell" (Hollis and Smith, 1991, 1992, 1994). Some solutions ultimately weigh in on one side or another. Wendt's conception is mostly structural, and Giddens' conception has been criticized as overly voluntaristic (Archer, 1990: 78).

No "solution" is perfect, but some seem to provide more explanatory leverage than others. One important problem with Giddens is his ultimate compression of structure and agency. Giddens transcends the structure/agency dichotomy by "making the two elements mutually constitutive, but the tightness of this mutual constitution prevents examination of their interplay. In turn, this precludes specification of their relative importance at any time, how they interact, and with what determinate kinds of consequences" (Archer, 1990: 83). According to Taylor, "to conflate structure and action is to rule out from the start the possibility of explaining change in terms of their interaction *over time*" (Taylor, 1989: 149). To address this problem, Archer offers a "morphogenetic approach" to structure and agency which incorporates time[8] to enable

---

[8] Advocates of historicized IPE also incorporate time, drawing upon Braudel's three-dimensional notion of social time (short time spans of day-to-day events, ten to fifty-year cycles, and the *longue durée* spanning centuries). This also focuses on the question of change, and sensitizes analysts to the variable mutability of structures (Amoore *et al.*:

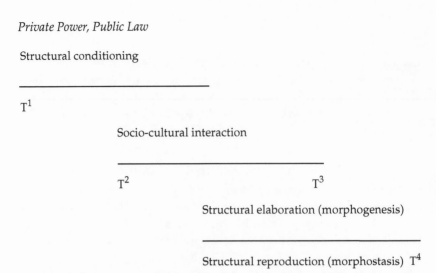

Figure 1.1: The basic morphogenetic/static cycle with its three phases (Archer, 1995: 157)

examination of the mechanisms and processes at work in mutual constitution (Archer, 1982; 1990; 1995). Her term "morphogenesis" comes from "morpho," shape, and "genesis" indicating that the shaping is the product of social relations. Thus "morphogenesis" refers to "those processes which tend to elaborate or change a system's given form, state or structure. Conversely, morphostasis refers to those processes in complex system-environmental exchanges which tend to preserve or maintain a system's given form, organisation or state" (Archer, 1995: 166). Arguing that structure and action operate on different time intervals, Archer highlights two core assumptions: "that structure logically predates the action(s) which transform it, [and] that structural elaboration logically postdates these actions" (1982: 467). Figure 1.1 illustrates the morphogenetic cycle.

The advantage of Archer's framework is that it allows the analyst to tease out which factors are doing the explanatory work at different phases of the process of mutual constitution. In this respect the morphogenetic approach provides a useful organizing methodological device. Incorporating the variable of time also introduces a dynamic

2000). This perspective is perfectly compatible with Archer's conception of time. However, critics do not accept that adding the variable of time solves the agency–structure problem in any sense. "The fundamental problem with morphogenesis is that it does not make sense of how we *integrate* structures and agents into a *single* story ... Morphogenesis does not specify how structures and agency are to be combined" (Hollis and Smith, 1994: 250).

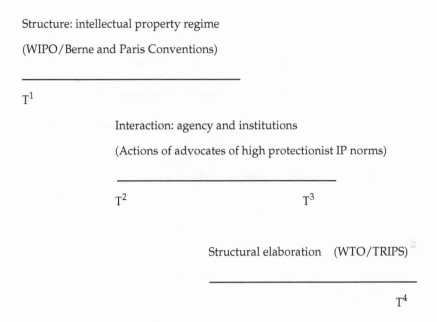

Figure 1.2: Morphogenetic cycle 1

element that focuses on the processes of change. This approach gives both structure and agency analytic autonomy; its analytic dualism is "artificial and methodological" (Archer, 1982: 477). More specifically, Archer's approach emphasizes the embeddedness of agency; for example, during $T^2$ and $T^3$ "(where prior structures are gradually transformed and new ones slowly elaborated)...there is no period when society is *un-structured*" (Archer, 1995: 157–158, emphasis in original). To apply Archer's framework, one must identify the relevant structures, investigate the processes of interaction, and specify the mechanisms that link structures and agents (Archer, 1990: 88). As she points out, "although all three lines are in fact, continuous, the analytical element only consists in breaking up the flows into intervals determined by the problem at hand" (Archer, 1982: 468). One is ultimately forced to make choices about where to slice into time, where to start one's analysis. Figure 1.2 illustrates how a morphogenetic perspective maps onto the TRIPS case.

Figure 1.2 identifies the structure at $T^1$ as the pre-TRIPS intellectual property regime described earlier in this chapter. The agents in my story had nothing to do with the creation of *this* structure; it was the object that their interaction sought to change. Structures vary in their depth and mutability. Examples of deep structures include sovereignty and capitalism. These are more difficult and take longer, even centuries, to change. At the next level lie entities like constitutions. Changing these may take decades. Finally, some structures are shallower, more malleable and can be changed relatively quickly (e.g., tax rules, Archer, 1990). The depth of the pre-TRIPS IP regime lies close to the midpoint of the spectrum, more like constitutions than either capitalism or tax policy. Property rights are the central norm underpinning the market system; "property rights establish a variety of nonstate actors (such as firms or classes) and their interests (such as attaining capital or maximizing income)" (Klotz, 1995: 16). Intellectual property rights are a subset of the central norm of capitalism. They are a subset of one particularly important component of late-twentieth, early-twenty-first-century capitalism and are embedded in the deep structure of global capitalism. For the private sector activists touting high protectionist IP norms, the problem of the pre-TRIPS structure was its limited scope (both in terms of subject matter covered and geography) and strength (enforcement).

Moving to the next line of the figure, interaction: agency and institutions, it is important to note that the action "initiated at $T^2$ takes place in a context not of its own making" (Archer, 1982: 470); this captures the notion of structured agency. While before $T^1$, the pre-TRIPS IP regime was constructed by agents (Sell and May, 2001), at the beginning of my story (as depicted above) this construction presented itself as a structure with which agents had to deal. Thus a construction at one time appears as a constraint at another. Structures do not present constraints only; they provide opportunities as well. Thinking about the codetermination of structure and agency as a process of change over time, involves "the capacity for strategic and tactical action on the part of significant actors cognizant of the potentiality of structures not only to constrain policy but also to provide opportunities for evolutionary action" (Carlsnaes, 1992: 262). Agency, in Archer's rendering, can exert a temporal and a directional independent influence between $T^2$ and $T^3$; "it can speed up, delay or prevent the elimination of prior structural influences" and it can "exercise a directional influence upon the future cultural definition" of [in this instance] property rights, "thus affecting the substance of elaboration at $T^4$" (Archer, 1982: 470). In the first cycle of the TRIPS story agents sped up the extension of IP rights through their actions, as demonstrated later by the counterfactual case, and succeeded in redefining them as a trade issue. This had a profound effect on both the substance and form of the structural elaboration of the IP regime as WTO/TRIPS. In turn,

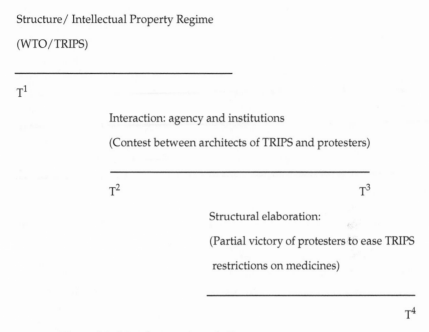

Structure/ Intellectual Property Regime

(WTO/ TRIPS)

———————————————————————

$T^1$

Interaction: agency and institutions

(Contest between architects of TRIPS and protesters)

———————————————————————

$T^2$                                                    $T^3$

Structural elaboration:

(Partial victory of protesters to ease TRIPS

restrictions on medicines)

———————————————————————

$T^4$

Figure 1.3: Morphogenetic cycle 2

this structural elaboration became the new structure, confronting actors at $T^1$ of the second cycle depicted in Figure 1.3.

In this cycle, WTO/TRIPS, which was the social construction of actors in the prior cycle, becomes the structure initiating the post-TRIPS cycle. The structure confronted those who did not participate in the construction of this public international law as a constraint. Suddenly, practices that had been acceptable before, such as keeping medicines off-patent, became unlawful. The conditioning influence of structure in this phase "divid[ed] the population (not necessarily exhaustively) into social groups working for the maintenance versus the change of a given property, because the property itself distribute[d] different objective vested interests to them at T2" (Archer, 1982: 469). This nicely captures the polarized politics of the post-TRIPS process. Dizzy with success, the TRIPS architects worked hard to extend property rights further and ensure enforcement of TRIPS, while the unwitting "victims" of TRIPS gradually mobilized to demand a change in this structure. The conditioning effects of structure were both constraining, but also facilitating. The overreach of TRIPS presented formidable constraints, but also opened up space for a reconsideration of such a broad and deep extension of IP rights. As will be discussed in greater detail in Chapter 6, the protestors have not *eliminated* the structural constraints that TRIPS presents but they have succeeded in softening some of its worst effects. That is no small achievement in light of the comparative resources deployed by their opponents.

The TRIPS story was hardly inevitable; things did not have to happen this way. For example, the process leading up to the adoption of new copyright treaties in the WIPO in 1996 looked very similar to the TRIPS story.[9] These negotiations were located in the very same changing structure of global capitalism. Many of the same players were active in these negotiations, including many of the same firms and same governmental officials such as Bruce Lehman (assistant secretary of commerce and commissioner of patents and trademarks). Interested private sector actors had persuaded US government officials to promote their cause of expanding the scope of copyright protection. They also worked closely with their European counterparts to press for a strong agreement covering digital property, forging a consensus that high-protectionist norms would enable their industries to flourish in the global marketplace. As in TRIPS, framing copyright as a trade and competitiveness issue strengthened the hand of the IP activists who favored high-protectionist norms. However, in the end, the outcome was quite different than in TRIPS in so far as those advocating high-protectionist norms were stymied. The resulting treaties, unlike TRIPS, affirmed a public-regarding approach to copyright in the digital environment by emphasizing the need to balance the rights of authors with the public interest in access to information. As Samuelson points out, the WIPO Copyright Treaty's affirmation of the value of "a balanced public policy approach to copyright in the digital environment suggests that predictions of the end of copyright – that is, its displacement by trade policy in the aftermath of TRIPS – may have been premature" (Samuelson, 1997: 375).

What was different? For one thing, this time those with the high-protectionist agenda faced vocal and powerful opposition by skilled articulators of an alternative position. Executives from companies such as Sun Microsystems, Netscape, and lobbyists representing nongovernmental organizations such as the International Council of Scientific Unions and the American Library Association teamed up to

[9] This account is based on Samuelson, 1997: 369–449.

highlight concerns with the high-protectionist draft treaties. They lobbied the Congress, the Clinton administration, various national delegations in Geneva, and WIPO-sponsored regional meetings, and participated informally as observers and lobbyists in the negotiations. Their alternative position revolved around the well-established legal norm of "fair use" as a counterpart to the proposed extension of information providers' rights. Fair use is the doctrine that permits limited uncompensated use of a copyrighted work for educational purposes or for scientific research. It seeks to balance public access to information for technical and scientific advance with the copyright holders' right to the work. "In the end, none of the original US-sponsored (high-protectionist) digital agenda proposals emerged unscathed from the negotiation process, and at least one – the proposed database treaty – did not emerge at all" (Samuelson, 1997: 374–375). Thus, an effectively mobilized opposition armed with a compelling alternative framing of the issue was able to rewrite the ending of what had promised to become another TRIPS story. The process makes a difference.

In the American TRIPS story, structures constituted newly powerful agents and altered institutions in ways that compounded these agents' power. At the same time, these agents altered institutions in ways that compounded and amplified the agents' power, American power, and structural power to alter outcomes for others. Institutional change empowered IP owners, and intellectual property owners drove further institutional change. But that is not the end of the story. The TRIPS Agreement has also helped to constitute new actors who oppose the global property rights regime, and who are changing the game yet again and altering the political landscape over which this contest will continue to be fought. Indeed, we are already seeing the consequences of this – not only in the post-TRIPS negotiations on the digital copyright agenda but in the increasingly effective protests against overly broad IP rights in pharmaceutical and agricultural products. For instance, the HIV/AIDS crisis in Thailand and sub-Saharan Africa has provided an opportunity for an alternative framing of pharmaceutical patent "rights" as a public health issue rather than a trade issue.

Theoretically, this study is centrally concerned with the origin of preferences and the relationship between agents, institutions, and structures. It speaks to enduring questions about the origin of norms, state power, and non-state actors and addresses the fundamentally political issues such as who is making the rules, who wins, who loses, and why. My aim, however, is not to develop a broad social theory of international political economy. I seek to employ theory to highlight and explain one of the most consequential developments in contemporary international political economy. Practically, the book tells an important story about how IP rights have evolved. It is motivated by a conviction that IP rights, as embodied in TRIPS, have been extended too broadly. While endorsing IP rights in principle, believing that they are both necessary and important, I maintain that the balance between private rights and public access has shifted too far in favor of private rights at the expense of the public weal.

## Organization of the book

Chapter 2 argues that TRIPS was a product of structured agency and presents the theoretical framework that guides the analysis. Changes in the structure of global capitalism animated competitiveness concerns among American policymakers. The private sector IP activists employed both direct and indirect power to ensure their desired outcome. However, their efficacy must be viewed in a broader context in so far as they crafted their advocacy to respond to competitiveness concerns that preoccupied US government officials. Chapter 3 provides an historical perspective, tracing the evolution of US IP policies and highlighting shifting conceptions of the role of IP rights. It examines the evolution of the courts' perspectives and the changing domestic environment for IP rights-holders. Chapter 4 shifts to the legislative and executive branches and addresses US competitiveness concerns and private sector lobbying. It describes the context within which private sector actors pushed for a trade-based approach. Chapter 5 examines the mobilization of a transnational private sector consensus in support of TRIPS, and the negotiations culminating in the adoption of the 1994 Agreement. Chapter 6 documents industry dissatisfaction with the final TRIPS Agreement, focusing on the "5 percent" it did not get. The chapter addresses recent efforts to strengthen global enforcement of IP rights and emergent controversies over these rights in the post-TRIPS era. On the one hand, the United States, at the behest of the private sector TRIPS architects, is pursuing an aggressive post-TRIPS strategy both bilaterally and multilaterally to accelerate the adoption and enforcement of TRIPS abroad and to ratchet up the levels of protection. On the other, new stakeholders have emerged to challenge the levels of protection afforded by TRIPS. A vibrant international social movement has emerged to oppose the breadth of coverage and has begun framing IP rights in a more public-regarding manner. In particular, the devastating AIDS crisis in Thailand and sub-Saharan Africa has become a flashpoint for sharp political battles over IP rights. Chapter 7 examines private power in comparative perspective by analyzing the private sector role in the new issues in the Uruguay Round (investment, services, and financial services). While TRIPS and the Financial Services Agreement both reflect significant triumphs for private sector activists, the record in these other agreements is more mixed. Finally, the chapter presents conclusions and explores the broader theoretical and policy implications of this analysis.

# 2    Structure, agents, and institutions

My argument draws upon insights of the morphogenetic approach to structure and agency to explain the adoption of the TRIPS accord and the establishment of a new global IP regime. This discussion highlights the structured nature of agency, as mediated by institutions. Focusing on agency alone and offering a "bottom-up" causal explanation would make "no allowances for inherited structures, their resistance to change, the influence they exert on attitudes to change, and crucially . . . the delineation of agents capable of seeking change" (Archer, 1995: 250). The TRIPS accord is the social construction of privileged agents whose interests were mediated through the US state. The knowledge and ideas that the IPC promoted were powerful elements in this process. The IPC's technical expertise, the framing skills of the IPC's advocates, and the cognitive appeal of the IPC's diagnosis and prescriptions help to provide the explanatory link between agents and structures.

This is a case with complex causality. I will break the argument down into discrete segments in order to clarify the mechanisms at work. The chapter begins by summarizing the overall argument. The first part of the chapter focuses on the structure of global capitalism and its effects on US institutions and on agents' interests. It also discusses the relevance of the structure of the international system for understanding this case. Having explored the causal effects of structure on institutions and agents, the chapter then offers a simple counterfactual to highlight the importance of agency. The chapter then analyzes the direct and indirect power of the private sector IP activists. The final section introduces the second morphogenetic cycle underway in the aftermath of TRIPS.

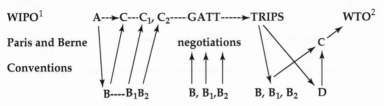

Old International Intellectual Property Regime:

New Global Intellectual Property Regime

WIPO[1]

Paris and Berne Conventions

Morphogenetic cycle 1                    Morphogenetic cycle 2

Figure 2.1: The argument
A = antecedent condition, the structure of global capitalism
B = independent variable, private sector activism (US)
$B_1$ = independent variable, private sector activism (Europe)
$B_2$ = independent variable, private sector activism (Japan)
C = intervening variable, institutional change in the United States
$C_1$ = intervening variable, institutional change in Europe
$C_2$ = intervening variable, institutional change in Japan
D = mobilized opposition to private sector activism
Dependent variable = New Global Intellectual Property Regime
[1] World Intellectual Property Organization
[2] World Trade Organization

## Structures, agents, and institutions

My argument combines structural, institutional, and agent-based explanations with a focus on contingency and concrete problems that decisionmakers at various levels sought to solve. The relevant structures, as depicted in Figure 2.1, are global capitalism and the international system. Beginning with the far left part of the diagram, the old international IP regime should be viewed as embedded in the larger structure of global capitalism. As discussed in Chapter 1, it is a subset of property rights. Therefore the old regime is embedded in (A), the antecedent condition. In Chapter 1 I examined the causal force of structure in *creating* the agents. In this chapter I examine the *effects* of structure on *institutions* and on the agents' *interests*. The first arrow, moving from (A) to (C), indicates the structure's effects on institutions. I argue that the structure of global capitalism fostered institutional change in the United States. The state adopted policies designed to increase its own and its firms' abilities to compete in the global economy. As will be discussed in subsequent chapters, these changes were evident in all branches of government.

The arrow moving from structure (A) to agents (B) indicates the structure's effects on the agents. As discussed in the introduction, changes in the structure of global capitalism constituted new agents of particular importance. Whereas, in the past, manufacturing interests were relatively powerful domestically, the structure of global capitalism delivered high-technology actors to the forefront of business regulation. Beyond this, it shaped their substantive interests by revealing new strains between the old system of IP protection and technological change. The IP activist agents sought to close the gap between the two. The arrow moving from agents (B) to institutions (C) indicates the agents' effects on the institutions. This highlights the important role that private sector activism played in institutional change at the domestic, international, and ultimately global levels. Private sector actors engaged in proselytizing and consensus building activities at every conceivable level.

For purposes of this book I have restricted my scope largely to an examination of the American process. I opted for depth over breadth, not least of all because the impetus for this new global IP regime came from the United States and its leading firms. Thus I do not explore the processes linking European and Japanese private sector activism with institutional change in Europe and Japan.[1] These undoubtedly are important but will not be covered here.

As depicted in Figure 2.1, I have identified TRIPS as the end of the first morphogenetic cycle. The right side of the diagram seeks to capture important elements of the vibrant contestation over IP rights. Chapter 6 is devoted to the second cycle which is still in progress. It is not exhaustive, omitting the WIPO digital treaties,[2] for example, but is meant to explore the continuing interplay between structure and agency in the wake of TRIPS. The very fact of TRIPS has spawned new actors who are mobilizing to contest the high protectionist agenda that won so handily in the TRIPS negotiations. This contestation is as much a part of the new global IP regime as the negotiated rules administered by the WTO. TRIPS is not merely an incremental change in international regulation, but rather the embodiment of a new "constitutive principle" in

---

[1] For an authoritative account of the European role in TRIPS, see D. Matthews (2002).

[2] "WIPO Copyright Treaty," CRNR/DC/94, Geneva: World Intellectual Property Organization, <http://www.wipo.int/eng/diplconf/distrib/94dc.htm>; WIPO Performances and Phonograms Treaty," CRNR/DC/96, Geneva: World Intellectual Property Organization.

**A**
**Old intellectual property regime (WIPO/Berne and Paris Conventions)**
**[subset of A]**

---

**T1 Structural conditioning**

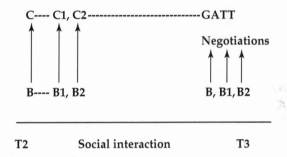

C---- C1, C2------------------------------GATT

Negotiations

B---- B1, B2             B, B1, B2

---

T2          Social interaction          T3

**WTO/TRIPS**

---

**Structural elaboration   T4**

Figure 2.2:  Morphogenetic cycle 1
A  = antecedent condition, the structure of global capitalism
B  = independent variable, private sector activism (US)
$B_1$ = independent variable, private sector activism (Europe)
$B_2$ = independent variable, private sector activism (Japan)
C  = intervening variable, institutional change in the United States
$C_1$ = intervening variable, institutional change in Europe
$C_2$ = intervening variable, institutional change in Japan
Dependent variable  =  WTO/TRIPS

so far as it creates new international property rights that create or define new forms of behavior and generate structures (Dessler, 1989: 455; Burch, 1994: 37–59). In short, it reconstitutes both agents and structures, reproducing and transforming them, and thereby redefines winners and losers. In this sense, it is not an endpoint but rather another beginning.

Figure 2.2 illustrates the first morphogenetic cycle, which culminated in the adoption of the TRIPS agreement. The introductory chapter presented this concept in a general way; the following discussion provides greater specific detail about the mechanisms driving the process.

The structure of global capitalism (A) provided a permissive condition for the TRIPS agreement. The actions of the agents (B) were necessary but not sufficient conditions for the TRIPS outcome. The institution of the US state (C), embedded in this broader structure, mediated between domestic private sector actors and international institutions. The efficacy of the private sector activists was conjunctural and context dependent. "Economic arrangements are established by social bargains and perpetuated through social institutions; they are neither natural nor inevitable and must therefore be analyzed in a contingent social setting" (Wilks, 1996: 40). Agents' interests are refracted by the state and projected onto the international system. If the US state were not so powerful in the international system, its domestic agents would have had less impact in the multilateral arena. If US policymakers had not been facing new challenges arising from changes in the structure of global capitalism, they would not have been so receptive to the private sector IP activists' efforts. If the particular agents pressing for a tough multilateral agreement were not so powerful within the United States, their actions would have been less effective. Archer captures this complexity in more general terms: "voluntarism has an important place in morphogenesis but is ever trammelled by past structural and cultural constraints and by the current politics of the possible" (1982: 470).

One can consider the agent as the proximate or immediate cause, who is embedded in larger and larger structures, including material causes, state institutions, and the structure of global capitalism, that both constrain and empower. Regarding the structures relevant to TRIPS, only a relative handful of agents was powerful. Structural power is "the power to choose and to shape the structures of the global political economy within which other states, their political institutions, their economic enterprises, and (not least) their professional people have to operate" (Strange, 1987: 565). The TRIPS outcome constitutes structural power, the power to shape the environment and redefine options for others (Palan and Abbott, 1996: 138; Strange, 1996). If we examined migrant farm workers or American textile workers as agents in the context of the Uruguay Round we would be telling a story of powerful constraints and powerless agents. The story to be told here emphasizes the empowering features of structure that made *these* corporate agents particularly efficacious. According to Granovetter, actors' "attempts at purposive action are...embedded in concrete, ongoing systems of social relations" (1985: 487). Therefore, it is necessary to illuminate the relationships between agents and structures and the mediating role of the state as an institution.

## Structure's effect on institutions

Chapter 1 provided the broad outline of TRIPS' embeddedness in global capitalism and that structure's effects in delivering specific actors to the forefront of regulation. This section looks more closely at the effects of these changes on US state institutions and policy orientations.

Four important aspects of globalization that have altered market structure are, "the globalization of finance, the internationalization of production, the changing role of technology, and the politics of deregulation" (Palan and Abbott, 1996: 20). These changes led to the rise of a competitive state strategy – "a set of policies that are explicitly aimed at improving the climate for business ... and hence at enhancing the 'competitive' advantage of such countries in the global economy" (Palan and Abbott, 1996: 6). Competitiveness concerns in the United States animated a number of significant policy changes relevant to the politics of intellectual property. US policymakers were preoccupied by US "decline," as reflected in both trade and budget deficits. The United States sought to enhance the ability of its corporations to compete in global markets.

The globalization of finance facilitated market expansion, and by the 1980s market access became the clarion call of US competitiveness. Worries over US trade deficits elevated the importance of trade in US policymaking. Domestically, the United States shifted to supply side economics to provide the conditions for generating growth (Palan and Abbott, 1996: 4). Attendant policies included the relaxation of anti-trust enforcement, which paved the way for reinvigorated domestic IP protection. In so far as patents confer temporary monopoly privileges, a natural tension exists between IP protection and anti-trust. "Anti-trust rules that once sharply restricted the commercial exploitation of patents have been greatly liberalized" (Silverstein, 1991: 313–314). The increasing importance of high-technology sectors in the global economy heightened US interest in intellectual property as an important element of competitive advantage. As Reichman points out, "the growing capacity of manufacturers in developing countries to penetrate distant markets for traditional industrial products had forced the developed countries to rely more heavily on their comparative advantage in the production of intellectual goods than in the past" (1993: 176). In recent years, beginning in 1982 with the establishment of the Court of Appeals for the Federal Circuit (CAFC), the so-called "patent court," the United States has dramatically improved the legal environment for patent holders. The CAFC vigorously upholds patent holders' rights against infringers, and other US policies have extended the definition of patentable subject matter, and the scope and duration of patent rights.

The post-World War II US commitment to "free trade" had come under stress by the late 1970s and was eclipsed by the concept of "free-but-fair trade." Proponents of this position argued it was necessary to "level the playing field," or to reduce distortions emanating from other countries' trade practices – implying that in a perfect world the United States could continue to practice free trade, but others were preventing it from doing so. In principle, the fair trade policy is designed to promote freer trade worldwide by opposing protectionism at home, enforcing individual cases brought under US trade law to counter "unfair" foreign practices, and negotiating bilateral and multilateral agreements to reduce trade barriers (Greenwald, 1987: 234). The US government "began to reevaluate its policy of benign neglect toward United States investment abroad" and focused on the United States Trade Representative (USTR) "as the agency most receptive to industry concerns and in the best position to coordinate efforts by the United States Government to develop responses" (Gadbaw, 1989: 228). By 1979 the USTR became the lead agency addressing investment issues and using trade measures as tools to combat restrictive investment practices abroad. It began to employ market access for developing countries as a bargaining chip in exchange for investment liberalization abroad.

The internationalization of production, characterized by a "post-Fordist"[3] regime of accumulation, empowered a new set of domestic corporate actors. Post-Fordism implies reduced political power for high-wage labor, and reduced bargaining power for industries still based on the Fordist model in industrialized countries. Industries in decline as a result of aggressive import competition from low-wage labor sites

---

[3] The French Regulation school of political economy popularized the term post-Fordism, which describes "the decline of the old manufacturing base and the growth of 'sunrise,' computer-based industries . . . an economy dominated by multinationals, with their new international division of labour and their greater autonomy from nation-state control; and the 'globalisation' of the new financial markets, linked by the communications revolution" (Hall, 1988; quoted in Amin, 1994: 4; see also Bernard in Stubbs and Underhill, 1994: 216–229; Cox, 1993).

enjoyed reduced political power. High-technology, IP-based, industries eclipsed formerly powerful sectors, such as steel and textiles.

In the Uruguay Round so-called "sunset" industries, for example, textiles, lost out to those industries that presented themselves as the leaders of the next wave.[4] These industries of the IPC – for example, pharmaceutical, entertainment, computer software – were in a good position in so far as they were vigorous exporters that enjoyed positive trade balances. While the US economy was hurting, these US businesses were prospering abroad. To secure a TRIPS agreement, the negotiators had to make trade-offs with other parts of the Uruguay Round agenda. For example, the Multi-Fibre Arrangement (MFA), which for years had provided US textile producers some import protection from low-wage producers, will now be phased out. There was "a recognition that without a deal on TRIPs, ratification of the Uruguay Round package in the US Congress was unlikely given the political weight of the US industries supporting strong IPR discipline" (Hoekman and Kostecki, 1995: 157; Mowrey, 1993: 369).

## Structure's effects on agents' interests

Structural change can alter agents' interests if such changes render existing institutions less useful or cause new harms that did not exist under the previous structure. Technological changes altered the preferences of capitalists who had benefited from the old system of IP protection. Operating within a cultural and ideational commitment to radical free market policies, they sought not reproduction of the existing system but rule change. A number of factors led US companies to embrace a more comprehensive strategy soliciting government help in protecting their intellectual property.

Two particularly important structural (and material) changes that shaped these activists' interest in securing a stronger IP regime were the development of new technologies and the increasing value of intellectual property. Technological changes made it cheap and easy for others

---

[4] In a formal sense this is true in so far as negotiators agreed to a timetable for dismantling the Multi-Fibre Arrangement, which provided import protection for US textile manufacturers. In fact, implementation of this negotiated phase-out has been slow and the subject of much criticism from developing countries. Furthermore, even while the older sectors lost out in formal negotiations, *de facto* political support continued in the form of increased use of unilateral anti-dumping measures and most recently in President Bush's spring 2002 support for US steel protection.

to copy expensively developed IP-based goods. Software, videos, and compact discs could be reproduced by virtually anyone with access to the requisite and widely available copying equipment. Yet, at the same time, the costs of innovation were soaring. Research and development (R & D) costs escalated, and greater investment in R & D was required for firms to continue to develop new products in a highly competitive marketplace. Further, technological innovation had produced new types of intellectual property, such as semiconductor chips, software codes, and biotechnological inventions that did not easily fit traditional IP categories.

Intellectual property-based products played an increasing role in international trade. Advances in communication technologies effectively created a global marketplace. Firms having global reach and extensive IP portfolios stood to gain staggering amounts of licensing revenue if their products and processes were better protected. For example, in 1995 alone "US multinational manufacturing enterprises['] ... exports, as measured by royalties and licensing fees, amounted to about US $27 billion ... while imports amounted to only US $6.3 billion" (Ryan, 1998b: 2; see also Merges, 2000: 2190).

These changes presented both an obstacle and an opportunity for the IP activists. In general terms, "*all* structural influences ... *are mediated to people by shaping the situation in which they find themselves*" (Archer, 1995: 196, emphasis in original). Such influences can either "foster or frustrate 'projects'" (Archer, 1995: 198). In this instance, widespread copying of products and processes threatened to undercut the viability of IP-intensive firms' advantages. The magnitude of those advantages (potential and actual) increased incentives to take action. Together, these factors highlighted a fundamental incongruence between the old IP regime and the emerging IP-based marketplace. The mismatch exemplifies a central element of Archer's conception of the relationship between agency and structure (Archer, 1995: 215). While the IP producers clearly benefited from the old IP regime, the increasingly uneasy fit between it and structural changes in technology threatened to empower a new group of actors (imitators) at their expense and dilute the benefits of the existing system.

Such structural incongruities present distinctive "situational logics which predispose agents towards specific courses of action for the promotion of their interests" (Archer, 1995: 216). This is a case of what Archer calls a "contingent incompatibility" in which reproduction, or a continuation of the status quo, hinders the achievement of the agents' aims. To claim that structural incongruity "conditions oppositional action is merely to argue that such corporate agents are in a situation whose logic is to *eliminate* practices which are hostile to achieving their vested interests" (Archer, 1995: 331; emphasis in original). Therefore, the aggrieved sought to eliminate hostile practices. In this instance, structural conditioning predisposed agents to pursue changes to the old IP system. They sought new tools to *eliminate* the copying practices of others. They also sought to expand IP protection to cover new types of innovations. In their quest to preserve and extend their privileges, IP activists moved to close the gap opened by the new technologies facilitating appropriability and the new technologies that did not easily fit under the old system's definitions.

Intellectual property protection is an important form of market control; it is a state-sanctioned means of controlling competition. Rather than lobbying for something entirely new, or eliminating the old system altogether, the IP-based businesses responded to their perceived market crisis by seeking state help to change the existing system to address their problems. Their conceptual template was informed by the existing system, but also moved well beyond it in terms of depth, breadth, institutional extension, and conceptualization as a trade issue.

## The structure of the international system

Derived from traditional realist theorizing (Waltz, 1979; Krasner, 1991; Gilpin, 2000), the structure of the international system is an important component for analyzing global regulation. Realists focus on the distribution of state power across the international system. In intergovernmental negotiations, such as the multilateral Uruguay Round, only states have formal standing. No matter how actively engaged private sector actors may be, bargains are ultimately struck between states. Realist logic suggests that the more powerful the state, the more likely it is to prevail in negotiations. In the case of the new global IP regime, the structure of the international system was important in at least two ways. First of all, the United States was indisputably the most powerful state. Whether one believes that the United States is the "sole remaining superpower" or the first among equals in a shared functional hegemony with Europe and Japan, the United States had abundant negotiating power. And even in an interpretation of more evenly shared hegemony, the United States, Europe, and Japan are preponderantly powerful *vis-à-vis* developing countries who accounted for most of the initial resistance to a trade-based IP agreement. Second, US power clearly was not limited to the multilateral arena. The United States had engaged in extensive coercive economic diplomacy leading up to and during the Uruguay Round. The United States had been using access to its large domestic market as a coercive means to goad other countries into adopting and enforcing stricter IP policies.

## A simple counterfactual

With so many structural factors weighing in favor of these particular agents, one might argue that this explanation is overdetermined. One might wonder, "Who needs agency?" Yet, considering the counterfactual case – that is, if the IP activists had not exerted themselves in this arena – it is highly unlikely that there would be a TRIPS accord. The most likely outcome would have been a much narrower, resuscitated Anti-Counterfeiting Code – if that. Until the IPC began lobbying its European and Japanese private sector counterparts, there was very little enthusiasm for or even interest in a comprehensive IP code. The IPC itself was surprised by how much it achieved; the TRIPS accord far surpassed the IPC's initial expectations.

Indeed, while the IPC's success underscores the structural possibilities that were made concrete by the IPC's actions, its surprise at its own success suggests two additional points. First, it shows that the agents themselves may not (and need not) fully recognize the extent of both structural impediments and structural possibilities in pursuing their actions. The IPC did not know ahead of time that its framing of intellectual property as a boon to free trade would work; its leaders were smart, but not clairvoyant. And second, we can only understand the IPC's success by examining factors that did not seem so obvious on the ground.

Imagine a world with no IPC. Holding other factors constant, what would the outcome have been? The most likely outcome would have been a narrow Anti-Counterfeiting Code restricted to border sanctions, authorizing customs officials to seize counterfeit goods. The push for an IP code in the GATT began in 1978, near the end of the Tokyo Round of negotiations. The Levi Strauss Corporation initiated an effort to combat foreign counterfeiting of its trademark blue jeans (Doremus, 1995: 149). Levi Strauss pressed its case with other trademark-sensitive firms (lobbying as the International Anti-Counterfeiting Coalition) and obtained the backing of the USTR for an anti-counterfeiting code. Owing in part to the eleventh-hour introduction of the proposal, the effort ultimately failed. By 1982, the United States, the European Community, Japan, and Canada had reached agreement on a draft proposal. Developing countries successfully resisted its adoption. In their preparations for the Uruguay Round, IP activists faced an uphill battle to convince both trade and IP specialists that the GATT was an appropriate forum for intellectual property (Gorlin, in Walker and Bloomfield, 1988: 171).

In 1986, at the outset of the Uruguay Round, several western delegations wanted to resuscitate the draft proposal to cover counterfeiting of trademarked goods. Their goal was to negotiate a narrow Anti-Counterfeiting Code *period* – leaving more comprehensive suggestions to later negotiating rounds (Emmert, 1990: 1339). In the early phases of the Round, meetings between American and European trade officials were dominated by debates over GATT's competence to deal with IP issues beyond trademark counterfeiting (Gorlin, in Walker and Bloomfield, 1988: 176). As one participant points out, when negotiators initially discussed intellectual property at Punta del Este

> the feeling was that this was going to be a sort of side issue . . . [The Anti-Counterfeiting Code] looked like it was in a form that could be adopted. The politicians and policy people could then exclaim, "Hooray, we're showing you that we're doing something." The scenario turned out to be surprisingly different than that.          (Jackson, 1989: 343)

The American IP activists, particularly the IPC, warned against quick adoption of an Anti-Counterfeiting Code fearing that, if adopted, it would end IP discussions in the Round and prevent the consideration of a more comprehensive code.

Jacques Gorlin, an economist, consultant and adviser to the IPC, worked hard to convince the IP section of the American Bar Association that IP interests would not be subordinated to trade interests. Some IP attorneys feared that linking intellectual property to trade would lead to horse trading and that intellectual property might get sacrificed for a deal on agriculture. Therefore, they initially preferred to avert the risk by leaving intellectual property out of the multilateral negotiations altogether. Gorlin addressed the IP section of the American Bar Association at its annual meetings and emphasized that using the trade card would, in fact, strengthen IP protection, and that the IP activists had no intention of trading it off for other issues, or weakening it in any way.[5]

---

[5] Author's interview with Jacques Gorlin, January 22, 1996, Washington, DC.

A -------------------➤ C -------------➤ Anti-Counterfeiting Code

Figure 2.3: The counterfactual case
A = antecedent condition, the structure of global capitalism
C = intervening variable, institutional change in the United States
Counterfactual dependent variable = Anti-Counterfeiting Code

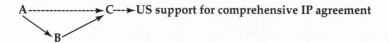

Figure 2.4: The actual case
A = antecedent condition, the structure of global capitalism
B = independent variable, private sector activism (US)
C = intervening variable, institutional change in the United States
Dependent variable = US support for comprehensive IP agreement

While France and the United Kingdom came to endorse the American quest for a broader IP code, other European countries, Germany in particular, were far more skeptical. As late as the Montreal mid-term review in December 1988, the Anti-Counterfeiting Code was a live option. Developing countries had finally come to endorse such a code as a damage limitation strategy – to prevent the expansion of GATT's purview of IP issues. Gorlin urged US negotiators to resist signing on to a "mediocre" Anti-Counterfeiting Code in the December 1988 Montreal GATT meeting and to hold out for a strong IP agreement that would benefit the United States much more (Gorlin, in Walker and Bloomfield, 1988: 175). American negotiators were persuaded by this rationale, and contrary to initial expectations, IP issues took center stage at the Montreal meeting. As Jackson suggests, "intellectual property has manifested how very effective private interests in the United States can move the government, and indeed basically move governments of the world forward in such a way that... going into the Montreal meeting we suddenly found intellectual property to be one of the two or three key issues of the negotiation" (1989: 343–344).

Yet the mediating role of the US state was also critically important. The IPC's activities notwithstanding, there would be no TRIPS accord if the United States had not changed its domestic attitudes toward strong IP protection. The US state, embedded in the context of the changing structure of global capitalism, redefined its interests and adopted a competitive strategy that made it particularly receptive to the IPC's policy advocacy.

Thus far, I have described the changing structure of global capitalism and the resultant changing institutional context of the United States. These produce expectations for the promotion of a dramatically strengthened multilateral IP regime as embodied in TRIPS. I have also identified the agents and their interests. What remains to be explained is the process by which private actors constructed complementarity between state and private interests, and how private interests became enshrined in public international law. Despite the facilitating conditions described in previous sections, there was nothing automatic about this process. While the member corporations of the IPC were structurally privileged by virtue of their role in the United States and the global economy, their potential for influence had "to be made a reality by conscious political action" (Augelli and Murphy, 1993: 132).

As Palan and Abbott point out, "capitalist enterprises need the state to provide ... the political and social conditions of accumulation" (1996: 36). The state structures private sector participation and access to decision makers: "it is within options set out by the state that interest groups organize and influence policies and their implementation" (Woods, 1995: 170). Some actors are more privileged than others, and state institutions often favor particular interests. Corporate actors employ both direct power, by lobbying, and indirect power, by establishing the normative context, in pursuing their aims. In order to reveal the process by which private interests become public one must examine the substance and power of discourse, the advocates' framing skills, and the "fit" between the message and the audience. Complementarity between state and private interests is ultimately constructed.

## The difference that agency makes

Structural conditions do not determine agency. Archer identifies two types of agency. Primary agents have neither organized nor articulated their interests and do not participate strategically in shaping or reshaping structure. By contrast, corporate agents "are aware of what they want, can articulate it to themselves and others, and have organized in order to get it" (Archer, 1995: 258). However, they must resent the status quo or recognize the potential of action before they mobilize to change the existing structure. Corporate agents "pack more punch in defining and re-defining structural forms, and are key links in delimiting whether systemic fault lines (incompatibilities) will be split open (introducing

43

[change]) or will be contained (reproducing [the status quo])" (Archer, 1995: 191).

In order to be successful, corporate agents need organization, access to resources, and a number of powerful players who resent the status quo. In terms of IP protection, businesses in disparate sectors were feeling the pinch in different ways and in different arenas by the late 1970s and early 1980s. Agricultural chemicals producers, book publishers, software producers, video and music entertainment providers, and non-generic pharmaceutical manufacturers were experiencing the incongruity between technology and the old system of IP protection on a daily basis. However, they had to be organized into a self-conscious grouping for the pursuit of shared aims.

Mobilizing others for action requires both material and discursive strategies to draw attention to the underlying congruence of interests or to construct congruence. Adversely affected industries began by lobbying separately; patent interests and copyright interests engaged in parallel but unconnected political action. Over time, and with the help of several key individuals (e.g., Edmund Pratt, John Opel, and Jacques Gorlin), these different groups realized that they were seeking the same goal – heightened IP protection. They came to lobby together, so that patent interests testified on behalf of copyright interests and vice versa. Archer refers to this congruence of goals as "superimposition," in which corporate agency points in the same direction. This superimposition at the domestic level was extended as the IPC went on to craft superimposition transnationally.

Structural incongruities may spur action, but discursive strategies can help solidify it, render it coherent, and legitimate it. While structural disjunction created incentives to alter rules governing IP protection, corporate interest groups developed new arguments to justify the desired changes. In this case, the IP activists' discursive strategy was to link intellectual property to trade. In this respect, structural conditioning crystalized "new corporate agents who not only [were] organized but [became] ideationally articulate" (Archer, 1995: 315).

The IPC sought a multilateral agreement to strengthen global protection of its members' intellectual property. In the past, companies viewed IP piracy as a local problem and tended to utilize foreign investment as leverage to negotiate separately with host country governments. US government involvement was minimal and *ad hoc*; companies occasionally would solicit the assistance of various US embassies as problems arose. Increasingly, firms were uncertain about the

Figure 2.5: The argument (Part 1)
A = antecedent condition, structure of global capitalism
B = independent variable, private sector activism (US)
Dependent variable = institutional change (US)

extent to which foreign governments would protect US-held intellectual property.

In the face of this uncertainty, the private sector intellectual property activists, who in the early stages acted through their industry associations, sought to enlist government support to preserve and improve their competitive position. This is depicted in Figure 2.5.

They began their quest by seeking US government support in pressuring foreign governments to adopt and enforce more stringent IP protection. They sought, and won, changes in US domestic laws (as discussed in Chapter 4). They urged the US government to get tough on foreign violators of US-held IP rights. They were encouraged by the elevated role of the USTR and its sympathetic stance toward industry concerns. The government's new focus on market access issues and the trade deficit was gratifying, in so far as some of the countries that posed the biggest piracy problems were heavily dependent upon trade with the United States, such as Brazil, China, South Korea, and Thailand (Gadbaw, 1989: 228).

IP activists redefined inadequate IP protection abroad as a barrier to legitimate trade. Adding inadequate enforcement of US IP rights abroad as actionable under existing trade statutes, such as 301, brought intellectual property under the normative umbrella of trade policy. Private sector IP activists effectively cast IP rights as equivalent to general property rights, hence essential to free trade. Behavior that once was tolerated was now redefined as objectionable and unfair. Linking IP to trade and advocating this conception for the multilateral trading order, the IPC was able to appeal to an existing international institution, GATT, and emphasize the benefits of the new approach not just for the IPC but for the world trading system as a whole. As one member of the IPC remarked:

> We in industry need to articulate the important market access and domestic growth aspects of intellectual property protection... It is critical that US companies work to stress the importance in public policy debates of intellectual property protection to the health of the international trading system. (Bale, in Walker and Bloomfield, 1988: 123)

The IPC offered an agenda that advocated expanding global economic integration. The IPC packaged its prescriptions as being good for America and for the health of the global trading system.

The IPC lobbied the government to support and promote a multilateral IP agreement through the GATT, eschewing the traditional venue, the World Intellectual Property Organization (WIPO), because WIPO lacked enforcement powers and was dominated numerically by less developed countries. Transnationally, the IPC member executives bypassed their industry associations and directly engaged their European and Japanese private sector counterparts to press for a TRIPS agreement in the GATT. The transnational leadership of these US-based corporations was decisive in the achievement of the TRIPS accord. The transnational private sector coalition seeking to globalize its preferred conception of IP policy needed GATT to further and legitimize its goals, monitor compliance, and enforce policy.

The agents in this case operated at multiple levels in pursuit of their goals. They were active at the domestic level, pushing for changes in US legislation. Transnationally, they mobilized a private sector coalition supportive of their vision of a trade-based IP regime. They actively pressed their case in international organizations prior to and during the Uruguay Round. They visited government and private sector representatives in countries known for lax IP protection and enforcement. They pleaded their case for a tough multilateral IP instrument to governmental officials in other industrialized states. In short, they used every available access channel to make their views known and to champion their cause.

## Direct and indirect power of the private sector

In capitalist economies, two types of corporate power are noteworthy. Corporations exercise direct, instrumental power when they mobilize resources and pressure. A second, equally important, type of power is indirect and normative. Their provision of information and expertise, their lobbying activities, and exploitation of institutional access reflect direct power, while their "mobilization of bias" and construction of actors' meanings and interests reflect indirect power (Wilks, 1996). Indirect power rests on the general societal acceptance of the corporation as "the dominant and essentially beneficial institution of economic life. That acceptance is manifest in the political weight given to the view of business groups... and the economic weight given to the market performance of such companies" (Wilks, 1996: 45). I will discuss each of these in turn.

The government relies on information provided by corporations. Large transnational corporations are able to provide government officials with potentially useful information about foreign countries. In intellectual property, multinational corporations and their industry associations consistently have provided detailed information about foreign governments' failures to provide adequate IP protection. Corporations have committed considerable resources to expose IP piracy abroad. Furthermore, to determine the scale and scope of foreign piracy, the government has had to rely on loss estimates provided by affected firms. For example, the first official quantitative estimates of distortions in US trade stemming from inadequate IP protection abroad was based on data collected by the International Trade Commission (ITC), which sent out questionnaires to affected industries. Firms interested in a trade-based approach to intellectual property had plenty of incentive to overestimate the losses, especially "knowing that the ITC report would be used by politicians and economists in Washington when they debated whether or not IP protection should become a major issue in international trade negotiations" (Emmert, 1990: 1324–1325). Subsequent independent estimates suggested that the ITC figures were wildly inflated (Gadbaw and Richards, 1988).

The private sector can provide expertise in issue areas not well understood by government. In this regard, intellectual property is especially unusual. Unlike other attorneys, most IP lawyers possess highly technical backgrounds in science, engineering, chemistry, or biochemistry. IP lawyers are privileged purveyors of expertise. The government had to rely on IP experts, typically corporate counsel, who were also advocates, to translate the complexities of IP law into political discourse and make clear the connection between intellectual property and international trade. In the case of intellectual property "technical knowledge was inextricably bound up with a commitment to promote its protection. This gave leading firms in the IPC a decisive advantage over states and other actors in the Uruguay Round negotiations" (Cutler, Haufler, and Porter, 1999: 347).

The IPC member corporations and their industry associations waged an extensive lobbying campaign. They pressed the Congress and successive administrations (Reagan, Bush, and Clinton) to recognize the "critical importance to the United States of trade in goods and services dependent upon intellectual property protection worldwide, and... to help forge the necessary legal tools enabling our trade negotiators to convince foreign nations to take action against massive and debilitating piracy and counterfeiting of US...products" (US Senate, 1986a: 162–164). They packaged their ideas as problem solvers – that support for their robust export industries would help the United States out of its perceived economic decline. They successfully pressed for changes in US trade laws that would institutionalize their desired link between trade and intellectual property. Through amendments to the trade acts in 1979, 1984, and 1988, Congress progressively responded to the demands of the IP lobby, and strengthened the link between IP protection and trade. As Jacques Gorlin, adviser to the IPC, commented, "the transformation of intellectual property into a trade issue and the development of a trade-based approach to improving the protection of intellectual property could not have occurred had the US government and the US private sector not worked closely together" (Gorlin, 1988, in Walker and Bloomfield: 172). The consensus-building process drew upon expertise (identifying the problem, providing information and loss estimates), framing skills (translating arcane IP issues into new instruments of trade policy), and the cognitive appeal of the solutions advocated.

Another important manifestation of the IP activists' direct power was their institutional access through the Advisory Committee for Trade Negotiations (ACTN),[6] constituted by the Executive Branch to solicit private sector views on trade policy. As the top oversight committee of the private sector advisory system for multilateral trade negotiations, ACTN is managed by the USTR in cooperation with the Departments of Commerce, Agriculture, Labor, and Defense (Ostry, 1990: 21–22). The president appoints its members, who played a major role in devising a trade-based IP strategy. The ACTN proved to be an important vehicle for the globalization of the private interests of its member corporations.

Throughout the 1980s, the increasingly vocal IP lobby played a larger role in the formation of US trade policy. Two corporate executives, Edmund Pratt of Pfizer Pharmaceutical and John Opel of IBM, had long been lobbying the US government to get serious about IP violators abroad. Both Pratt and Opel participated in the US-based International Anti-Counterfeiting Coalition (to protect trademarked high fashion and luxury goods) at the end of the Tokyo Round of GATT negotiations. Beginning in 1981, Pratt chaired the ACTN. Pratt and Opel pursued

---

[6] In 1988 ACTN was renamed the Advisory Committee on Trade Policy Negotiations (ACTPN).

parallel efforts during 1983 and 1984 to advance their specific IP concerns to the administration. Another advocate of strong levels of IP protection, John Young, CEO of Hewlett-Packard (and later, founding member of the IPC and the International Intellectual Property Alliance) chaired the president's Commission on Industrial Competitiveness. In December 1984, the Commission issued a special report (as an addendum to the 1983–1984 Commission's Report) describing the impact of poor intellectual property protection on US competitiveness (Gorlin, 1988, in Walker and Bloomfield: 173). In 1984, the USTR requested private sector input on including intellectual property in the upcoming GATT Round. Opel commissioned Jacques Gorlin, an economist who served as a consultant to ACTN and subsequently the IPC, to draft a paper for the USTR outlining a trade-based approach for intellectual property.

Gorlin played a role that is difficult to overestimate. He was the chief architect of the discursive and negotiating strategy that the IPC pursued. Agency is a collective concept, but individuals can make a significant difference in promoting agents' agendas (Archer, 1995: 187). Gorlin articulated a coherent new vision for enveloping IP protection in a trade context and demonstrated impressive intellectual entrepreneurship in connecting the two issues in a very specific way. Gorlin's paper (Gorlin, 1985) became the basis for the multilateral IP strategy that corporations soon pursued. Gorlin's paper provided concrete proposals for a multilateral IP agreement, emphasizing minimum standards of protection, dispute settlement, and enforcement, and suggested strategies for consensus building. ACTN created an eight-member Task Force on Intellectual Property Rights, which included Opel, Fritz Attaway, Vice President and General Counsel of the Motion Picture Association, and Abraham Cohen, President of the International Division of Merck & Company, Inc. (at that time America's largest pharmaceutical corporation). Consultations with the private sector, ACTN's task force, led to Cabinet level discussions on intellectual property and trade in July 1985 and resulted in the government's decision to include intellectual property in the upcoming multilateral negotiations (Simon, 1986: 503). In October 1985, this task force presented its report to ACTN and its recommendations appeared to be lifted wholesale out of Gorlin's paper (USTR, 1985; 1986).

Significantly, Edmund Pratt, CEO of Pfizer, was the Business Roundtable's leader in 1988 as trade and intellectual property began to dominate the US agenda. Pratt was selected to represent the private sector at the Uruguay Round trade talks. Pratt was an adviser to the US

Official Delegation at the Uruguay Round in his capacity as chairman of ACTN. This was auspicious because the private sector had no official standing at GATT. Thus the state, through ACTN, conferred power upon particular agents to advance their IP agenda in multilateral negotiations, underscoring the link between state interests and the private sector.

Corporations also pursue normative power, or the construction of the normative context. This normative context defines right and wrong, and distinguishes fair from unfair practices. It also points to which sets of competing ideas are likely to find favor. In this case, the private sector activists' "expertise and control over information privileged [their] position in the determination of the norms governing the intellectual property regime and enabled the private sphere to shape the definition of the public interest of the United States" (Cutler, Haufler, and Porter, 1999: 350). As Sikkink (1991) has pointed out, particular economic ideas are more likely to prevail – that is, to be supported, adopted, and implemented by policymakers – if they resonate with the broader culture and are considered to be legitimate. As Archer suggests, "the whole point of a material interest group adopting ideas is quintessentially public – to inform and unify supporters or to undercut opponents argumentatively" (Archer, 1995: 306). The IPC's policy advocacy responded to concrete problems facing policymakers in a contingent social context in which US policymakers were trying to respond to changes in the structure of global capitalism.

In cognitive terms, economic ideas perform four basic functions: a cathartic function, which apportions blame; a morale function, which provides a vision of the future; a solidarity function, which provides a rallying device or a basis for building coalitions; and an advocacy function, which stresses empowerment (Woods, 1995: 173–174). The particular ideas promoted by the IPC laid the blame for the United States' growing trade deficit on an outside enemy (foreign "pirates"). Placing the blame for the United States' trade woes on foreign countries' unfair practices helped to sharpen policy options in a way that an extended round of introspection could not. Policymakers were spared the arduous task of evaluating the extent to which US trade problems were the products of either its own or its firms' bad choices. The morale functions of the IPC's policy advocacy were apparent inasmuch as the IPC promised a more robust future for US competitiveness and promoted their member corporations as vibrant industries capable of leading the United States out of its economic doldrums. The IPC agenda also included a solidarity function; the IPC industries united behind a trade-based conception of

IP protection, which became a rallying device for mobilizing a powerful group of industries that could present themselves as part of the solution to the United States' trade woes. They elevated intellectual property to the top tier of the US trade agenda in a way that would permit the United States to maximize its leverage via access to its huge domestic market. Promoting the instrument of trade leverage for resolving disputes over IP protection, the IPC was able to emphasize an avenue that gave the United States a clear advantage, especially *vis-à-vis* developing countries whose access to the US market is imperative for their long-term economic development. Therefore, the ideas and solutions promoted by the IPC captured the imagination of US policymakers as both feasible and politically beneficial.

The private sector activists displayed impressive framing skills in presenting their case to the government and their foreign counterparts not merely by making the link between intellectual property and trade, but by the very terms they used to describe their position. Historically, patent rights were considered to be "grants of privilege." Over time this notion has given way to the notion of "property rights" in intellectual goods. The language of rights weighs in favor of the person claiming the right. The language of privilege weighs in favor of the person granting the privilege. By wrapping themselves in the mantle of "property *rights*" the private sector activists suggested that the rights they were claiming were somehow natural, unassailable, and automatically deserved. They were able to deploy "rights talk" (Weissman, 1996: 1087) effectively in part because they were operating in a context in which property rights are revered; "rights talk" resonated with broader American culture. It is easy to imagine this rhetoric falling flat in a culture that did not hold property rights so dear, or one that balanced them more sharply against competing sets of rights. Their indignation at those violating these "rights" was further underscored by their claims that so-called violators were "pirates." This evocative language highlighted wrongdoing, when in fact many of the activities they decried as "piracy" were absolutely legal in national and international law.

The way that activists frame issues is important (Baumgartner and Jones, 1993; Braithwaite and Drahos, 2000; Cobb and Ross, 1997; Jones, 1994; Litfin, 1995; Risse, 2000), and invoking well-established legal norms and discourse can boost the activists' effectiveness. In the TRIPS case "rights talk" and the rhetoric of "free trade" worked. However, opponents of the activists' agenda can also deploy legal norms to their advantage. For example, in the WIPO digital treaties negotiations discussed in the Introduction, challengers of the TRIPS-style high-protectionist agenda invoked the well-established norm of "fair use" in copyright in order to ensure more balance in the public interest. Similarly, in the ongoing deliberations over IP rights in the context of the sub-Saharan African HIV/AIDS crisis, "public health" is emerging as an increasingly effective counter-framing to the high-protectionist activists. As Chapter 3 will demonstrate, for much of the twentieth century US courts regarded patent "rights" as "monopolies" and thereby subject to the disciplining effect of anti-trust law. At least since the days of Theodore Roosevelt, "monopoly" has had a negative connotation in American culture; it is only recently that patents have escaped that almost automatic association.

In fact, the TRIPS accord stood out in the Uruguay Round agenda because it was not about freeing trade, but extending more protection (Hoekman and Kostecki, 1995: 152). Borrus has characterized the US approach to intellectual property as "quite defensive, trying to hold ground by increasing intellectual property protection" (1993: 376). It is ironic that in the context of both competitiveness and IP debates extending monopoly privileges could be marketed as "freer trade." But conditions of uncertainty create new opportunities to redefine interests, despite the fact that some versions seem to defy logic and come from the wrong side of Alice in Wonderland's Looking Glass. Indeed, the international public policy manager for Hewlett-Packard Company defended his quest as follows:

> Intellectual property protection is the only valid type of 'protectionism' being pushed in Washington now because it is really not traditional protectionism at all. Instead, it is at the heart of an open trading system, and those companies that support the strengthening of the trading system and oppose protectionist approaches are the same ones that need and support better intellectual property protection.
>
> (Bale, in Walker and Bloomfield, 1988: 123)

This rendering only makes sense in the broader context of the policies of the so-called "competition state." This concept assumes that states are increasingly organizing themselves to compete for market share, encourage investment, and achieve economic growth (Strange, 1987, 1996; Cerny, 1995).

One of the most crucial aspects of the IPC's indirect power was its mobilization of its European and Japanese counterparts to develop a consensus on substantive norms for international IP protection. Substantive

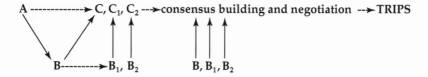

Figure 2.6: The argument (Part 2)
A = antecedent condition, the structure of global capitalism
B = independent variable, private sector activism (US)
$B_1$ = independent variable, private sector activism (Europe)
$B_2$ = independent variable, private sector activism (Japan)
C = intervening variable, institutional change in the United States
$C_1$ = intervening variable, institutional change in Europe
$C_2$ = intervening variable, institutional change in Japan
Dependent variable = TRIPS

norms "represent an understanding between the major actors about the main content of agreements or policies" (Wilks, 1996: 49). The social skills of agents matter a great deal in this process. Intellectual entrepreneurs like Gorlin helped to provide the template to unite disparate actors in a single course of action. His 1985 paper set a negotiating agenda, framed IP issues as trade issues and aggregated interests. As Fligstein points out, "this is what strategic actors must do that is most important. They must find a way in which to join actors or groups with widely different preferences and help reorder those preferences" (Fligstein, 1997: 400). As Lou Clemente, VP General-Counsel of Pfizer, Inc. and founding member of the IPC remarked, "I think the overriding significance of [the IPC] is that it has been able to join together with our colleagues in electronics, in the traditional copyright fields, the chemical industry, and so on, to present a united front on behalf of strong intellectual property protection" (C.L. Clemente, 1988, in Walker and Bloomfield: 134). This phase of the process is depicted in Figure 2.6. This process was "not just about the construction of shared meanings, but [also] about power and actions taken in producing... current arrangements" (Fligstein, 1997: 404).

From the time of its formation in March 1986, the IPC only had six months before the upcoming September Punta del Este meeting. IPC members immediately contacted their counterparts in European and Japanese industry. In June 1986, the IPC met with the Confederation of British Industries, the Bundesverband der Deutschen Industrie (BDI) in Germany, the French Patronat, and through them, with the Union of Industrial and Employers' Confederations of Europe (UNICE).

UNICE is the official representative of European business and industry in European institutions; it is composed of thirty-three member federations from twenty-two countries. In July, the IPC went to Japan and met with the Japan Federation of Economic Organizations (Keidanren hereafter). Keidanren is a private, non-profit economic organization representing virtually all branches of economic activity in Japan.

In these meetings, the IPC stressed that the issue of intellectual property was too important to leave to governments.[7] The group argued that industry needed to decide upon the best course of action and then tell governments what to do. The IPC convinced their European and Japanese counterparts of the merits of a trade-based approach by emphasizing their shared experience and common plight. The IPC stressed the high costs of IP piracy, and the successes that it had achieved through bilateral trade negotiations. The IPC succeeded in forging an industry consensus with its European and Japanese counterparts, who agreed to work on it and pledged to present these views to their respective governments in time for the launching of the Uruguay Round. As Pratt noted, this joint action by the US, European, and Japanese business communities represented "a significant breakthrough in the involvement of the international business community in trade negotiations" (quoted in Drahos, 1995: 13). UNICE and Keidanren successfully advanced their new cause to their governments. By the launching of the new trade round in September, the United States, Japan, and Europe were united behind the inclusion of an IP code in the GATT.

The IPC, UNICE, and Keidanren agreed to continue to work together to devise a consensual approach to an IP code at the GATT. Industry representatives met in October and November 1986, and worked on producing a consensus document to present to their respective governments and the GATT Secretariat. Participants made a concerted effort to "honestly represent all forms of intellectual property and all industries concerned" (Enyart, 1990: 55). In June 1988, this "trilateral group" released its "Basic Framework of GATT Provisions on Intellectual Property" (IPC, Keidanren, and UNICE, 1988). This document was strikingly similar to Gorlin's 1985 paper, covering minimum standards of protection, enforcement and dispute settlement provisions, and became the basis of the eventual TRIPS agreement. It was a consensus document that included compromises. For instance, the US research-based

[7] This paragraph is based on the author's interview with Gorlin, January 22, 1996, Washington, DC.

54

pharmaceutical industry was not completely satisfied with the compulsory licensing provisions, but the IPC conceded the issue to keep the Europeans and Japanese on board. Having produced this consensus proposal, the IPC, Keidranen, and UNICE had to go home and sell the approach to other companies and industries (Enyart, 1990: 55). This process was not at all difficult for the IPC, which faced a very receptive home government; the US government sent out the June 1988 proposal as reflecting its own views.[8]

The private sector's normative power was consolidated and institutionalized in so far as it "elevated its own self-interest to the status of a substantive norm" and established "understandings about what is proper, natural and legitimate" that reflected "the interests of the big corporate players" (Wilks, 1996: 49–50).

In the TRIPS negotiations the IPC had a potent ally at the Uruguay Round in Edmund Pratt of Pfizer, who was an adviser to the US Official Delegation at the Round in his capacity as chairman of ACTN. The IPC worked closely with the USTR, the Commerce Department, and the Patent and Trademark Office (PTO). A 1988 IPC report stated that "this close relationship with USTR and Commerce has permitted the IPC to shape the US proposals and negotiating positions during the course of the negotiations" (Drahos, 1995: 13).

The adoption of TRIPS marks the end of the first morphogenetic cycle. "The process is not endless; the very fact that Structural and Cultural Elaboration takes place signals that some alliance has won out to a sufficient degree to entrench something of the change it sought and thus to re-start a new cycle of interaction embodying this change as part and parcel of its conditional influences" (Archer, 1995: 322). Expressing satisfaction with the final 1994 TRIPS agreement Gorlin said that the IPC got 95 percent of what it wanted.[9]

## The new global intellectual property regime

The triumph of the IPC was the triumph of a small fraction of the private sector. Structural factors tipped the scale in the direction of the privileged agents and their preferred policies, but it took the actions of agents to ensure this outcome. This case demonstrates how agents transformed the structure through their actions. The TRIPS accord redefines

[8] Author's interview with Gorlin.
[9] Author's interview with Gorlin; I will be discussing the "5 percent" that the IPC did not get in Chapter 6.

winners and losers and the WTO institutionalizes a more aggressively liberal world trading order. This expanded approach is now a structural feature that either constrains or empowers agents. The TRIPS component of the WTO empowers the IPC. But, at the same time, opponents of TRIPS have mobilized to confront what they perceive to be its excesses.

TRIPS, like the previous IP regime, was socially constructed but in this cycle confronts actors as an object or a structure. TRIPS as a structural feature ($T^4$ of the first cycle, $T^1$ of the second cycle), exerts conditioning effects by dividing the population into those in favor of it and those opposed to it. TRIPS is a specific instance of the more general phenomenon that Archer identifies. At this point in the cycle *TRIPS is there*, to be exploited, defended, and perhaps extended by those who favor it; but for those who are negatively affected by it, "the problem is how to get rid of [it] or deal with [it]" (Archer, 1982: 461). The distributional effects of TRIPS create new corporate agents as formerly "primary agents" come to resent TRIPS. Vested interest groups supporting TRIPS actually spawn "differentiation and ideational diversification as part and parcel of the *pursuit* of vested interests which is better pictured as an exercise in accumulation than the protection of fixed assets" (Archer, 1995: 263–264). The "noisy public process" of discourse and issue framing in defense of TRIPS identifies the vested interest group with a position that others can come to oppose (Archer, 1995: 306, 315).

This time newly activated corporate agents deploy organizational and discursive strategies to confront the consequences of TRIPS. At the time of the TRIPS negotiations most people had no idea what the agreement would mean for their lives. Yet an agreement so broad, so sweeping, so deeply intrusive into domestic regulatory systems, was bound to touch many people. Additionally, the fact that the TRIPS architects wasted no time in reaping the fruits of their victory, demanding rapid enforcement and even TRIPS-plus[10] implementation, hastened the process whereby formerly "primary agents" became corporate agents. It quickly became apparent that this agreement was going to hurt many more people than it would help, at least in the short run; and that the price was not going to be paid in dollars alone but also in human lives. In the face of the HIV/AIDS pandemic many people came to believe that the apparent requirements of TRIPS were unconscionable.

[10] TRIPS-plus refers to standards that either are more extensive than TRIPS standards, or that eliminate options under TRIPS standards (Drahos, 2001: 793).

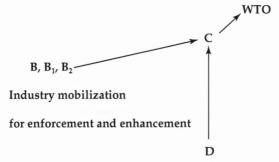

TRIPS

**WTO**

**C**

**B, B₁, B₂**

**Industry mobilization**

**for enforcement and enhancement**

**D**

**Mobilization of opposition**

Figure 2.7: The argument (Part 3)
B, B₁, B₂ = private sector activism (US, Europe, and Japan)
C = OECD governments
D = mobilized opposition to private sector activism
Dependent variable = New global intellectual property regime

In this case, consumer and health groups on the front lines of the HIV/AIDS pandemic mobilized to protest the high cost of HIV/AIDS drugs, the subsequent lack of access to the drugs, and the dangers of overly strong intellectual property protection as embodied in TRIPS. They presented an alternative framing of intellectual property as a public health issue, not a trade issue. Suddenly the struggle over TRIPS became competitive and created a new political context for the consideration of IP issues.

TRIPS' supporters sought to protect and defend TRIPS, whereas consumer advocacy and public health groups mobilized to oppose and dilute (if not eliminate) it. Just as structure created and delineated new agents in the first morphogenetic cycle leading to TRIPS, TRIPS delineated new agents in the form of the most deeply and adversely affected and their advocates. As Drahos points out, "during the TRIPS negotiations international NGOs and African states were not significant players. The two most striking features in terms of actors involved in the post-TRIPS scene has been the engagement of international NGOs in TRIPS issues and the leadership of the Africa group on health and biodiversity issues" (Drahos, 2002: 26). The new element in the political equation was the mobilized opposition to the TRIPS' architects. This is depicted in Figures 2.7 and 2.8.

With the exception of initial developing country resistance, opposition to TRIPS emerged rather late – after its adoption. This implies that

**WTO/TRIPS**

[subset of A]

---

**T1 Structural conditioning**

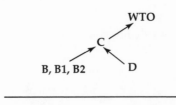

---

**T2 Social interaction**          **T3**

**Partial victory of protesters to**

**ease TRIPS restrictions on**

**medicines (e.g., Doha Declaration;**

**Global Fund)**

---

**Structural elaboration? (ongoing) T4**

Figure 2.8: Morphogenetic cycle 2 (incomplete; in progress)
A = antecedent condition, the structure of global capitalism
B = independent variable, private sector activism (US)
$B_1$ = independent variable, private sector activism (Europe)
$B_2$ = independent variable, private sector activism (Japan)
C = intervening variable, institutions in the United States, Europe and Japan
D = mobilized opposition to private sector activism
Dependent variable = Doha Declaration and new intellectual property regime

while TRIPS cannot be "undone" in any direct sense, the fight over loopholes, alternative interpretations of vague language, and perhaps, most importantly, effective resistance to further expansion of global intellectual property rights lies ahead. This suggests some limits to the type of governance that TRIPS' architects had in mind, but it also opens up the possibilities for more balanced and democratic governance of intellectual property. The deck still is stacked in favor of a commercial, as opposed to social, agenda but the access to medicines campaign has had an impact and is gaining significant momentum. Its most recent triumph was the WTO member countries' endorsement of the Declaration on the TRIPS Agreement and Public Health.[11]

## The rest of the book

Chapters 3 and 4 cover part one of my argument as depicted in Figure 2.5. They describe and explain institutional change in the United States. Chapter 3 provides an historical analysis of IP policy in the United States and demonstrates how IP policy has always been embedded in broader public policy issues. It particularly focuses on the judiciary. Chapter 4 examines institutional changes in the executive and legislative branches adopted in the wake of the Watergate scandal that increased private sector access to trade policymaking. It explores the United States' growing concern with competitiveness in the early 1980s, and the role of industry associations in changing domestic IP laws. These domestic changes are noteworthy because a number of provisions in these laws reappeared in the final TRIPS agreement. Chapter 5 addresses part two of the argument, as depicted in Figure 2.6. It addresses issues of agency more directly by documenting the activities of the private sector advocates of high protectionist norms. It focuses on the IPC, the mobilization of a transnational private sector consensus, and the negotiations which ultimately led to the adoption of the TRIPS Agreement. Chapter 6 examines the new global IP regime, the second morphogenetic cycle, as depicted in Figures 2.7 and 2.8. It highlights the tension between commercial and social agendas in the wake of TRIPS. Finally, Chapter 7 offers a comparative perspective on this case and examines implications of the argument.

[11] "Declaration on the TRIPS Agreement and Public Health," WT/MIN(01)/DEC/2,20 November 2001. http://www.wto.org/english/thewto_e/minist_e/min01/mindecl_trips_e.htm

# 3  US intellectual property rights in historical perspective

I argue that the recent globalization of intellectual property rights originated in the United States. This chapter provides historical background of US IP protection, underscoring just how recent and dramatic the US commitment to stronger IP protection has been. It has effectively reversed about 75 years worth of policy skepticism over the merits of strict IP protection. The chapter discusses the formation of the Court of Appeals for the Federal Circuit (CAFC) in 1982 and its role in changing the domestic environment for patent holders. Several landmark court cases, *Devex* v. *General Motors* and *Kodak* v. *Polaroid*, highlight the extent of this change. Furthermore, governmental concerns over competitiveness in the 1980s led to changes in anti-trust policy, documented here, that redounded to the benefit of IP owners. Overall, the historical trends point to a dramatically improved domestic environment for IP owners, and a noteworthy redefinition of US interests in IP protection. These domestic changes paved the way, and provided much of the substance, for the ultimately successful US quest to globalize its new commitment to strict IP protection.

## US intellectual property rights in historical perspective

The United States included intellectual property in the Constitution, Article I, Section 8, which authorized Congress to "promote the progress of Science and the useful Arts by securing for limited times to Authors and Inventors the exclusive right to their respective Writings and discoveries." The emphasis on "useful Arts" underscores the commercial intent of the legislation and the utilitarian rationale behind it. IP rights were devised to create incentives for innovation and risk-taking. This is consistent with both Benthamite and Lockean notions of property: "with property rights people have an incentive to labour and industry will prosper" (Drahos, 1996: 201).

## Copyrights

The United States passed its first Copyright Act in 1790, which gave citizens and residents a copyright for fourteen years, renewable for an additional fourteen if the author was still alive. During the depression of the 1830s, which ravaged the American book trade as much as it did other economic sectors, cheap magazines and newspapers proliferated and indiscriminately reprinted works of foreign authors without even the pretense of acknowledgment (Feather, 1994: 154). The reprinters' activities were perfectly legal under US copyright law, which provided no protection for authors not living in the United States.

These practices prompted a group of British authors to petition the US Congress for copyright protection in 1836. They found a sympathetic audience in Senator Henry Clay of Kentucky, who presented the British petition to both the House of Representatives and the Senate. Faced with ardent opposition from a number of American publishers, Clay attempted to mollify the opposition by incorporating a provision "which was to bedevil the American position in international copyright for the rest of the century and beyond" (Feather, 1994: 158). This provision, which came to be known as the "manufacturing clause," would make the "granting of copyright to foreign authors dependent upon their books being manufactured in the United States" (Feather, 1994: 158). While the law did not pass, the so-called manufacturing clause was resuscitated and incorporated in the Chase Act of 1891 and was not permitted to expire until 1986.

The 1790 Federal Copyright Act, and its successor of 1831, included a provision that copyrights could only be acquired through registration. The law required authors to register their work first, by depositing a copy of the title page with the Register of Copyrights in Washington, and second, after publication by sending a copy of the book to the Library of Congress (Feather, 1994: 166). Years later, this domestic law proved to be inconsistent with the international agreement on copyright, the Berne Convention of 1886, which made the acquisition of copyright by the author/owner automatic upon authorized publication in any member state. Berne signatories could not require registration as a precondition for granting copyright. Therefore, the United States was excluded from the Berne Convention.

A group of publishers formed the American Copyright League in 1884 to press for domestic and international copyright reform. The exclusion of the United States from the Berne Convention provoked the League in 1887 to undertake a vigorous lobbying effort to change US law in conformity with Berne. Between 1886 and 1890, Congress considered numerous copyright bills but the Democrats opposed each and every one. Democratic supporters, primarily in the South,

> were bitterly antipathetic to any measure which would open up Amer-ican markets to foreign competition, or ... increase the price of books, as many feared that it would. The opposition was not only political. The publishers of cheap reprint series were against it, and so too were the increasingly powerful trade unions in the printing industry who feared loss of work if the copyright in imported books were protected under American law. It was a concession on the last point which finally allowed the bill to pass, but the same concession caused the continued exclusion of the United States from the growing international consen-sus on copyright protection. (Feather, 1994: 168)

The final bill, the Chase Act of 1891, incorporated the manufacturing clause first suggested by Senator Clay in 1837. In order to appease the printing workers' unions, foreign authors could obtain US copyright protection only if their work was published in the United States not later than it was published in its country of origin; and foreigners' works had to be printed in the United States, or printed from type set in the United States, or from plates made from type set in the United States (Feather, 1994: 168). This manufacturing clause went directly against the principles of the Berne Convention, which forbade any law that required authors to publish their works in a particular country in order to obtain and protect their rights. Therefore, the United States continued to remain outside the international agreement until 1986, when the clause was finally allowed to expire.[1]

---

[1] Previously the United States had been instrumental in organizing the Universal Copy-right Convention. The UCC was adopted at a UNESCO conference in Geneva in 1952 and revised in Paris in 1971. It formalized the use of the universal copyright symbol (the circled 'c'). Though weaker than Berne, the UCC gave countries unwilling or unable to ratify Berne, such as the United States, some measure of international protection for their national authors. See Sell and May (2001).

## Twentieth-century copyright

In Jessica Litman's masterful survey of US copyright law (Litman, 1989), she reveals a pattern of incremental change in which private stake-holders draft narrow legislation that favors their interests. The context-specific nature of the legislation has rendered it inflexible and unable to adapt to technological change. Therefore, each time a new technology appears, whether player pianos or computer software, the process repeats itself to the detriment of the public weal. Narrowly tailored, industry-specific provisions are injected, and copyright owners receive broader and more expansive rights. Litman documents the process of negotiated bargains among industry representatives that has resulted in a striking expansion of copyrightable subject matter. As Litman points out:

> the dynamics of inter-industry negotiations tend to encourage fact-specific solutions to inter-industry disputes. The participants' frustration with the rapid aging of narrowly defined rights has inspired them to collaborate in drafting rights more broadly. No comparable tendency has emerged to inject breadth or flexibility into the provisions *limiting* those rights. (Litman, 1989: 333; emphasis added)

The legislative process has tended to exclude the public and thereby has privileged the private interests of authors and owners at the expense of the public interest in the use and reuse of copyrighted information (Aoki, 1996: 1310).

Over time, the scope of subject matter eligible for copyright protection has broadened considerably. For example, as Cornish points out, "the major computer lobbyists in the United States pressed for computer programs to be protected by accretion, that is, by treating them as literary works within traditional norms of copyright; and they now have persuaded much of the world to adopt this approach" (Cornish, 1993: 55). Under TRIPS computer programs are protected as "literary works." While some users of copyrighted information have protested this expansion of copyright, the recent trend has been to protect more rather than less.[2]

The debate over semiconductor chip protection was hotly contested, and exemplified how new technologies complicate the identification of

[2] For an exception to this trend, see the discussion of the victories of the interoperable developers, such as Sun Microsystems, over the advocates of high-protectionist norms, such as IBM and Microsoft, in Band and Katoh (1995). For the high-protectionist norms advocates' position see Clapes (1993).

intellectual property. In the early 1980s American semiconductor chip manufacturers, faced with escalating competition from Japanese producers, sought to gain protection of the design structure (or "architecture") of semiconductor chips (mask works). They bemoaned the inadequacy of existing IP regimes to protect their products. While they initially sought to obtain patent protection, their chips often failed to meet the requisite standards of novelty and inventiveness (Drahos, 1997). Therefore, they sought protection by accretion into the broader copyright regime. However, user groups, such as the American Association of Publishers (AAP), successfully resisted this effort. The AAP represented a broad group of industries that uniformly opposed copyright protection for semiconductor mask works, "viewing the proposed terms a serious breach of fundamental copyright principles" (Doremus, 1995: 159).

The semiconductor industry reached a consensus to abandon its copyright initiative and instead devised a *sui generis* solution. The Semiconductor Chip Protection Act of 1984 provided an entirely new form of IP protection based in part on copyright, and embodying reciprocity. The Act protected both the mask works, which are fixed in semiconductor chips, and the chips themselves. The Act provided for a short-term, 10-year protection against copying the chip design, and provided such protection only to those foreign nationals whose countries had adopted a similar law. While this was a domestic law, the international ramifications were made quite clear from the outset. The United States broke new ground by extending protection to mask works, and incorporating extensive transition provisions to facilitate reciprocal protection by other countries (Sell, 1998: 136). The TRIPS agreement also includes this *sui generis* protection.

## Patents

Throughout most of the nineteenth century, America was a net technology importer. As Merges points out:

> some technology was obtained despite foreign intellectual property-type claims. For example, in the early days of steam engine technology, Britain forbade the export of engines, parts, and skilled personnel. The US imported all three regardless. Recognition of British rights might have yielded a net benefit to the US, but that is doubtful. The decision was made in the US that at that stage of economic development, the best policy for the US was lax enforcement of foreign intellectual property. (Merges, 1990: 245)

This preference for weak protection changed in the latter half of the nineteenth century when US firms began to achieve significant technological breakthroughs. Thomas Edison's incandescent carbon filament lamp is but one of the more prominent examples. US firms, such as the Edison Company, pressed for strong IP protection in the negotiations over the Paris Convention in 1883.

The evolution of US patent policies was deeply intertwined with anti-trust.[3] The economic power of patents reached its zenith in the *laissez-faire* era at the end of the nineteenth century and the beginning of the twentieth. The Supreme Court elevated patent power in its decision in *Henry* v. *A. B. Dick & Co.*[4] in 1912. The A. B. Dick company owned a patent for its mimeograph machine. The company sold its machine with a tag license that required purchasers to buy A. B. Dick's ink, even though the ink was not protected by a patent. This is known as a tying clause whereby the patentee requires purchasers to buy an unpatented article; in anti-trust parlance this is a form of vertical restraint. The Supreme Court condoned this practice and held that a patentee "could extract whatever price or other concession he chose as a consideration for granting a patent license, including the purchase of unpatented articles to be used in conjunction with a patented machine" (Kastriner, 1991: 6). The Court reasoned that had the patentee kept the invention to himself, "no ink could have been sold by others for use upon machines embodying that invention" (244 US 1 (1912) at 33; quoted in Kobak, Jr., 1995).

However, this patent power was short lived. The passage of the Sherman Anti-trust Act ushered in an era of anti-trust dominance, beginning with the Court overruling the *A. B. Dick Case* "with its heavy hand suppressing the patent law," that was to last seventy-five years (Kastriner, 1991: 6). Throughout most of the twentieth century patents were considered to be monopolies rather than necessary incentives for innovation. The concept of patent misuse first arose in 1917, and found its inspiration in Section 3 of the 1914 Clayton Act which expressly forbid tying clauses. In 1917 the Supreme Court reversed the *A. B. Dick* ruling and in *Motion Picture Patent Co.* v. *Universal Film Mfg. Co.*[5] "struck down the tying arrangement between a patented movie projector and the use of unpatented film sold by the patentee" (Kastriner, 1991: 18). The Court reasoned that "tie-ins allowed the patent owner to obtain

---

[3] Commonly known as competition policy outside of the United States.
[4] 244 US 1 (1912).     [5] 243 US 502, 518 (1917).

*de facto* 'monopolies' over non-patented claims by extending their patents to cover non-claimable items" (Kobak, 1995: para. 5).

From that time forward, the Court continued to strike down tying arrangements as being inconsistent with the overriding public policy of promoting free competition. Patent rights were construed as monopolies, market power was presumed and these rights were subordinated to the dominant anti-trust policy. The concept of patent misuse reached its zenith in a series of cases in the 1940s, including the *Mercoid*[6] cases and *Morton Salt Co.* v. *G. S. Suppinger Co.*[7] As Kobak suggests, these decisions "alarmed the patent bar ... [because] misuse became a *per se* defense that an infringer could successfully use to escape all liability. In this respect it proved to be a real windfall for patent infringers" (1995: para. 7). Referring to the doctrine of patent misuse, William Nicoson complained that "in this welter of opportunity for judicial absolution, it must be a dull rascal indeed who cannot make patent piracy pay" (1962: 92, quoted in *Harvard Law Review*, 1997: at note 21).

This anti-patent environment, characterized by vigorous anti-trust enforcement and judicial attacks on the scope and validity of patents, led US businesses to question the economic value of patent protection. More often than not, the courts presumed patents to be invalid, and patentees were criticized for setting monopoly prices for inventions that were already in the public domain (Dreyfuss, 1989: 6). Would-be domestic competitors had little to fear from infringing behavior. For example, in 1976 when Eastman Kodak sought to develop an instant camera to compete with Polaroid, its development committee issued an internal directive that stated: "Development should not be constrained by what an individual feels is potential patent infringement" (quoted in Silverstein, 1991: 307).

Since patents were frequently held to be invalid and infringers faced low penalties that usually amounted to payment of a royalty, US businesses sought other means of protection from competition, such as trade secret protection, government subsidies combined with high secrecy levels (in defense industries), and "voluntary" export quotas (for the automobile industry) (Silverstein, 1991: 291). However, not all industries could take advantage of these alternative forms of protection and the demise of the US patent system throughout the 1940s and until the early 1980s had deleterious effects in sectors such as consumer electronics. In

---

[6] *Mercoid*, 320 US 661; *Mercoid Corp.* v. *Minneapolis-Honeywell Regulator Co.*, 320 US 680 (1944) (sustaining anti-trust liability); and *Mercoid* 320 US at 669.
[7] 314 US 488 (1942).

this environment "few American businesses were willing to undertake the financial risks of commercializing new technologies" (Silverstein, 1991: 305). Therefore, while US firms pioneered technologies such as the transistor, the video cassette recorder, and the integrated circuit, other countries, most notably Japan, successfully commercialized these US inventions. In fact, by the late 1960s Japan came to dominate the global consumer electronics market.

The lax US domestic patent environment began to change in 1980 and the Supreme Court signaled a new attitude toward patents. In its ruling in *Dawson Chem. Co.* v. *Rohm & Haas Co.*,[8] the Court stated that "the policy of free competition runs deep in our law ... but the policy of stimulating invention that underlies the entire patent system runs no less deep" (quoted in Kastriner, 1991: 20). For the first time since the *A.B. Dick* case, the Supreme Court placed the public policy of supporting patent rights on an equal footing with the public policy of supporting free competition, and "effectively ended the era of anti-trust dominance over patent law in the eyes of the judiciary" (Kastriner, 1991: 20). The rights of owners of intellectual property became more important as these owners were increasingly likely to deliver economic development and competitiveness objectives valued by the US government.[9]

## The creation of the "patent court"

Another important development in the changing judicial approach towards patents was the establishment of the Court of Appeals for the Federal Circuit (CAFC) in 1982. The Court was established as part of the United States' most comprehensive judicial reform. In important respects, the establishment of the CAFC has had unintended consequences that have redounded to the benefit of patent holders and have had a profound effect on the dramatic changes in US policy on intellectual property. The CAFC has resulted in a significant increase in the economic power of patents. While concern for innovation animated some of the debate leading up to the creation of the CAFC, its origins lie in the more pedestrian concerns of docket management and uniformity in the law.

The origins of the CAFC go back to the early 1970s when the appellate court structure became seriously overloaded and many areas of the law lacked national uniformity. Most patent cases were heard in

---

[8] 448 US 176 (1980).    [9] I thank Chris May for urging me to clarify this point.

the various regional circuit courts of appeals, and the Supreme Court was the only court "capable of rendering authoritative declarations of national law" (Lever, 1982: 186). With the appellate system under untenable pressure, with a five-fold increase in court filings between 1962 and 1981 – from just under 5,000 cases to over 26,000 cases (Lever, 1982: 186, note 30), and mounting docket congestion at the Supreme Court, a 1972 study group – the Freund Committee – recommended the creation of a National Court of Appeals. That same year, Congress created the Hruska Commission to evaluate the appellate system and recommend changes. Like the Freund Committee, it also recommended a National Court of Appeals. The Hruska Commission highlighted the inability of the appellate court system to definitively adjudicate issues of national law, which had the effect of rendering the law uncertain and unpredictable. An undesirable consequence was rampant and costly forum shopping among the circuit courts of appeal; the Hruska Commission concluded that the problem was most acute in the area of patent law. While the two groups' proposals went nowhere, the insights provided by the Hruska Commission resurfaced in subsequent reform deliberations.

The Justice Department revisited the issue of judicial reform in 1977, and in 1978 issued a memorandum that ultimately became the basis for the creation of the CAFC. The memorandum called for a merging of the Court of Claims and the Court of Customs and Patent Appeals to create a single forum for patent cases. Congress vigorously debated the proposed establishment of the CAFC for several years. Congress passed the bill creating the Court in March 1982 and President Reagan signed it into law on April 2, 1982.

The debates over the creation of the CAFC are instructive in so far as they provide insight into the diagnosis of the "patent problem" and anticipate the proposed benefits of such a court. The central problem that CAFC advocates identified was uneven application of patent law in the various circuit courts. Some circuits favored infringers, whereas others favored patentees. For example, between 1945 and 1957, a patent was nearly four times more likely to be enforced in the Seventh Circuit than in the Second Circuit (Dreyfuss, 1989: 7). Infringers scrambled to have their cases heard in the lenient circuit courts, whereas patentees fought to have their cases heard in the stricter Fifth, Sixth, and Seventh Circuits. Forum shopping, and requests to have patent infringement appeals transferred to different circuits, injected considerable uncertainty into patent litigation. When 250 US companies engaged in industrial research were surveyed by the Industrial Research Institute on the question of a single patent court, the vast majority of respondents indicated that the uncertainty, complexity, and inconsistencies in patent enforceability eroded the full economic value of the patent (Lever, 1982: 198 at note 61). In this convoluted legal environment patents could not be considered sufficient incentives to invest in research and development (Dreyfuss, 1989: 7). Furthermore, forum shopping increased the length and cost of litigation, and made it difficult for patent attorneys to advise clients.

The stakes rose sharply after the 1972 Supreme Court decision in *Blonder-Tongue Laboratories Inc.* v. *University of Illinois Foundation* which barred a patent owner from re-litigating patent validity against a new defendant: "This meant that a patent owner had only 'one bite at the apple'; if the case were tried in an anti-patent forum, the owner stood to lose not merely the one lawsuit but his entire patent" (Silverstein, 1991: 309). In this high stakes and inherently unpredictable environment, proponents of a CAFC argued that a single court would eliminate forum shopping and inconsistent court rulings, provide more uniformity in patent law and thereby facilitate innovation by reducing doubt as to what protection is available for inventions (Lever, 1982: 198–199).

Opponents of the CAFC questioned the extent to which inter-circuit conflict existed, and argued that claims of forum shopping were exaggerated. They also raised concerns that a patent court, like any specialized court, might be prone to isolation and susceptibility to special interest groups (Lever, 1982: 202). If the court were to become either pro-patent or anti-patent, the dangers of concentrated judicial decisionmaking power could have a negative impact on the law (Lever, 1982: 203–204). In the end, supporters of the CAFC addressed most of the objections raised by opponents. Most importantly, they were able to dispense with fears attendant to specialized courts because the CAFC's docket would not be limited to patents alone but would encompass tariff and customs law, trademarks, technology transfer regulations, and government contract and labor disputes (Lever, 1982: 204).

Since the CAFC's establishment in 1982, decisions of the court have not only consolidated technical and legal criteria for determining patent infringement, but have raised substantially the level of damage and royalty compensation awarded to successful patent-owner litigants. The activation of the CAFC has ushered in a more vigorous approach to the enforcement of patent holders' rights. The CAFC's decisions have reflected a more pro-patent approach and have supported higher damage awards than the decisions of previous Courts of Appeal. The CAFC has invigorated the presumption of validity of patent rights, "making the challenger's case harder to sustain" (Dreyfuss, 1989: 26). Parties challenging the validity of a patent now have "the burden of establishing invalidity by 'clear and convincing' evidence" (Kastriner, 1991: 11). Under the CAFC, references to patents as "monopolies" have all but disappeared (Kastriner, 1991: 9).

In terms of enforcement, the CAFC has raised the costs of infringement substantially. The CAFC has enabled patentees to receive much higher compensatory damages by adopting new methods of computing lost profits or reasonable royalties; it has awarded patentees lost profits from the sale of related goods and allows patentees to include the drain on human and financial resources in calculating lost profits (Dreyfuss, 1989:19). Permanent injunctions against infringers are now available to patentees immediately upon successfully establishing validity and infringement at trial (Kastriner, 1991: 12). Overall, the CAFC has been a good court for patentees (Dreyfuss, 1989: 26).

The Supreme Court has also contributed to this improved legal environment for patent holders. In 1982 the Court handed down a landmark decision in *General Motors* v. *Devex*. Prior to the *Devex* decision, in infringement cases in which the patent owner prevailed, interest would be awarded from the date of infringement (as opposed to the date of judgment) *only* in exceptional cases. Under the old system successful litigants could not expect compensation based on damages from the date of actual infringement, but only from the much later date of the court's decision. *Devex* reversed this, and now prejudgment interest is common in infringement cases in which the patent owner prevails. Furthermore, since the *Devex* holding, numerous patent infringement awards have included "staggering" amounts of prejudgment interest (Whipple, 1987: 110).

Two CAFC decisions, in 1983 and 1986 respectively, have had additional important effects. In *Smith International* v. *Hughes Tool* (1983), the court emphasized that since a patent right is the right to exclude others, courts should feel free to grant permanent injunctions once a patent has been held valid and infringed. This signaled a further shift in public policy in favor of patent holders in so far as the court ruled that "public policy favors 'protection of rights secured by valid patents,' adding that 'public policy favors the innovator, not the copier'" (Kastriner, 1991: 13–14). This is clearly a far cry from the earlier judicial suspicion of the monopoly aspects of patent rights.

However, the CAFC perhaps made its greatest mark in its 1986 decision in *Polaroid Corp.* v. *Eastman Kodak*. Polaroid was suing Kodak for infringing Polaroid patents for instant cameras. The US District Court of Massachusetts found that Kodak had indeed infringed the Polaroid patents and, relying on the *Smith International* case, issued an injunction barring Kodak from further infringement. Kodak protested and argued that the injunction would force it to lay off 800 workers and cause it to lose its $200 million investment in the plant (Kastriner, 1991: 14). Nonetheless, the District Court awarded Polaroid the injunction. Finding that Kodak's infringement had been "willful and deliberate, the court left open the possibility of assessing treble damages, costs and attorney's fees totaling more than $1 billion against Kodak" (Silverstein, 1991: 306). The CAFC affirmed all aspects of the District Court's decision. As Silverstein points out, "what made American business sit up and take notice . . . was that the outcome effectively restored to Polaroid a virtual monopoly over the United States market in instant photography" (Silverstein, 1991: 307). The Kodak–Polaroid case was widely regarded as the most striking instance of an increasingly pro-patent sentiment in US courts. The case demonstrated that "a successful patent infringement case can eliminate a competitor from a business, as well as costing the infringer over a billion dollars in damages and related costs," and signaled to businessmen that infringement is "no longer an economically feasible option" (Kastriner, 1991: 15).

The decisively pro-patent trend of the court raises some of the issues of regulatory capture that initial opponents of the CAFC feared. However, the picture is somewhat more complex than simple regulatory capture in so far as the court may well be influenced by broader public policy concerns. The preceding historical discussion has underscored that the development of US IP law has hardly been immune to the broader economic and political climate. Whether it is the courts striking down patent rights in favor of anti-trust objectives, or the Congress retaining mercantilist elements in US copyright law to appease the printing workers' unions, the history of IP protection in the United States is both embedded in and reflects the prevailing climate. With regard to the pro-patent orientation of the CAFC, in the years since its founding there has been

> a major reorientation of national competitive policy and increased appreciation of the role of high technology in the nation's economy. These changes can be seen in anti-trust enforcement policy . . . and in the Supreme Court's new sympathy towards . . . protection of intellectual

property. Although the Patent Act has not changed dramatically in that time, it should not be surprising that the CAFC has geared its interpretation of the Act to the current climate.    (Dreyfuss, 1989: 27)

In short, "the CAFC's leanings towards patentees may not be so much evidence of capture as recognition of national priorities" (Dreyfuss, 1989: 28, at note 174).

## Intellectual property and anti-trust

This resurgence in patent rights in the 1980s was intertwined with a relaxation of formerly stringent anti-trust policies. As demonstrated above, anti-trust law used to foster the view that IP rights created monopolies and therefore conflicted with anti-trust law. Throughout the 1980s anti-trust law increasingly recognized that IP rights, including patent rights, do not *necessarily* "confer monopolies or even market power in any relevant market" (Webb and Locke, 1991: at note 29). The US Department of Justice underscored this position as follows: "market power or even a monopoly that is the result of superior effort, acumen, foresight, or luck does not violate the anti-trust laws. The owner of intellectual property is entitled to enjoy whatever market power the property itself may confer" (US Department of Justice, 1988: S-16).

The Reagan Administration expressed concern about US industries' ability to compete more effectively in world markets and codified its more permissive approach to anti-trust in the Antitrust Division's Merger Control Guidelines of 1982. Reflecting the influence of the Chicago school of economics the new guidelines abandoned a populist focus on market structure in favor of the Chicago school's focus on price theory. In this view anti-competitive business practices are those that reduce output and increase prices; business practices that expand output are pro-competitive (Sell, 1998: 158). In contrast to earlier approaches, according to the Chicago school, "high levels of market concentration and the exercise of market power may be indicative of efficiencies" (Eisner, 1991: 105). The 1982 guidelines presented an expanded definition of relevant markets; this had permissive effects. The guidelines allowed the introduction of non-structural factors, such as foreign competition or the possession of a new technology that was important to long-term competitiveness (Eisner, 1991: 198). The Justice Department argued that "anti-trust laws should not be applied in a way that hinders the renewed emphasis on competitiveness" (Hoff, 1986: 19).

With regard to intellectual property, guidelines issued in 1988 rescinded the "Nine No-Nos" embodied in the 1977 Justice Department guide for licensing practices (US Department of Justice, 1977). The 1977 guide had listed nine *per se* illegal practices that included tying arrangements and other restrictions a patentee might try to impose on a licensee that are not directly related to the patented item or process.[10] In the early 1980s the Justice Department abandoned the Nine No-Nos in favor of a rule of reason approach, because in line with the new thinking many of the "no-nos" were reinterpreted as either innocuous or pro-competitive (Webb and Locke, 1991: at note 24). Under the rule of reason approach, practices are not prohibited outright but are subjected to analysis first, for actual anti-competitive effect, and second, the practices' possible contribution to pro-competitive benefits.

No longer do authorities *presume* that IP owners possess requisite economic power to invite anti-trust scrutiny (Hayslett, 1996: 381). Instead, both the administrators and the courts have adopted the view that an IP owner has no relevant market power (in terms of anti-trust) if close substitutes exist for the product or process. This more flexible approach, when coupled with broader definitions of what constitutes a relevant market, redounds to the benefit of the licensor, in comparison to the pre-Chicago approach. As Hayslett suggests, focusing on the role of substitute goods expands the relevant market

> in a way that reduces the likelihood of intellectual property rights securing monopoly power. For example, if an inventor held a patent on staplers, the agencies would not automatically presume that the inventor possessed influential monopoly power because paper clips, butterfly clips, tape, and other potential substitutes compete with staplers for shares of the paper-fastening market. (1996: 385)

The consequence of this new thinking was to remove most IP licensing from anti-trust scrutiny. Under the Reagan administration, "the executive agencies viewed the economic incentives provided by intellectual property rights as legitimate means of extracting the full economic benefit from innovation. Intellectual property rights acted as a 'magic trump

[10] The guidelines declared the following nine practices as *per se* illegal [meaning they were absolutely prohibited]: tying arrangements; assignment of exclusive grantback of improvements; restraints on the resale of a licensed product; restrictions on the licensee's freedom to deal in goods and services not covered by the patent; requirements of exclusivity in license grant; mandatory package licensing; conditioning grant of license on licensee's agreement to pay royalties not reasonably related to sales; restricting sales of unpatented goods made by a patented process; and dictating the price the licensee can charge for the licensed product. See Webb and Locke (1991: note 23).

card' allowing many previously suspect arrangements to proceed without challenge from the FTC or DOJ" (Hayslett, 1996: 382). The 1980s has been referred to as an "anything goes era" for IP licensing arrangements (Yurko, quoted in Hayslett, 1996: 382, note 33).

The 1980s ushered in a re-dedication to a conception of intellectual property as a system to protect and exclude, rather than one based on competition and diffusion. Notably, the former conception is embodied in TRIPS. Changes in the domestic environment for IP protection were embedded in a broader set of concerns raised by the changing structure of global capitalism. Competitiveness concerns animated a number of significant changes in US policymaking and its institutions. Policy changes, such as the relaxation of formerly stringent anti-trust policies, facilitated an environment more favorable to IP owners. Institutional changes such as the creation of the CAFC paved the way for IP owners to promote their private interests. This era fortified the perceived connection between competitiveness and intellectual property. The *Kodak* case brought American jurisprudence full circle, back to the *A.B. Dick* philosophy championing protection, exclusion, and opportunities for extracting monopoly rents. It symbolized the emergence of US patent law out of an era of judicial skepticism that characterized much of the twentieth century. The signals were unmistakable, and the trends captured by the case alerted US business that patents would be upheld and could be counted on as valuable economic resources.

# 4    The domestic origins of a trade-based approach to intellectual property

While Chapter 3 focused on domestic rights of IP owners, this chapter focuses on the domestic evolution of the linkage between intellectual property and trade. Here, the action shifts from the judiciary to the Congress and executive branch as firms and industry associations began lobbying for firmer guarantees that their IP rights would be recognized abroad.

In the United States, the private sector has been remarkably successful in politicizing IP protection. As a result of concerted action by industry associations (such as the PMA, and the Motion Picture Association of America), US policymakers have explicitly linked IP protection to trade in Section 301 of the US Trade and Tariff Act. At the behest of these private sector actors, the US has vigorously pressured violators of such property rights abroad by threatening trade retaliation under Section 301. This trade-based conception of IP rights has been incorporated in regional trade pacts such as the North American Free Trade Agreement and the Caribbean Basin Initiative. Finally, representatives of industry associations also succeeded in initiating and mobilizing support for a global IP agreement (TRIPS).

Whether industry representatives sit across the table suggesting specific revisions in foreign countries' draft legislation, avail themselves of the US Section 301 machinery, play the Generalized System of Preferences (GSP) trump card, compile reports of the latest violations and estimates of lost revenue, conduct raids on pirated goods abroad, or monitor compliance in a vigilant effort to keep the pressure on, they have become important players in the crusade for the worldwide protection of their valuable intellectual property.

This chapter examines the domestic political processes that led to the elevation of a previously arcane, technical issue – intellectual property –

to an issue perceived to be of fundamental national importance. I examine the mobilization of like-minded industry associations, and their role in the formation of the US policy preference for linking IP protection to international trade. Private sector actors have played a major role in catapulting the previously arcane issue of IP protection to the top tier of the US trade agenda, and have been able to enlarge the range of options for both themselves and US policymakers by linking IP protection to international trade. This increasingly powerful lobby includes the following private sector groups: the International Intellectual Property Alliance;[1] the Pharmaceutical Manufacturers Association; the Chemical Manufacturers Association; National Agricultural Chemicals Association; Motor Equipment Manufacturers Association; Auto Exports Council; Intellectual Property Owners, Inc.; the International Anti-counterfeiting Coalition; and the Semiconductor Industry Association.

The chapter describes the context within which the push for a trade-based approach to IP protection emerged. Forming this context were institutional changes that expanded private sector access to trade policymaking, policymakers' concerns over a burgeoning trade deficit, and a domestic debate over industrial policy that was sparked by fears of Japan's economic might. The chapter outlines the revisions in US trade laws, specifically Sections 301 and 337 in 1979 and 1984, and highlights previous shortcomings in these laws from a private sector perspective as well as the private sector lobbying efforts. The 1988 amendments to the US Trade and Tariff Act are discussed, and the extent to which these amendments responded to private sector demands examined. Overall, it highlights the domestic side of the building momentum that led to the US push for TRIPS.

## The 1974 amendments to the Tariff Act and the eroding consensus on US GATT obligations

As early as 1974 the United States adopted amendments to the IP provisions of the 1930 Tariff Act. Although the US Trade Act of 1930 included an IP protection section (No. 337), industries that complained of violations were dissatisfied with its lack of effective remedy. In 1974, the United States amended Section 337 to render it "a more useful action for domestic industries" (Kaye and Plaia, 1981: 465). The political pressure

---

[1] An umbrella organization of trade associations, for a list of members see: http://www.ilPa.com

for the 1974 revisions came from traditional protectionist groups, such as the steel industry and the agricultural sector.

The amendments transferred from the president to the International Trade Commission (ITC) the authority to issue orders excluding importation of foreign goods that violated the rights of US IP holders. This change was meant to provide a more impartial venue for the pursuit of claims under Section 337. In addition, the amendments required the ITC to complete investigations within one year. In the past, Section 337 investigations had often dragged on for many years, during which the violations could continue unabated to the detriment of complainants. With the new deadline, the advantage shifted from the accused to the complainant in so far as it left the respondent very little time to prepare its case (Kaye and Plaia, 1981). These amendments were mild compared to what followed in 1988, but between 1974 and 1981 Section 337 became "one of the most utilized laws in combating activities alleged to be unfair competition in international trade" (Kaye and Plaia, 1981: 465).

The Trade Act of 1974 also incorporated Section 301, allowing the president to deny benefits or impose duties on products or services of countries unjustifiably restricting US commerce. This Act gave the USTR authority to administer the procedures. Essentially a political statute, this was intended to provide the executive branch with the flexibility to exert leverage over other countries to eliminate practices detrimental to US commerce. Petitioners filed eighteen cases seeking Section 301 redress between January 1975 and July 1979. Yet, during that entire period, "the United States took no retaliatory actions under Section 301 and terminated only six cases through satisfactory bilateral resolution. From the United States' point of view, the majority of these cases were never satisfactorily resolved" (Coffield, 1981: 384). Therefore the 1974 revisions did not achieve the intended results, and Congressional frustration began to mount.

The 1974 Trade Act also amended Section 252, that gave the president authority to restrict imports from countries found to be unjustifiably or unreasonably restricting US exports (Bliss, 1989). Originally, Section 252 imposed no time limits and required only that the president "provide an opportunity for a public hearing upon request from interested parties" (Bliss, 1989: 504). Section 252 also required the president to act in conformity with US international obligations, for example, the GATT. But owing to Congressional dissatisfaction with the GATT dispute settlement procedures, the US Congress sought to sever this connection between US trade policy and its GATT obligations. In the words of the

1974 Senate Finance Committee Report, "the Committee felt it was necessary to make clear that the President could act to *protect US economic
interests whether or not such action was consistent with the articles of an out-
moded international agreement initiated by the Executive 25 years ago and
never approved by Congress*" [emphasis added] (Coffield, 1981: 383).

## Trade amendments in 1979 and the increasing role of the private sector

Throughout the 1960s and 1970s, US businesses became increasingly active and involved in trade policymaking. Institutional changes that the
House of Representatives adopted in the wake of the Watergate scandal
paved the way for private actors to play a larger role in shaping trade
policy. The decentralization of power in Congress and the opening up
of legislative procedures made trade policymaking much more transparent. New House procedural rules made markups of bills open to the
public, and "offered new opportunities for special interests to press their
proposals" (Destler, 1992: 69).

The amendments to Section 301 enacted in the Trade Agreements Act
of 1979 allowed "private parties to take a significant and public step to
enforce existing international trade agreements" (Fisher and Steinhardt,
1982: 575). It established the right of private petitioners to seek government redress and made Section 301 "a potentially powerful weapon
for a US industry aggrieved by foreign trade practices" (Fisher and
Steinhardt, 1982: 599). One of the key features of the 1979 amendments
required the federal government "to take account of the views of the
affected industry, effectively establishing a cooperative relationship between public and private sectors" (Fisher and Steinhardt, 1982: 605). In
the process of preparing for consultations and dispute settlement proceedings under 301, "the USTR [United States Trade Representative]
is required to 'seek information and advice' from the petitioner and
the appropriate private sector representatives" (Fisher and Steinhardt,
1982: 605, note 176). Throughout the process of a 301 investigation, the
USTR is expected to continue its consultations with the petitioner and
other relevant private sector actors. Thus, the 1979 amendments significantly enlarged the scope of private sector participation in trade
policy.

By the late 1970s, a different group of private sector players emerged
favoring generic, versus sector-specific, trade legislation (Odell and
Destler, 1987). Generic trade legislation is designed to combat the full

panoply of unfair practices of foreigners rather than to provide sector-specific trade protection. Historically, the United States has had an effective anti-protectionist coalition, consisting of: "(1) US companies which use or sell imported goods; (2) firms with large export interests; (3) those policymakers in Congress or the Executive Branch who oppose protection for ideological or pragmatic reasons" (Bayard, 1990: 326). With the rise of export interests has come a novel approach to trade remedies. According to Jagdish Bhagwati:

> if they sell in other markets ... they can ... ease the pressure of competition on themselves by asking for, not higher import barriers against others, but lower import barriers by others ... It is also in keeping with the general multinational ethos and interests of achieving a freer world trading regime. It has the added advantage that one might be able to fit into the 'unfair trade' framework, if applied at the level of products, firms and industries. (Bhagwati, 1982: 452)

In the late 1970s agricultural chemicals producers – Monsanto Agricultural Company, FMC, and Stauffer – acting through the US government, engaged in bilateral talks with the Hungarian government in a quest to end the piracy of agricultural chemicals and strengthen Hungarian intellectual property laws (Enyart, 1990: 54). The private sector mobilization process began modestly in the late 1970s within the agricultural chemicals industry in these negotiations with the Hungarians. The initial efforts began within companies such as Pfizer, FMC, IBM, and Du Pont. Activists, such as Enyart (at that time, executive director of international affairs for Monsanto Agricultural Company), within those companies persuaded corporate managers to dedicate resources to change foreign IP laws (Enyart, 1990: 54). The mobilization process gained momentum as the agricultural chemicals industry joined forces with the US-based International Anti-Counterfeiting Coalition (organized to protect trademarks in luxury and high fashion goods), and the Copyright Alliance to press for changes in US trade policy.

In 1982, at the behest of various US corporate interests whose intellectual property constituted valuable assets, the United States embarked on a series of bilateral consultations with Hungary, Korea, Mexico, Singapore, and Taiwan on their patent, trademark, and copyright laws. These bilateral consultations were an important step in the evolution of the United States' new approach. The government thought that this bilateral pressure was productive because Hungary, Taiwan, and Singapore indicated a willingness to ensure more vigorous protection.

Former assistant general counsel of the USTR, Alice Zalik, points out that having US trade officials (rather than IP administrators) conduct these discussions with their foreign counterparts rendered the talks more effective because trade officials have more power to change policy (1986: 200). Through these early successes, both the US government and the activist firms realized that linking trade and IP protection could produce results. Enyart emphasized that these early bilateral consultations convinced a large segment of US-based high-technology and creative industries that exploiting intellectual property and trade linkage was fruitful (1990: 54).

A number of developments in the late 1970s and early 1980s contributed to the increased influence of private sector export interests in US trade policy and support for a new approach to trade. These included: macro-economic changes, such as the US trade deficit and increasing pressure on the United States to be globally competitive; and the "de-industrialization" school of economic theory popularized by, among others, Lester Thurow (1985), Robert Reich (1983), Ira Magaziner (Reich and Magaziner 1982), and John Zysman and Stephen Cohen (1987). I will discuss briefly each of these in turn.

The growing US trade deficit led to a new approach to trade policy. Growing trade deficits, especially with Japan, engendered frustration in Congress. Advocates of a new approach to trade underscored the perceived lack of reciprocity between the United States and Japan, and laid the blame for America's trade woes abroad. Advocates argued that the United States was at a marked disadvantage *vis-à-vis* Japan due to the relatively open US market as opposed to Japan's relatively closed market. The 97th and 98th Congresses (1981–1983) expressed growing frustration with the trade deficit, and Senator John Danforth of Missouri, among others, introduced a number of bills "intended to pressure US trading partners into providing equivalent opportunities for US exporters. Foreign countries would be given a choice between reducing their trade barriers to the levels imposed by the United States or facing the prospect that US barriers would be raised in retaliation" (Lande and van Grasstek, 1986: 38). Between 1980 and 1985, the US trade deficit increased by 309 percent – from $36.3 to $148.5 billion (Hughes, 1991: 177). The trade problem was exacerbated by an overvalued dollar that made US exports less competitive. During Ronald Reagan's first term as president, the administration largely ignored this aspect. Not until 1985, under the Plaza Accords agreement, did the administration begin to address the problem.

However, the 1985 realignment of the dollar was no panacea. Bhagwati suggests that the Plaza Accords' failure to remedy the trade deficit shifted the political focus to trade policy (1989: 443). Trade policy suddenly became the focus of US aspirations to remain globally competitive. According to Susan Strange, the US preoccupation with competitiveness strengthened the hand of firms in shaping government policy (1991: 45).

In response to the perception that the United States was in danger of losing the "race," both politicians and academics highlighted the fear of the United States' imminent deindustrialization. For example, during the 1984 presidential campaign, "Walter Mondale invoked images of Americans reduced to flipping hamburgers at McDonalds while the Japanese overwhelmed the country's industries" (Bhagwati, 1989: 445). John Zysman and Stephen Cohen, participants in the Berkeley Roundtable on International Economics, published a popular book exposing the myth of the postindustrial economy and emphasizing that the United States must not lose its manufacturing base (Zysman and Cohen, 1987). The "manufacturing matters" thesis elevated the support of US-based manufacturers to a matter of national interest, and advocated industrial policy as a possible solution implying selective protection of core economic sectors. In a crude sense, this "if-you-can't-beat-them-join-them" approach indicated the erosion of the traditional US postwar preference for free trade and economic liberalism.

## Linking trade and intellectual property: the 1984 amendments

Several other US developments in IP protection were overt in their intended international dimension, and the trend beginning in the early 1980s gained momentum. The United States began to expand its newly invigorated pro-patent approach to encompass international trade. As the former assistant general counsel of the USTR argued, "the economic harm done to our industries today by the lack of adequate intellectual property laws abroad is staggering...Our companies find that they must compete with the unauthorized copies not only in the source country but in third countries as well" (Zalik, 1986: 199). Industries felt the pain, and US industry representatives initiated a series of measures to try to reverse this trend.

Throughout the 1980s the increasingly active private sector IP lobby played a larger role in the formulation of US trade policy. As discussed in Chapter 2, Edmund Pratt, CEO of Pfizer Pharmaceutical, and John Opel, CEO of IBM, had long been lobbying the US government to get serious about IP violators abroad. Pratt and Opel had been active in the US-based International Anti-Counterfeiting Coalition at the end of the Tokyo Round of GATT negotiations. Pratt was primarily concerned with patent protection for pharmaceuticals, whereas Opel's focus was copyright protection for computer software.

From 1981, Pratt chaired the Advisory Committee for Trade Negotiations (ACTN), which provides an official channel for business people to provide private sector consultation to the president. The president appoints its members, and they played a major role in devising a trade-based IP strategy and in shaping US trade policy. The ACTN argued that investment obstacles, and in particular weak intellectual property protection, had to be put on the trade agenda. Further, the committee recommended that USTR create a new post – assistant trade representative for investment – which was established in 1981 (Ryan, 1998b: 68). Pratt and Opel pursued parallel efforts during 1983 and 1984 to advance their specific concerns to the administration. Their efforts helped to catalyze and sharpen a resurgent governmental focus on high technology and competitiveness.

In a 1983 national address, President Reagan avowed his commitment to maintaining US technological superiority into the twenty-first century. Yet,

> when asked for its program, the White House admitted that the President's pledge was a last minute addition without backup papers. This vacuum did not survive for long, however; the private sector emerged with a series of initiatives intended to capture the renewed political attention to United States technological leadership. In virtually every program advanced, both trade and intellectual property issues featured prominently. (Gadbaw, 1989: 234)

Largely as a result of private sector input, the President's Commission on Industrial Competitiveness, chaired by John Young, president and CEO of Hewlett-Packard and founding member of the Intellectual Property Committee, issued its 1983–1984 report which included an addendum outlining the effects of weak IP protection abroad on US competitiveness.

The US government first officially linked IP protection and international trade in 1984. According to Emery Simon, then at USTR, "trade and intellectual property began to merge in 1984" (quoted in D'Alessandro, 1987: 433 note 116). In January 1984, Gerald J. Mossinghoff, in his capacity as assistant secretary of commerce and commissioner of patents and trademarks, delivered a strong statement outlining the relationship between patents, trademarks, and international trade. He underscored the vital link between IP protection and innovation, and American industry's capacity to compete globally. He concluded by stating that, "there is widespread bipartisan agreement that the protection of intellectual property worldwide is a critically important factor in expanding trade in high technology products. This Administration is committed to strengthening that protection as an integral component of our service to US trade and industry" (Mossinghoff, 1984). In a classic example of the "revolving door" between government and the private sector, Mossinghoff left the government to become president of the US-based Pharmaceutical Manufacturers Association (now called Pharmaceutical Research and Manufacturers of America) in 1985 – one of the most active associations pressing for the linkage of intellectual property and trade.[2]

Most significantly, Mossinghoff's statement signaled an end to the previous piecemeal treatment of US-held intellectual property abroad. Prior to late 1984 government agencies dealt with IP problems on an *ad hoc* basis; US embassies offered to help companies as problems arose (Zalik, 1986: 200). Bipartisan support for this newly integrated approach emerged over a ten-year period in which private actors played an increasingly large role in focusing government attention on IP protection.

Private sector lobbying intensified throughout 1983 and 1984. During this period the private sector dominated the debate over high technology and competitiveness (Gadbaw, 1989: 235). For example, Pratt of Pfizer was active in Washington rallying others to the cause of incorporating intellectual property into the trade agenda. He called upon the membership of the PMA and the CMA to lobby vigorously for stronger

---

[2] Other prominent examples of the "revolving door" phenomenon include: Alan Holmer and Judith Hippler Bello. Holmer, formerly Deputy United States trade representative, succeeded Mossinghoff as president of PhRMA in late 1996. Holmer then appointed Bello, formerly acting general counsel of USTR, as PhRMA's executive vice president for policy and strategic affairs. Harvey Bale left the USTR in 1987, after twelve years, to become PMA vice president (Kosterlitz, 1993: 398). Emery Simon, formerly of USTR, left the government and became the executive director of the Alliance to Promote Software Innovation (APSI), and in 1996 was named counselor to the Policy Council of the Business Software Alliance (representing IP maximalists, esp. Microsoft). Tom Robertson, formerly a senior attorney in the office of the general counsel of USTR, became Microsoft's Asian regional counsel, based in Hong Kong. For further examples of the revolving door between government and the pharmaceutical industry see Novak (1993) and Engelberg (1999: esp. note 56).

IP protection (Ryan, 1998b: 69). The PMA emerged as one of the strongest, best-organized campaigners for using US trade leverage to secure stronger IP protection abroad. While the PMA and CMA shared a focus on patent and trade secret protection, the copyright industries began to mobilize for stronger protection as well.

The Motion Picture Association of America (MPAA), headed by Jack Valenti, lobbied particularly hard. In the early 1980s Valenti became an outspoken critic of copyright piracy abroad. He argued for bilateral trade pressure on countries engaging in widespread piracy of American motion pictures. His association successfully lobbied for an IP provision in the Caribbean Basin Economic Recovery Act (CBERA)[3] of 1983, stipulating that those countries pirating US copyrighted products would be denied non-reciprocal tariff waivers on their imports under the Generalized System of Preferences (GSP). Inspired by the motion picture industry's strategy, American book publishers also looked to the CBERA as a way to curb book piracy in the region. Cooperation between the entertainment and publishing industries emerged to pressure the government to incorporate IP protection in its trade policy and was instrumental in the 1984 amendments to the Trade and Tariff Act (Ryan, 1998b: 70). This interindustry mobilization expanded with the creation of the International Intellectual Property Alliance (IIPA).

In 1984 the IIPA was founded to promote copyright interests. Quickly the IIPA emerged as a powerful and effective lobbying arm representing over 1,500 corporations "whose annual output exceeds five percent of the US Gross Domestic Product" (Liu, 1994: 102). It coordinates policy positions based on shared concerns of its members, tracks copyright policies abroad, provides detailed information on foreign copyright practices and infractions, testifies before Congress, and publishes influential reports that it delivers to Congress and the USTR. Nicholas Veliotes, president of the Association of American Publishers and founding member of the IIPA, stated that the member organizations of the IIPA:

> came together in this umbrella organization to press Congress and the Administration *first*, to recognize the critical importance to the United States of trade in goods and services dependent upon intellectual property protection worldwide, and *second*, to help forge the necessary legal tools enabling our trade negotiators to convince foreign nations to

[3] Also known as the Caribbean Basin Initiative, Public Law 98–67, title II. Approved August 5, 1983, 19 U.S.C. 2701 *et seq.*

take action against massive and debilitating piracy and counterfeiting
of U.S. . . . products representing the best of American creativity.

(Senate 1986a: 162, 164)

IP issues continued to gain increasing attention. For example, in June
1984 a US mission spent two weeks engaged in consultations on commercial counterfeiting with government officials in Taiwan and Singapore (US Department of Commerce, 1984: 1–2). The USTR, the State
Department, the Patent and Trademark Office, the Copyright Office,
and twenty private sector participants representing ten industry associations participated. The participants discussed counterfeiting problems
in pharmaceuticals, chemicals, copyrighted materials, and trademarks.
They reportedly made little progress, but the trip was important in so
far as it brought together IP advocates representing both copyright and
patent interests. Representatives of the MPAA and the International
Anti-Counterfeiting Coalition participated in discussions of draft revisions of Taiwan's copyright law, and agreed to meet with Taiwanese officials to discuss specific issues in the future. The Commerce Department's
memo emphasized that it expected "the continued close involvement of
the industry associations . . . in all follow-up activities" (US Department
of Commerce, 1984: 2). Enyart points out that the Taiwanese negotiations were striking in the breadth and diversity of US industry repre-
sentation, and that this expansion of actively involved private sector
representatives was further reinforced by coalition work on the IP components of the Trade Act of 1984 (Enyart, 1990: 54). On this trip, in
discussions between the US government's participants and the private
sector representatives, the industry associations involved indicated that
they would press even harder in the administration and Congress for
legislation that would, for example, make adequate protection of intellectual property a precondition for eligibility under the Generalized
System of Preferences (US Department of Commerce, 1984: 2). The private sector began to see the GSP as an attractive trump card in light
of the fact that these two recalcitrant countries were, at that time, GSP
beneficiaries.

Congress adopted new amendments in the Trade and Tariff Act of
1984[4] that directly responded to the demands of the IP lobby and incorporated a trade-based conception of IP protection. While "the major
impetus for the 1984 changes . . . came from service and investment industry representatives" (Hughes 1991, 184), the focus on intellectual

[4] Trade and Tariff Act of 1984, Public Law 98–573, October 30, 1984.

property was driven by increasingly well-mobilized private sector patent and copyright interests.

For the first time, the amended act included the failure to adequately protect intellectual property as actionable under Section 301. The language of the 1984 Act identified as "unreasonable" acts, practices or policies that deny "fair and equitable provision of adequate and effective protection of intellectual property rights" even though the act, policy, or practice does not violate "the international legal rights of the United States." "'Unjustifiable' includes any act that... denies protection of intellectual property rights" (Hughes, 1991: 184–185). The Section permits industries, trade associations, and individual companies to petition the USTR to investigate actions of foreign governments. The 1984 amendments gave the USTR authority to initiate cases on its own motion. This was designed to lessen the prospect of retaliation against an industry or company filing a 301 complaint. The amendments also included IP protection as a new criterion for assessing developing countries' eligibility for non-reciprocal trade concessions under the Generalized System of Preferences (GSP) program. This reflected the CBERA precedent and the lobbying efforts of the entertainment, publishing, and pharmaceutical industry associations.

As Baik suggests, "protection of US intellectual property rights became a dominating issue only after a few firms and industry organizations initiated an intellectual property lobby... Through astute marketing of their demands, the lobby could gain broad support from the business community and elicit support even from liberal trade-oriented Congressmen" (1993: 147 note 56). These private actors were in a good position in so far as they represented vigorous export industries that enjoyed positive trade balances. For instance, in a document presented to the House Energy and Commerce Committee on behalf of the IIPA, Vico Henriques pointed out that, "whereas the United States experienced a massive merchandise trade deficit in 1982, the copyright industries earned a trade surplus for this country of over $1.2 billion. This is only a fraction of what could have been earned if adequate and effective copyright protection were available" (IIPA, 1985: 80–81).

They were able to present their industries as part of the solution to America's trade woes, as opposed to being part of the problem. They successfully argued that foreign pirates, particularly in East Asia and Latin America, were robbing them of hard-earned royalties. They pushed hard for a trade-based approach to IP protection. Despite the fact that these private organizations had been busy trying to persuade foreign governments of the importance of providing adequate IP protection, they argued that without the "muscle" and backing of the US government their efforts would continue to achieve weak results.

## Dissatisfaction with the 1984 amendments

Despite the substantial legislative victories that the private sector lobbyists had won in the 1984 amendments, the IP lobby accelerated its activities and kept intellectual property on the front burner of trade policymaking. The lobbyists felt they needed to educate Congress and the executive branch on the importance of intellectual property and its relationship to both trade and competitiveness. Now that the Trade and Tariff Act had more statutory bite, especially for intellectual property, the IP lobbyists pressed the government to take action. In 1985, in his testimony before Congress on behalf of the IIPA, Vico Henriques argued that the US government must curtail or rescind trade benefits under the GSP and CBERA, "unless countries that permit piracy show significant and tangible improvements in both their copyright laws and their efforts to enforce those laws" (House, 1985: 75). Henriques expressed his dissatisfaction with the failure of the government to take strong action in the wake of the 1984 amendments to the Trade Act. He agreed that the government had begun to acknowledge the scope of the problem, but had yet to do much about it. In his response to Henriques, Representative Wyden stated:

> My free-trade credentials are about as impeccable as anybody in the Congress ... But the impression I get both from you and our other witnesses is that our Government negotiators just don't understand how serious the problem is. They just don't seem to be getting the message. It's my perception that unless our negotiators use the tools that they have got in front of them ... the administration is literally inviting a whole new wave of protectionist legislation ... I hope that because of your good work and your testimony, that the administration gets the message ... We don't see an adequate response by the administration to ensure the fair trade that we need ... You have really given an education particularly to this member.        (House, 1985: 128)

Wyden's response suggests the effectiveness of Henriques' testimony and his recognition of a politically viable alternative to overtly protectionist trade policies.

Mossinghoff, former US Commissioner of Patents and Trademarks, testified before the House Energy and Commerce Committee in his capacity as president of the PMA in July 1985: "The PMA was one of the first advocates for a trade law that would allow private industries to bring complaints against a foreign sovereignty for the violation of trade agreements" (Liu, 1994: 107). Mossinghoff urged Congress to get serious about using GSP leverage against violators of US-held intellectual property. He stated: "Argentina, Mexico, Brazil, South Korea, Taiwan, and Yugoslavia account for over 50 percent of the GSP benefits. All have very significant deficiencies in intellectual property protection for pharmaceuticals, the correction of which would substantially improve the market share of US pharmaceutical companies" (House, 1985: 189). In accompanying documents submitted to the Committee, Mossinghoff detailed the scope of the industry's problems abroad and asked the government to take the PMA's concerns into account when assessing the renewal of GSP applicability. The PMA had already submitted these documents to the USTR and the Generalized System of Preferences Subcommittee. Mossinghoff's remarks emphasized that GSP recipients remained unconvinced that the United States was prepared to take punitive action, despite the inclusion of IP protection as a new criterion for GSP renewal (House, 1985: 220).

Jack Valenti, president of the MPAA, echoed Henriques' and Mossinghoff's sentiments in his testimony to the Senate Finance Committee in May 1986. He bemoaned the paltry results of the past bilateral talks and submitted an IIPA report in conjunction with his testimony that called for amendments in the GSP renewal policy. The IIPA surveyed ten countries, nine of which were GSP beneficiaries, and argued that, "the United States Trade Representative should make it known to these countries that . . . unless significant improvements are made . . . their GSP beneficiary status is in jeopardy" (IIPA, 1986: 159). According to the report, "since the passage of the Trade and Tariff Act ten months ago, with the exception of Taiwan, we have at the most heard only indications that improvements will be made. Delay can no longer be excused; the resolve of the US to combat piracy must be made crystal clear" (IIPA, 1986: 158). In an exchange with Senator Danforth, who pointed out that Valenti was "one of the people who got [him] into the issue"[5] of intellectual property, Valenti indicated that the 1984 law did not constitute a credible threat. Danforth raised the GSP issue and asked Valenti: "Do you think we should say, in effect, that it is true back in 1984

---

[5] Quotes in these two paragraphs from discussion following Statement of Jack Valenti to Senate Finance Committee, S361–88.4, May 14, 1986, pp. 170–171.

we were crying wolf, but we are not crying wolf anymore; we are actually going to withdraw GSP status because of piracy?" Valenti replied, "Absolutely" (Valenti, 1986: 170–171).

In fact, Valenti was deeply involved in a protracted series of discussions with Korea regarding its failure adequately to protect intellectual property in 1985. As Valenti pointed out, "in Korea, where they have one and a half billion dollars worth of GSP, there is some pain there... And I've just come through a long and tortuous negotiation under a 301 filing with the Republic of Korea... They understood what I was talking about" (Valenti, 1986: 170–171). He recommended that the United States be willing to cut off violators, and further, that the USTR issue a list of priority countries that violate acceptable standards of IP protection. Finally, he advocated the adoption of amendments that would establish firm deadlines and mandate a retaliatory response in the absence of negotiated progress. Nicholas Veliotes, president of the Association of American Publishers, raised similar concerns before the Senate Finance Committee (Senate, 1986a: 162, 164). Thus private sector actors pressed for additional forms of leverage to secure developing countries' commitment to the protection of US-held intellectual property.

The sentiments of these private actors found more formal expression in the reports of the Advisory Committee for Trade Negotiations' Task Force on Intellectual Property Rights. The heavy hitters of the private sector campaign to secure better IP protection abroad were well represented on the Task Force. Among the participants in the eight-member Task Force were: the CEO of IBM, John Opel; Vice President and Counsel of the Motion Picture Industry Association, Fritz Attaway; and president of the International Division of Merck & Company Inc. (at that time America's largest pharmaceutical corporation), Mr. Abraham Cohen. In its report to the Advisory Committee of October 1985, the Task Force recommended that the United States pursue a trade-based approach. As stated in the report: "the growing economic importance of intellectual property to all industries and the inadequacies of the present IP system... have led the US private sector to seek a trade-based response" (USTR, 1985: 2). The report endorsed US efforts to incorporate IP rights into the GATT framework.

In March 1986, the Task Force's report focused on US bilateral and unilateral efforts. It endorsed a carrot and stick approach by supporting efforts to provide technical training to foreign officials in IP issues, while at the same time strengthening US trade leverage over reluctant foreign governments. Among the sticks, of course, were making the renewal of GSP benefits contingent upon the effective protection of intellectual property, and the strengthening of Section 301.

The Task Force also underscored the crucial role that the private sector had played in the expansion of the trade-based approach. According to the report, "the US IP-based industries have already displayed a significant catalytic and stimulative role in defining IP as a trade issue and in having US trade officials accept IP as part of their agenda" (USTR 1986, 8). The Task Force emphasized the continuing importance of private sector–government dialogue for shoring up domestic consensus on a trade-based approach.

Between 1984 and 1988 the private sector did not limit itself to testifying before Congress and meeting with officials from countries profiting from the unauthorized exploitation of US-held intellectual property. For example, beginning in 1984 the MPAA sent representatives to a number of Latin American countries and conducted raids of video shops, destroyed counterfeit tapes and urged the local governments to provide stronger enforcement measures (D'Alessandro, 1987: 432). In addition, the private sector was busy pursuing Section 301 actions against foreign governments.

A 1985 Section 301 case targeted South Korea for its inadequate protection of US-held intellectual property. As a consequence of the bilateral negotiations, the Korean government acquiesced in 1986 by enacting product patent protection for pharmaceuticals and improved enforcement procedures. Mossinghoff, PMA's president, stated that, "the Korean case was a major step forward and set an important example of what could be accomplished using trade instruments to achieve intellectual property objectives" (Mossinghoff, 1991: 76). The IIPA and the PMA continued to monitor Korea's performance. That same year, the MPAA filed a Section 301 petition against Korea. Valenti was prominently involved in the ensuing consultations with the Korean government.

In 1987 the PMA initiated a case against Brazil for its lack of patent protection for pharmaceutical products. This was the first case that resulted in trade retaliation by the United States under the 301 provisions. After Brazil refused to alter its policy the United States placed a $39 million tariff on imports of Brazilian pharmaceuticals. Brazil filed a GATT complaint over US trade retaliation, but it "withdrew its complaint when the sanctions were dropped [in summer 1990] in exchange for Brazil's patent commitments" (Mossinghoff, 1991: 77).

The United States first invoked the GSP provisions of the 1984 Trade and Tariff Act in a case against Mexico in 1987 and denied Mexico GSP benefits for Mexico's failure to offer protection to pharmaceutical products. The Mexican government had long held that the availability of affordable pharmaceuticals was a matter of the public interest. Therefore, it persisted in its refusal to enact pharmaceutical product patent protection, and lost $500 million in GSP benefits (Mossinghoff, 1991: 76).

## The 1988 Omnibus Trade and Competitiveness Act

Pressures for a trade remedy for America's economic woes reached a strident climax in the form of the proposed Gephardt Amendment of 1986–1988. This amendment, targeted at countries running a trade surplus with the United States, would have mandated an annual trade surplus reduction of 10 percent. Mandatory tariffs and quotas would have been employed against recalcitrant states. At this juncture US trade policy was at a crossroads between the pursuit of "fair trade" or outright protectionism. Industry associations presented a politically viable alternative to protectionism that was more compatible with the United States' post-World War II penchant for free trade. Their alternative was a better fit between the United States' self-professed values and its postwar policies.

The protectionist nature of Gephardt's proposal alarmed many; multinational corporate interests were especially opposed to it due to the danger of trade wars. US export interests did not relish the idea of trade contraction. Gephardt's proposed amendment "provided the impetus for enactment of Super 301" (Ashman, 1989: 149). The specter of protectionism mobilized like-minded industries in opposition and led to the 1988 adoption of the Omnibus Trade and Tariff Act and the revisions of Section 301. This Act was a compromise to defuse protectionist pressure. As Fisher and Steinhardt have argued, "Section 301 can serve as a safety valve in the formulation of trade policy in a democratic society by releasing pressures which might otherwise result in more extreme solutions from Congress" (1982: 579).

In 1988 the trade-based approach for IP protection was further strengthened by Amendments to the Trade and Tariff Act. Since 1985, private sector groups and an increasingly convinced Congress had been pressuring the administration to use Section 301 more vigorously. Congressmen bemoaned the fact that the Executive Branch shied away from trade retaliation "because of the desire to use trade to barter for other non-trade issues" (Bello and Holmer, 1988: 1).

On August 23, 1988 Congress enacted H.R. 4848, the Omnibus Trade and Competitiveness Act. Designed to pry open foreign markets and secure higher standards of protection for US-held intellectual property, this bill "directly assist[s] the export-oriented element of the anti-protectionist forces. US government efforts to open foreign markets... through Section 301 ... [are] the quid pro quo for US exporters' support for free trade" (Bayard, 1990: 326). The new Section 301 is generic, versus sector-specific, trade legislation. Under the prior law, "the foreign country had no incentive to correct its broader, national trade-restrictive policies. ... Super 301 target[s] the entire web of impediments, not the sector-specific strands" (Ashman, 1989: 148). The Omnibus Bill included several new amendments that directly responded to the specific requests of the private sector.

First of all, the new bill effectively transferred substantial authority from the president to the USTR. According to Representative Bill Richardson of New Mexico, this change is "intended to enhance USTR's position as the lead trade agency and to make it less likely that trade retaliation would be waived because of foreign policy, defense, or other considerations" (quoted in Bello and Holmer, 1988: 3 note 10). In effect, this change codifies the elevated niche that trade has come to occupy in US foreign policy – that trade interests should *not* be subordinated to issues traditionally conceived of as "high politics." The 1988 Act transfers to the USTR authority under Section 301 "not only to determine whether foreign government practices are unfair, but also to take action" (Bello and Holmer, 1988: 8). According to Julia Bliss, "the transfer of authority follows the trend towards a less flexible process, one mandating action" (Bliss, 1989: 514). This is exactly what the private sector had hoped for.

The 1988 Trade Act also strengthens the IP components that were originally incorporated in 1984. Now the USTR must annually identify IP priority countries (violators) and self-initiate investigations of priority countries within thirty days of identification. Furthermore, the USTR must determine the actionability of foreign activity and devise a policy response within six months of the initiation of the investigation. It must implement Section 301 action within thirty days of an affirmative determination. The tight time deadlines and requirement for the public identification of violating countries reflect the expressed desires of the private sector to toughen US resolve: "Consultations must now be initiated with the foreign government on the day the USTR decides to initiate a case" (Bliss, 1989: 518). The amendments require the USTR to make a determination in every case, whether or not retaliatory action is taken.

The process of compiling USTR reports to identify foreign trade barriers includes gathering information from private sector advisory committees. In addition, the USTR's methods to calculate the economic damage caused by foreign trade barriers rely extensively on estimates provided by the affected US industries. "Thus, corporations and individuals who stand to benefit directly from the finding or exaggeration of foreign trade barriers are also relied upon for information in determining the existence and impact of these barriers" (Lash, 1992: 14).

Consultation procedures to be employed in monitoring compliance and enforcing agreements with foreign governments were also amended under Section 306. The new procedures institutionalize the participation of the private sector. Under the new amendment, "before taking any action, the USTR shall consult with the petitioner and the domestic industry and provide an opportunity for public views" (Bliss, 1989: 519). Thus the participation of the industry associations has been increasingly institutionalized.

Another significant amendment under Section 337 of the Trade Act of 1988 strengthens the enforcement of IP rights. The MPAA, PMA, Computer & Business Equipment Manufacturers Association, and Intellectual Property Owners, Inc. actively had lobbied Congress for changes in Section 337. These industry associations succeeded in their quest to eliminate the injury requirement in IP rights investigations. Under the amended Section 337 complainants are no longer required to prove injury. As Newman points out:

> By not requiring proof of injury, complainants are spared the exercise required under prior section 337 practice, of establishing injury ... It is estimated that over half the total expenses of litigating section 337 cases were incurred in establishing the injury and other economic requirements ... The deletion of the injury requirement in investigations based on intellectual property violations represents a great new advantage to complainants.                                (Newman, 1989: 575–577)

With the 1988 amendments, complainants no longer have to demonstrate that their businesses are "efficiently and economically operated domestic industry." The MPAA sought this revision because under the old rule the International Trade Commission "was skeptical of mere marketing and sales efforts, licensing, and the ownership of intellectual property" (Newman, 1989: 578). Since much of the MPAA's business abroad constitutes these types of activities, the amendment gives its IP efforts a substantial boost. Finally, the time period for temporary relief proceedings was shortened "on the theory that an accelerated procedure would be more useful to complainants" (Newman, 1989: 574). Indeed, one of the main complaints about the old Section 337 was that as the proceedings dragged on the IP violations continued unabated to the detriment of the complainant. By passing these amendments the Congress sought to make the ITC investigations of IP violations "less costly and cumbersome" (Newman, 1989: 587).

Thus 1988 was a watershed year in the quest to strengthen a trade-based approach to IP protection. The private sector secured the changes that it sought, and proceeded to use these new weapons in its arsenal – swift retaliation and a more credible threat – particularly against newly industrializing and developing countries.

The private sector has been remarkably successful in its efforts to get the United States to adopt a trade-based approach to IP protection. Not satisfied with unilateral measures through US Trade Act amendments, representatives of various IP-based industries also pressed for bilateral and multilateral approaches. For example, on the bilateral front the PMA sought to ensure that the NAFTA agreement with Mexico incorporated strict IP protection standards. As Mike Privatera, the public affairs director for the US-based pharmaceutical company Pfizer Inc., noted, "The Mexicans gave us everything we wanted" (quoted in Neuman, 1992: 127).

While the evidence presented here is not exhaustive, it provides insights into the origin of the US preferences for a trade-based approach to intellectual property. The movement for a trade-based approach was embedded in the changing structure of global capitalism and attendant competitiveness concerns. Institutional changes such as increased private sector access to trade policymaking bodies paved the way for IP owners, especially corporate actors, to promote their private interests. Significantly, institutions mediated between changes in the structure of global capitalism and the private interests of the IP rights activists.

US preferences for a trade-based approach to intellectual property were the result of both the power of the various industry associations, and the specific ideas and policy prescriptions that they promoted. Mobilizing behind the trade linkage concept was a powerful group of industry associations that could present themselves as part of the solution to America's trade problems. These associations captured the imagination of American policymakers who sought to stave off an apparently impending protectionist approach to trade policy.

This trade-based conception of IP protection was reflected in amendments to domestic laws, and bilateral agreements. US-based industry associations availed themselves of opportunities afforded by changes in US trade policy, including the increased access for private sector representatives as well as heightened concerns over the trade deficit. Astutely marketing their demands, these industry associations captured the attention of US policymakers and presented a persuasive case to use trade policy in an effort to secure protection of IP rights abroad.

The activities of these private sector actors were critical to the fortunes of the multilateral efforts in the Uruguay Round. The United States advocacy of a stringent global IP agreement did not appear out of nowhere. Private sector actors painstakingly and relentlessly worked to change attitudes toward intellectual property, and to get the government to take concrete steps to institutionalize the new approach. The advocacy of the industry associations and a handful of well-connected corporate players was critical in developing support for a trade-based approach to intellectual property in a strikingly short period of time. However, taking these concerns to the next level – in the Uruguay Round – was the task of an even smaller, more focused group of advocates, the Intellectual Property Committee (IPC). Their story is the subject of Chapter 5.

# 5    The Intellectual Property Committee and transnational mobilization

> If war is much too important a subject to leave up to generals, as
> Bismarck said, the rules of international commerce are far too impor-
> tant to leave up to government bureaucrats.
>
>   James Enyart, director, International Affairs, Monsanto
>   Agricultural Company

In March 1986, six months before the Punta del Este meeting launching
the Uruguay Round of GATT negotiations, twelve corporate executives
of US-based multinational corporations formed the Intellectual Property
Committee (IPC).[1] The IPC sought to develop international support for
improving the international protection of intellectual property (patents,
copyrights, trademarks, and trade secrets). The IPC, in conjunction with
its counterparts in Europe and Japan, crafted a proposal based on existing industrialized country laws and presented its proposals to the
GATT Secretariat. By 1994, the IPC had achieved its goal in the Trade
Related Aspects of Intellectual Property (TRIPS) accord of the Uruguay
trade round. The United States, and ultimately the parties to the GATT
negotiations, accepted the particular vision articulated by the IPC. What
is new in this case is that industry identified a trade problem, devised a
solution, and reduced it to a concrete proposal that it then advanced to
governments. These private sector actors succeeded in getting most of
what they wanted from an IP agreement, which now has the status of
public international law.

In effect, twelve corporations made public law for the world. The
combination of the increasing openness of the US system to private

---

[1] Throughout the years 1986–1996, the IPC's membership fluctuated from eleven to fourteen corporations. In 1994, CBS, Du Pont, and General Motors no longer participated,
but Digital Equipment Corporation, FMC, Procter & Gamble, Rockwell International and
Time Warner did.

influence and the changing structural position of the United States in the world economy provided an opening for corporate influence. These were necessary, but not sufficient, conditions for the TRIPS outcome. As Mizruchi suggests, "the business community, despite its potential for power due to its huge accumulation of resources, will be a politically powerful actor only to the extent that it is capable of mobilizing as a politically unified force" (Mizruchi, 1992: 34). Powerful firms organized among themselves, through their industry associations, and with their European and Japanese counterparts to construct a transnational coalition favoring tough multilateral IP rules.

Domestically, the most active private sector participants were corporations working through their industry associations. By contrast, transnationally, US corporate executives bypassed their industry associations and directly engaged their European and Japanese counterparts to press for a TRIPS agreement in the GATT. The transnational leadership of these US-based corporations was decisive in the achievement of the TRIPS accord.

The first section of this chapter discusses the relationship between the private sector and the state. The second part addresses the formation of the IPC. Following that the chapter describes the IPC's efforts to mobilize its European and Japanese counterparts, and the development of a negotiating consensus. Lastly, the negotiating process at the GATT, and the outcome of the TRIPS accord are discussed.

The relationships between private sector actors and state policy are quite fluid. According to Strange, "states may provide a framework of legal rights and duties within which other actors influence outcomes. Or they may be merely the arena, the stage or circus roof beneath which the action is played out" (Strange, 1996: 70). Conceptually, the relationship between state and private actors can vary considerably; private actors may see the state as an adversary, an ally, or irrelevant to the pursuit of their interests. Private actors may succeed in altering states' interests to conform to their private interests, thereby making the state an ally. Private actors may prompt the state to expand the framework of legal rights and duties by "persuading others to share fundamental beliefs about society and economy or to decide what knowledge is sought for and acquired and by whom" (Strange, 1996: 70). In the IP case, firms began to see the state as an ally, once the state had accepted the private sector's trade-based conception of intellectual property. Private authorities saw the US government, and by extension the international institution of the GATT, as a potential ally in their quest to expand international rules covering intellectual property. In this case, private actors seeking to globalize their preferred conception of policy needed international institutions to further and legitimize the private actors' goals, monitor compliance, and enforce policy. Since these actors sought the protection of their intellectual property, the GATT ultimately facilitated the achievement of their goals and helped empower this transnational coalition at the expense of others who fundamentally disagreed with its position.

Private actors pursued their interests through institutionalized access channels. The private actors appealed to both the legislative and executive branches in their quest for globalizing IP protection. The state is not a neutral broker of interests, and it structures private sector participation. The state plays both a "dependent and intervening role, its initiatives [are] continually shaped by corporate preferences" (Lipson, 1985: 256). Corporations are not like other interest groups. The "playing field" is far from level. As Lipson points out, "major corporations play a structurally privileged role, including a hegemonic role in establishing political norms and public agendas" (Lipson, 1985: 222). The corporations that formed the IPC were even more privileged than most; for example, eight of the member corporations are among the top fifty US exporters (Aley, 1995: 73–76). They have access to resources unmatched by most other interest groups.

The sources of the IPC corporations' private authority are multiple and varied. Their prominent role in both production and knowledge structures gives them a larger voice as authority shifts from states to markets. States recognize these firms' sheer economic power, and confer authority upon them when they give them an explicit policymaking role. The private authority of leading firms in intellectual property derives "in part from their mastery of technology, in part from their financial resources and developed systems of marketing and distribution. But it has also depended on the support and collaboration of states in the promotion of an ideology of property rights" (Strange, 1996: 97). Their access to information and expertise gives them an additional source of authority.

Corporations perform many essential functions for government (Lindblom, 1977: 175), not the least of which is to provide information. Their structurally privileged position contributes to what Lindblom refers to as "impairment" in the marketplace of ideas (Lindblom, 1990). In intellectual property, multinational corporations and their industry associations consistently have provided information about foreign governments' failures to provide adequate IP protection. Availing themselves of private policy networks, such as private law firms based abroad, these corporations have been the source of detailed substantive information about IP laws, practices, and infractions. The corporations have been vigilant in monitoring compliance in targeted states and have contracted law firms to report back to them. Corporations have committed considerable resources to the exposure of rampant piracy of intellectual property abroad. To determine the scale and scope of foreign piracy, the government has had to rely upon cost estimates provided by affected firms. Government reliance on information provided by a self-interested private sector stacked the deck in that sector's favor.

A further resource the private sector can provide to government is expertise in relatively arcane issue areas. To a certain extent IP law is reminiscent of the Catholic Church when the Bible was in Latin. IP lawyers are privileged purveyors of expertise as was the Latin-trained clergy. IP law is highly technical and complex, obscure even to most general attorneys. The arcane nature of IP law gave additional advantages to the US IP lobby; its possession of technical and juristic knowledge was an important source of its private authority. The government relied upon IP experts, who were also advocates, to translate the complexities into political discourse and make clear the connection between intellectual property and international trade.[2] IP lawyers are socialized to promote the *protection* of international property and uphold the ideology of private property rights. Thus, even though there are IP lawyers in the US Commerce Department and the Patent and Trademark Office, they share a commitment to IP protection. Therefore, in this context, there is no neutral or objective group of civil servants in a position to counterbalance private demands.

When private actors need the state to promote their interests, they must present their interests in a way that appeals to policymakers in furthering the goals of the state. This is especially true in multilateral negotiations in which nation-states, not private actors, have standing. In this case, the IP lobby was particularly effective in translating their private interests into a matter of public interest. Conscious that the US government was increasingly worried about its burgeoning trade deficit and its ability to effectively compete internationally, the IP lobby astutely packaged its demands as a solution to America's trade woes. IP

---

[2] In some respects, this conception mirrors issues raised by the "epistemic community" literature yet my argument is broader. The relevant community of experts was hardly the image of scientists presenting their objective results in a persuasive manner. It included experts, advocates, lobbyists, and corporations who stood to gain quite a lot by prevailing.

advocates presented their industries as part of the solution and high-lighted their strength as competitive exporters. They emphasized that they were the industries of the future that would provide new American jobs into the next century. They further stressed that they were not seeking protection or special treatment of any kind, but sought the government's help in creating a more fair global trading order. Their success, in large part, was in their appeal to America's long-standing free trade ethos and in pitching their cause in a way that captured the imagination of American policymakers as politically feasible. The way that the IP lobby presented its case to both Congress and the Executive Branch underscores the relationship between ideas and interests. Their efforts led the US government to redefine its interest in intellectual property, and endorse a trade-based approach to the globalization of intellectual property. In this case, there would have been no multilateral TRIPS agreement without the concerted efforts of a handful of individuals. Prior to the 1986 Punta del Este meeting there was no enthusiasm for such an agreement outside the United States.

The story that follows illustrates the porous boundaries between domestic and international realms, public and private sectors, ideas and interests. This porousness reflects the complexity of a world in which multinational enterprises are the primary agents of internationalization, and are at the forefront of new forms of diplomacy and global regulation.

## The quest for a multilateral approach to intellectual property: the IPC

The private sector mobilization began modestly and gained momentum over time following a number of legislative successes. The scope of participation widened in 1984 under the umbrella of the newly created International Intellectual Property Alliance (IIPA hereafter).[3] The moving force behind the creation of the IIPA was the motion picture industry and its energetic association president, Jack Valenti. The IIPA was created in 1984 to promote copyright interests in the section 301 process, to educate trade negotiators and advertise the scale and costs of copyright piracy worldwide. (Not coincidentally, John Young, CEO of Hewlett-Packard, was among the founding members of the IIPA, and later, the

---

[3] The IPC and IIPA worked closely together, and many of the IPC members were quite active in their respective industry associations as well. However, I will focus my discussion primarily on the IPC.

IPC). Soon patent interests were testifying before Congress in favor of copyright and trademark interests, which had heretofore been engaged in separate efforts. The IP activists realized that advocating enhanced protection of all forms of intellectual property would help improve the climate for their particular interests, and thus they banded together and united behind the common cause.

The ACTN, led by Opel and Pratt, persuaded the USTR that intellectual property should be included in the GATT Round. Initially however, the copyright industries, unlike the patent interests, were not so enthusiastic about a multilateral GATT strategy. The computer software companies, including IBM, were not opposed to reforming the multilateral Berne Convention to incorporate computer software but were concerned about enforcement in developing countries. But the music, book, and film industries preferred the bilateral 301 strategy to press enforcement abroad. Valenti, of the MPAA, was a firm believer in the bilateral process and had been closely involved in successful negotiations with Korea among other developing countries. The IIPA also endorsed the bilateral approach as preferable for getting relatively quick results. GATT Rounds were notorious for their complexity; the copyright interests feared that their agenda might be watered down or traded away for other concessions. Most crucially, they feared losing their unilateral 301 option that they had worked so hard to obtain. It took substantial reassurance and several heated meetings hosted by USTR to get the copyright interests on board for the multilateral effort (see Ryan, 1998a: 562).

In 1984, the USTR requested private sector input on the issue of including intellectual property on the agenda of the upcoming GATT Round. Opel of IBM commissioned Jacques Gorlin, an economist who had served as a consultant to ACTN and subsequently the IPC, to draft a paper for the USTR outlining a trade-based approach for intellectual property. Gorlin's September 1985 paper, "A Trade-Based Approach for the International Copyright Protection for Computer Software" (Gorlin, 1985) became the basis of the multilateral IP strategy that corporations soon pursued.

A turning point in the private sector's quest for the globalization of its preferred trade-based conception of IP protection occurred in 1985. Gorlin's contribution was his synthesis and extension of the more *ad hoc* lobbying requests and position papers that corporations and industry associations had presented to Congress and the Executive Branch throughout the early 1980s. His document provided the contours of a possible multilateral agreement for the GATT, as well as suggested strategies for consensus building. Not surprisingly, in October 1985 the ACTN Task Force on Intellectual Property Rights presented its report to ACTN and its recommendations appeared to be lifted wholesale out of Gorlin's document (USTR, 1985).

Gorlin advocated a number of strategies, including: a campaign to educate IP experts on the economic aspects of the issues; US accession to the Berne Convention for the Protection of Literary and Artistic Works; the negotiation of an IP code with like-minded industrialized countries within the OECD or plurilaterally within the GATT, "to avoid the obstructionist tactics of the LDCs" (Gorlin, 1985: iv); recognition that the WIPO would need to be consulted, and its resistance to the establishment of an IP code at GATT overcome; and the continuation of complementary unilateral and bilateral efforts to combat piracy and weak enforcement abroad. According to Gorlin, the advantages of incorporating intellectual property into the multilateral trade regime would include availability of a dispute settlement mechanism, the use of linkage to other trade and investment issues, and the greater political leverage of trade officials. As Gorlin summarized, developing a trade-based code "would help deal with the problems of piracy that are caused by governmental actions such as substandard legal protection and enforcement, by providing a forum with higher visibility, a tradition of finger-pointing, and a willingness to get involved in dispute settlement" (Gorlin, 1985: 43). To build the necessary consensus, Gorlin advocated pursuing plurilateral simultaneous negotiations within the OECD and GATT.

In February and March 1986, USTR Clayton Yeutter asked Opel and Pratt for assistance in putting intellectual property on the Uruguay Round agenda.[4] Yeutter pointed out that the European, Japanese, and Canadian governments were not getting any industry pressure for intellectual property, and that without all of the big four on board (United States, Canada, Europe, Japan) there was no chance of an IP deal in the Uruguay Round. To develop an IP code, Pratt and Opel needed a core of committed and actively engaged companies with international connections to secure US governmental and foreign support (Enyart, 1990: 54). At this point, Opel and Pratt contacted their peers and convinced their fellow CEOs to form the IPC in March 1986. According to James Enyart, then director of international affairs for Monsanto Agricultural

---

[4] This section is based on author's interview with Jacques Gorlin, January 22, 1996, Washington, DC.

Company and founding IPC member, the CEOs provided adequate funding and human resources to the IP effort, and provided added momentum by directly contacting their corporate counterparts (Enyart, 1990: 54).

The IPC, rather than working through its respective industry associations, chose to bypass these associations in search of a quick consensus. The IPC sought rapid results. To maximize its impact it deliberately limited its membership, and insisted that member companies be represented by the top echelons of management to avoid cumbersome negotiations within the corporations. The IPC operated as a committee of the whole, and its streamlined structure was designed to get things done quickly. It represented a broad array of US industries – chemical, computer, creative arts, electronics, heavy and consumer manufacturing, and pharmaceutical industries. As Enyart points out, "no existing US trade group or association really filled the bill, we had to create one" (Enyart, 1990: 54).

The first step was to arrive at a consensus as a group. Representing pharmaceuticals, movies, and computers, for example, raised coordination challenges. According to Pratt, this group of "strange bedfellows" needed to define its objectives and strategies very clearly (Pratt, quoted in Ostry, 1990: 23). In fairly short order, the group resolved that the three critical aspects for an international IP agreement were: (1) a code of minimum standards for copyrights, patents, trademarks, and appellation of origin issues; (2) an enforcement mechanism; and (3) a dispute settlement mechanism.

That same month, March 1986, the ACTN's Task Force on Intellectual Property Rights issued a second report focusing on US bilateral and unilateral efforts (USTR, 1986). Like Gorlin's 1985 paper, it endorsed a carrot and stick approach by supporting efforts to provide technical training in IP issues to foreign officials, while also strengthening US trade leverage over reluctant foreign governments. Among the sticks were making the renewal of GSP benefits contingent on the effective protection of intellectual property and the further strengthening of Section 301. The Task Force also underscored the crucial role that the private sector had played in the expansion of a trade-based approach. According to the report, "the US IP-based industries have already played a significant catalytic role in defining IP as a trade issue and in having US trade officials accept IP as part of their agenda" (USTR, 1986). The Task Force emphasized the continuing importance of private sector/government dialogue for shoring up domestic consensus on a trade-based approach.

Domestically, the IPC was far from idle.[5] It contacted the US Chamber of Commerce and numerous industry associations to persuade them of the merits of a trade-based approach to intellectual property. These organizations adopted IPC positions and endorsed the overall multilateral strategy. For example, in July 1986, the Joint Working Party on IP issues and the GATT of the International Chamber of Commerce recommended the inclusion of intellectual property in the new GATT round (US Senate, 1986: 149). Since the IPC member corporations were among the most active in their respective industry associations as it was, this was not a particularly hard sell.

## IPC: mobilizing a transnational coalition; shoring up a consensus

Time was short; the IPC only had six months before the upcoming September Punta del Este meeting. From the time of its formation in March, the group wasted very little time in its quest to develop a pre-negotiation consensus with the Europeans and Japanese. IPC members immediately contacted their peers in European and Japanese industry. In June 1986, the IPC met with the Confederation of British Industries, the BDI in Germany, the French Patronat and through them, with the Union of Industrial and Employers' Confederations of Europe (UNICE).[6] In July, the IPC went to Japan and met with the Japan Federation of Economic Organizations (Keidanren).[7] The IPC hoped that a joint agreement between the United States, Europe and Japan would have a positive effect on curbing IP "theft" in developing countries.

Initially UNICE and Keidanren were lukewarm at best and balked at joining the IPC effort. As Pratt noted, these associations "feared that intellectual property was too new a subject to become part of the GATT, and they felt initially that intellectual property was...ill-suited to the Uruguay Round..." (Pratt, quoted in Ostry, 1990: 23). The Europeans and Japanese anticipated an already complex agenda for the Round, including issues of great salience, such as agriculture. They also were

---

[5] Ibid.

[6] UNICE is the official spokesman for European business and industry in European institutions; it is composed of thirty-three member federations from twenty-two countries with a permanent Secretariat based in Brussels.

[7] Keidanren is a private, non-profit economic organization representing virtually all branches of economic activity in Japan. It maintains close contact with both public and private sectors at home and abroad.

aware that developing countries were opposed to incorporating intellectual property into the GATT. The IPC embarked on a series of meetings with its European and Japanese counterparts to try to change their attitudes.

In these meetings, the IPC stressed that the issue of intellectual property was too important to leave to governments.[8] The group argued that industry needed to decide upon the best course of action and then tell governments what to do. The IPC emphasized that WIPO, while at that time charged with administering various IP conventions, was no longer adequate to the task. The problem, according to the IPC, was WIPO's identification with the special interests of developing countries. As a part of the UN system with a one-state one-vote process, WIPO was destined to uphold the interests of the majority of developing countries "who abet the theft of intellectual property" (Pratt, quoted in Ostry, 1990: 24). While recognizing the value of WIPO as a technical body involved with IP issues, the IPC argued that since intellectual property was essentially a trade and investment issue that it rightly belonged in the GATT.

The IPC also sought to persuade its European and Japanese counterparts of the merits of a trade-based approach to intellectual property by emphasizing their common plight, and asking questions such as, "Don't you have problems with Brazil too?" The IPC emphasized the high costs of IP piracy, and the successes that had been achieved through bilateral trade negotiations. The IPC explained and documented the extent of IP "theft" and underscored the threat that unauthorized use of intellectual property posed to the industrialized countries' future prosperity. Using the US International Trade Commission (ITC) figures that US firms had supplied, the IPC argued that US firms had lost $23.8 billion or 2.7 percent of sales affected by intellectual property. The IPC cited the ITC figures that US industry as a whole had lost between $43 and $61 billion in 1986 due to inadequate IP enforcement abroad (IPC, Keidanren, and UNICE, 1988: 12–13).

Finally, the IPC presented its own broad consensus that minimum standards, enforcement and dispute settlement mechanisms could be developed within GATT. A GATT-based solution could render IP infractions more transparent, incorporate direct consultation and mediation procedures for IP violations, and would improve upon existing

---

[8] Unless otherwise indicated, the next three paragraphs are based on author's interview with Gorlin.

arrangements in WIPO by providing for enforcement mechanisms. Additionally, the IPC pointed out that a GATT IP agreement, "by diminishing the need for unilateral retaliation . . . would do much to restore a sense of calm to trade relations" (Pratt, quoted in Ostry, 1990: 24).

The IPC succeeded in forging an industry consensus with its Japanese and European industry counterparts, who agreed to work on it and pledged to present these views to their respective governments in time for the launching of the Uruguay Round. Pratt noted that this joint action by the US, European, and Japanese business communities represented a noteworthy breakthrough in the international business community's involvement in trade negotiations (Drahos, 1995: 13). UNICE and Keidanren successfully advanced their cause to their governments in the short time remaining; by the launching of the new trade round in September, the United States, Japan, and Europe were united behind the inclusion of an IP code in the GATT.

At the outset of the Punta del Este meeting, some Western delegations still endorsed a more modest approach to intellectual property than that advocated by the IPC. They sought to revive a 1982 draft proposal on an Anti-Counterfeiting Code that had been developed in the wake of the Tokyo Round of GATT negotiations, and leave more comprehensive proposals on IP rights to later negotiating rounds. Indeed, the European and Japanese trade associations and their governments, IPC efforts notwithstanding, were not as committed to a broad IP agreement at the outset. They were unsure whether GATT was the most appropriate venue for IP issues, and there were a number of other pressing and salient issues at stake in the Round. However, over time the Europeans and Japanese came to abandon this more limited strategy "for fear that a successful Anti-Counterfeiting Code might take the momentum out of the negotiations for a broader, all-inclusive code" (Emmert, 1990: 1939).[9]

In the United States, the IPC worked closely with the IIPA to coordinate and promote their positions to the government. The Patent and Trademark Office (PTO) and USTR also worked closely together to push the US IP agenda. Mike Kirk, the chief US TRIPS negotiator, was "very supportive."[10] Throughout the process the IPC continued to consult with the US administration and Congress, and a 1988 IPC report

[9] The Germans were concerned about developing country opposition but were reassured when they asked the IIPA "how countries like Mexico could be persuaded not to oppose TRIPS. 'Don't worry about Mexico', they said. 'We've got them in our pocket.' Reference was made to their trade dependence" (Braithwaite and Drahos, 2000: 215).

[10] Author's interview with Gorlin.

indicated that the IPC's close relationship with commerce and the USTR permitted it to shape both US negotiating positions and specific proposals throughout the course of the negotiations (Drahos, 1995: 13). Indeed, a number of the IPC member corporations were represented in ACTN, or as formal advisers to the USTR on intellectual property matters (senior officials from PhRMA, and Pfizer, Inc., Dow, Johnson & Johnson, Merck & Co. Inc., du Pont, Monsanto, and Procter & Gamble) (Kosterlitz, 1993: 398; Weissman, 1996: 1076). While in Geneva, American trade negotiators frequently contacted the IPC, IIPA, and PhRMA; these groups provided careful and detailed analysis and proposals (Ryan, 1998a: 564; Ostry, 1990: 23). US industry, and the IPC in particular, had a potent ally at the Uruguay Round. Pratt was an adviser to the US Official Delegation at the Uruguay Round in his capacity as chairman of ACTN. This was auspicious because the private sector has no official standing at GATT. UNICE and Keidanren represented European and Japanese business in Geneva throughout the negotiation process.

The IPC, UNICE, and Keidanren agreed to continue to work together to devise a consensual approach to an IP code at the GATT. Industry representatives met in October and November 1986, and worked on producing a consensus document to present to their respective governments and the GATT Secretariat. During this process of devising a concrete proposal for a GATT code, participants worked hard to fairly represent the diverse forms of intellectual property and the various industries involved (Enyart, 1990: 55). In October 1987 the USTR in Geneva submitted its suggestions for achieving the negotiating objective of an IP agreement. By November 1987, the Europeans and Japanese tabled concrete negotiating proposals for an IP agreement, and thereby gave the TRIPS effort considerable momentum (Damschroder, 1988: 398).

In June 1988, this private sector "trilateral group" released its "Basic Framework of GATT Provisions on Intellectual Property" (IPC, Keidanren and UNICE, 1988) and presented it to all the Round participants. The contents were very similar to the concrete proposals of Gorlin's 1985 paper, and became the basis of the eventual TRIPS agreement. It advocated minimum standards, national enforcement measures, border measures to seize counterfeit goods, and dispute settlement mechanisms. As a consensus document, it included some compromises. For example, the US pharmaceutical industry was not entirely satisfied with the provisions on compulsory licensing; but the United States conceded the issue to keep the Europeans and Japanese on board. Furthermore, to induce the broadest possible participation in an IP agreement the European business groups urged preferential treatment for developing countries along with technical assistance and transition provisions (see IPC, Keidanren, and UNICE, 1988: 27). Having produced this consensus proposal, the IPC, Keidanren, and UNICE returned to their home countries to pitch the trilateral approach to other industries and companies (Enyart, 1990: 55). The IPC had no difficulty; indeed, the US government requested 100–150 copies of the June 1988 trilateral proposal and sent it out as reflecting its views.[11] Furthermore, the oft-noted differences in government–business relations in the United States, Japan, and Europe did not seem to make much difference in the ability of this Trilateral Group to secure governmental support for its proposals.

## The GATT negotiations and the TRIPS accord

Between 1986 and April 1989, IP issues stalled in the trade negotiations. The so-called "Group of Ten" developing countries, led by India and Brazil, vehemently protested the inclusion of intellectual property in the GATT.[12] Meanwhile, the United States increased the pressure by adopting new amendments to US trade laws. In 1988 the US strengthened its trade-based approach to intellectual property. Motivated by industry lobbying, Congress pressed the administration to use Section 301 more vigorously. The private sector secured the changes that it sought and proceeded to use these new weapons in its arsenal – swift retaliation and a more credible threat – particularly against newly industrializing and developing countries. Significantly, the recalcitrant Brazil immediately bore the brunt of the United States' aggressive strategy. The PMA initiated a Section 301 case against Brazil for its failure to provide patent protection for pharmaceutical products. After Brazil refused to alter its domestic IP policy, in 1989 the United States placed a 100 percent retaliatory tariff (totaling $39 million) on imports of Brazilian pharmaceuticals, paper products, and consumer electronics.[13]

In December 1988 trade negotiators met in Montreal for the midterm review of the Round. This meeting concluded with no formal agreements due to a deadlock over long-term agricultural reform and

[11] Ibid.

[12] These ten countries were Argentina, Brazil, Cuba, Egypt, India, Nicaragua, Nigeria, Peru, Tanzania and Yugoslavia.

[13] n.a. "Differences Over Code on Patents," *Latin American Regional Reports – Brazil*, RB-91–04 (London: Latin American Newsletters, May 2, 1991), p. 4.

intellectual property. The Trade Negotiations Committee (TNC) sought consensus on a framework of an IP agreement and a commitment to negotiate specific standards. The TNC made significant progress toward narrowing differences between contracting parties, yet in the end Brazil and India stood fast in opposition and "prevented attainment" of the mid-term review objectives (Stewart, 1993: 2268–2269).

Despite the fact that progress on the TRIPS negotiations had stalled, the IPC continued to pursue its multilateral efforts. The IPC worked to keep its business coalition together, and also focused its efforts on the GATT Secretariat. Intellectual property was a new issue for the GATT Secretariat. Some members of the Secretariat recognized the inherent tension between free trade and the monopoly privileges of intellectual property, yet did not systematically analyze TRIPS in this light but rather "responded to the 'imperatives of the negotiations'" (Drahos, 1995: 14). Furthermore, taking a page from the 1985 Gorlin paper, negotiators worked in enclave committees to achieve plurilateral consensus – just as the IPC had done in its discussions with its European and Japanese counterparts. The IPC replicated its consensus-building approach within the GATT, and two subgroups – a "Friends of Intellectual Property" group, and the Quad (the most powerful enclave committee) – significantly contributed to developing the TRIPS text (Drahos, 1995: 14).

By April 1989, leading developing countries had accepted that GATT could have jurisdiction in intellectual property, and that the TRIPS group could negotiate a comprehensive code of all trade-related aspects of IP rights. At the April 1989 Geneva meeting the delegations adopted a declaration endorsing continuation of the negotiating round and the applicability of GATT principles to intellectual property issues (Emmert, 1990: 1374). India continued to hold out until September 12, 1989 when it announced it had accepted in principle the international enforcement of trade-related IP rights within the Uruguay Round context. After this breakthrough the negotiations entered into a more intensive phase and a number of developing countries became more engaged in the process (Evans, 1994: 170).

There were several reasons that formerly intransigent developing countries went along. First of all, they were experiencing escalating pressure from the United States via Section 301 and GSP actions. Besides the Brazilian case, the United States also had targeted South Korea for 301 action. Many developing countries hoped that cooperation on TRIPS might ease the 301 pressure. In May 1988, East Asian NICs were officially dropped from the United States list of developing countries and became ineligible for GSP benefits. India had received considerable bilateral pressure from the United States to drop its opposition to the TRIPS agreement. While they initially posed the choice of forum as one between WIPO and GATT, developing countries came to realize that in reality the choice was between GATT and USTR (Ryan, 1998a: 566). Also, the United States, Canada, and Mexico had successfully negotiated NAFTA, which included stiff IP requirements.[14] Many Latin American countries, hoping eventually to join considered IP commitments as part of the admission price (Drahos, 1995: 15). For smaller countries that had not been targeted by 301 actions, NAFTA and the proliferation of similar regional trading blocs posed a different set of concerns that led them to support TRIPS and the Round as a whole. Not being parties to any preferential regional agreements, they came to endorse a strong liberalizing outcome to counter discriminatory trade practices emanating from the regional blocs, recognizing that broad market access was imperative for their economic well-being (Whalley, 1995: 305–326). Furthermore, developing countries received promises of greatly expanded market access for their agricultural products and textiles in exchange for agreeing to offer greater IP protection.

Another factor was the glaring asymmetries in experience and expertise on IP issues. India and Brazil had formulated numerous counterproposals during the negotiations, stressing issues such as the public interest, shorter patent terms, and the obligations of IP owners to "work" their inventions in developing countries. However, corporate counsel from US industry with extensive experience in intellectual property and licensing critically evaluated these proposals. As Drahos points out, "once they had passed an opinion the enclave committee structure within the GATT, groups like the IPC and IIPA, the business triumvirate and the developed countries coordinated to criticize and reject the proposals" (Drahos, 1995: 15). Drahos stresses that the rejection of the counter-proposals cannot be explained simply in terms of power, and that developing countries' representatives were novices with regard to intellectual property and licensing expertise. Authority deriving from technical and juristic expertise enabled industrialized country

[14] Notably the IPC was intimately involved in the NAFTA process as well. In Canada, a letter from the IPC to then-USTR was leaked that "included negotiating instructions and specific demands for inclusions in NAFTA to satisfy industry... The success of the US industry in securing patent provisions in NAFTA was... summarized by Edgar G. Davis, former vice president of Eli Lilly... Davis boasts that putting the patent provisions in NAFTA was 'a master stroke, [demonstrating] what an industry that has its act together can accomplish'" (Weissman, 1996: 1082).

negotiators to "pull rank" and subject developing country negotiators to "the disciplining effect of expert knowledge" (Drahos, 1995: 15).

Thus, by 1989 developing country resistance had finally been overcome. By the end of 1989 negotiators reached a consensus that developing countries should be allowed a grace period to implement measures to permit them to conform to an IP agreement. The TRIPS negotiating process shifted from the North–South impasse to hard bargaining over specific provisions between the Europeans and Americans, and the Americans and the Japanese.

While the IPC, UNICE, and Keidanren had reached broad consensus on the substance of a multilateral IP agreement as reflected in their trilateral document, differences emerged over details of specific provisions. "North–North" issues dominated the remaining negotiations. Essentially, the Europeans pressed the Americans to accept some European features of IP policy, and the Americans challenged areas of difference between American and Japanese practices (Stewart, 1993: 2313). The EC played a leading role in trying to bridge differences outstanding as of January 1990 and was the first to submit a comprehensive draft text during this new phase of negotiations (Evans, 1994: 171).

Throughout 1990 the United States and the European Community clashed over exceptions to patentable subject matter. The US, Japanese, Nordic, and Swiss proposals offered no exceptions. The European Community's and developing countries' draft proposals included exceptions for "inventions that would be contrary to public policy and health, plant or animal varieties or the biological processes for their production" (Stewart, 1993: 2273). Those listed by the European Community and developing countries (ultimately incorporated in TRIPS as Article 27(3)) were seen as a direct challenge to the booming US biotechnology industry. American biotechnology interests have argued that without patent protection for their products and processes they are hard pressed to attract venture capital for their businesses. While US law permits the patenting of life forms,[15] for example, the infamous "Harvard mouse," the idea of patenting life forms is distasteful on moral grounds in much of Europe, and the Catholic Church, which is very strong in a number

[15] In the landmark case *Diamond v. Chakrabaty*, 447 US 303 (1980) the Supreme Court ruled that a live, genetically altered microorganism could be patented. This precedent-setting case has led to the expansion of rights to own living organisms. In 1987 Harvard researchers Philip Leder and Timothy Stewart won a patent on a transgenic mouse; they developed a strain of mice for cancer research by inserting a cancer gene into mouse egg cells.

of European countries, looks down upon such practices.[16] Furthermore, the very idea of patenting a life form raises controversial questions about invention, novelty, and the suitability of patenting products of nature. The TRIPS agreement follows the European Patent Convention of 1973, which permits the patenting of microbiological but not macrobiological processes; so micro-organisms and non-biological and microbiological processes are protected, but higher organisms are not (Reichman, 1993: 192–193).

The European Community and Switzerland also bargained hard for protection for geographical indications, including appellations of origin. Driven by the wines and spirits' interests in France, Italy, Spain, and Switzerland the Europeans sought to provide for narrow definitions of "geographical indications" whereby, for instance, only wines made from grapes grown in Bordeaux could be called "Bordeaux." The United States called for protection of "non-generic" appellations of origin, for example, arguing that "champagne" is generic due to its common usage. The Europeans sought to include measures states could take to prevent geographical indications from becoming "generic." By mid-1990 the TRIPS negotiations were stalled while the United States and the European Community tried to reach agreement on these issues.

In May 1990 the United States, the European Community, Japan, Switzerland, and India (on behalf of a group of fourteen developing countries) tabled separate drafts, presenting five different structures and no common way of conceiving of institutional arrangements for implementation (Evans, 1994: 171). Ambassador Lars Anell of Sweden, chairman of the TRIPS negotiating group, then prepared and presented his own draft text of the status of work toward an agreement in July 1990. With this document he sought to provide a clear picture of the state of the negotiations. The TRIPS negotiating group continued to meet throughout 1990 in preparation for the Brussels Ministerial Meeting of December 1990 which was to conclude the Round. Negotiations intensified throughout the second half of 1990. The Brussels Draft TRIPS Agreement reflected the negotiations as of November 22, 1990 and demonstrated considerable progress. The remaining unresolved issues included: moral rights, copyright protection for computer programs, protection for

---

[16] European and Japanese biotechnology firms have coped with their more restrictive legislative environments by establishing alliances with US firms to conduct research and develop products in the United States. A number of German firms have relocated their research facilities in the United States where the legal and political climate is more hospitable (Tancer, 1995: 159).

performers and broadcasters, length of protection for sound recordings, and whether plant varieties should be protected, and if so, by patents or otherwise, application of TRIPS into the GATT, and the strength of the dispute settlement procedures (Stewart, 1993: 2276).

Yet on December 7, 1990, the Uruguay Round negotiations collapsed in Brussels in a deadlock over agricultural subsidies between the European Community, on the one hand, and the United States and the Cairns group of agricultural exporters on the other. Since TRIPS progress was linked to the progress of the Round as a whole, the agricultural stalemate slowed down the TRIPS momentum. This spelled an end to the so-called "green room" process in which thirty-five countries or so engage in "horse trading."[17] In April 1990 the Latin Americans walked out. At this point, GATT director general Arthur Dunkel took over the process. He instituted a "ten on ten" (ten developed and ten developing countries) informal working group to examine the draft text with the aim of addressing each country's initial concerns (Evans, 1994: 173). There would be no more horse trading, but Dunkel took stances on controversial issues for countries to react and respond to. The Round was restarted and the TRIPS negotiating group resumed its meetings in late June 1991. According to Gorlin, 1991 was a tense time in the negotiations. The IPC deliberately ceased its lobbying activities and left the process to official US negotiators. The IPC did not want to seem underhanded, or acting behind the backs of the US negotiating team. Agriculture and services were particularly thorny issues. In the second half of 1991 most of the TRIPS negotiating action now shifted from the formal negotiations to the informal "Quad" group (United States, European Community, Japan, and Canada) and bilateral meetings, because at this point the major differences were between the Europeans, Americans, and Japanese (Stewart, 1993: 2280).

Some of the major outstanding issues involved copyright, and the IIPA and MPAA were particularly concerned with the French system of video levies,[18] and music interests objected to Japan's compact disc

---

[17] Paragraph based on author's interview with Gorlin.

[18] Also known as "collective licensing," this refers to the distribution of fees as compensation to authors of a copyrighted work. In the French system, for example, consumers are charged a small royalty on the purchase of blank videotapes and video recorders. This royalty is then divided up into four parts, one-fourth goes to the author to compensate for losses incurred by home taping. The IIPA and MPAA object to the provision in French law whereby foreign companies can only collect from the author's fund; according to the IIPA and MPAA this practice violates national treatment by discriminating against foreign copyright owners (Stewart, 1993: 2280–2281).

rental industry. The IPC testified before Congress on the Japanese practice; Pratt argued that Japan's rental business is "in effect, a license to make...piratical copies" (Pratt, quoted in Stewart, 1993: 2281–2282). US industry sought language giving record companies the right to prohibit commercial rental.

The Japanese, and Keidanren in particular, were wary of US and European proposals to extend too much copyright protection to computer software under Berne. This concern reflected the view that Japanese software was less sophisticated than American and European software. The Japanese argued for clarification that such protection would not be extended to an "idea" or "procedure"; they were particularly opposed to copyright protection for algorithms (Matsushita, 1992: 94; Correa, 1994: 545). The final draft agreement stipulates that protection is not extended to ideas, procedures, methods of operation or mathematical concepts (1994, TRIPS: Art. 9(2)).

The GATT talks resumed in September 1991, but the parties still had not reached agreement. In November, TNC chairman Dunkel distributed his overview of the negotiations, *Progress of Work in Negotiating Groups: Stock-Taking.*[19] He identified three groups of issues requiring agreement: (1) level and nature of IP standards, for example, patent term, whether wines and spirits should be granted extra protection under geographical indications, for copyrights the nature of protection of computer programs and the issue of rental rights; (2) grace periods for developing countries; and (3) institutional framework for international implementation.

Eager to save the Round and move the negotiations forward, in December Dunkel produced a draft comprising the results of the negotiations in each sector. This draft included a new TRIPS text that "provided an arbitrated resolution to issues undecided by the negotiators" (Stewart, 1993: 2282). Dunkel presented his draft to negotiators and proposed that the so-called "Dunkel Draft"[20] be rejected or accepted as a whole. For the next two years, the Dunkel Draft was roundly criticized for its inadequate treatment of IP rights. In the United States the IPC, the IIPA, PhRMA, the MPAA all testified as to its shortcomings before Congress, and continued to pursue aggressive 301 strategies through the

---

[19] GATT Doc. No. MTN.TNC/W/89/Add. 1 (November 7, 1991).

[20] Agreement on trade-related aspects of intellectual property rights, including trade in counterfeit goods (Annex III) in Draft final act embodying the results of the Uruguay Round of multilateral trade negotiations, GATT Doc. No. MTN.TNC/W/FA (December 20, 1991).

USTR. Their specific complaints will be discussed in more detail below, but they all opposed the transition provisions, or grace periods, for developing countries. However, these complaints must be placed in their proper context. Referring to the pharmaceutical industry, Weissman points out, "the industry's vociferous opposition to a ten-year transition period obscured how much it had won. It had completely seized control of the terms of the debate. The disputed issue was no longer whether the rest of the world should or would adopt strict patent rules but *when* it would" (Weissman, 1996: 1084–1085, emphasis added). According to Evans, a combination of negotiation fatigue, sunk costs, a sagging world economy, and fears of looming protectionism prompted negotiators to bring the Round to a conclusion (Evans, 1994: 174). Negotiating parties finally reached agreement on the so-called "Dunkel Draft" and the Uruguay Round was successfully concluded on April 15, 1994.

The IPC succeeded in getting most of what it wanted in the TRIPS (Trade Related Aspects of Intellectual Property, Including Trade in Counterfeit Goods) agreement in the Uruguay GATT round. According to Gorlin, except for the lengthy transition periods for developing countries, the IPC got 95 percent of what it wanted.[21] The IPC was particularly pleased with the enforcement provisions. The industry representatives' demands are reflected clearly in the final agreement. For example, the TRIPS agreement affirms the principle of national treatment and Article 33 mandates a twenty-year minimum period for exclusivity of patent rights from the date of filing the patent application.[22] Chemical and pharmaceutical producers gained by the provision in the TRIPS agreement that reverses the former burden of proof in process patent infringement cases; before the burden of proof of infringement rested with the patent holder, now the alleged infringer must demonstrate that the process used is substantially different (Kent, 1993: 179; TRIPS, Art. 34). Furthermore, the agreement restricts the issuance of compulsory licenses by forbidding exclusive licenses and sharply reducing the conditions for and scope of such licenses (TRIPS, Art. 31). This is significant, because, in the past, a number of developing countries reserved the right to issue exclusive compulsory licenses – authorizing a third party to work

[21] Author's interview with Gorlin.
[22] See: Office of the US Trade Representative, The 1994 General Agreement on Tariffs and Trade, Annex 1(C), "Agreement on Trade-Related Aspects of Intellectual Property, Including Trade in Counterfeit Goods," August 27, 1994, Articles 3(1), 27(1), and 33 of the TRIPS Agreement. This patent term was also included in the Trilateral Group's July 1988 agreement (IPC, Keidanren, and UNICE, 1988: 36).

an invention and excluding the property owner from exploiting the resource. Policymakers in developing countries suspected that many foreigners filed patents solely to block the use of the patented invention in the country or to promote importation of that article by the patent holder. In order to protect themselves from paying above-market rates for patented technology due to an import monopoly, many developing countries believed that the threat of exclusive compulsory licensing was a powerful tool for ensuring that foreign IP holders put their intellectual property to productive use rather than abuse their monopoly rights. This tool is no longer available to TRIPS signatories. The compulsory licensing provisions followed the EC conditions for such licensing, which are somewhat more forgiving than the outright prohibition that the US pharmaceutical industry preferred.

One issue of particular concern to the US negotiators was "moral rights." In copyright, the Berne Convention covers both "economic rights" and "moral rights." Continental-European law incorporates "moral rights" which permit the author to "claim authorship of the work and object to any distortion or mutilation which would be prejudicial to his honor or reputation" (Correa, 1994: 543–544) even *after* the author has transferred his economic rights. By contrast, US law only recognizes economic rights. When the United States acceded to Berne in March 1989 its implementing legislation omitted reference to Article 6$^{bis}$ which covers moral rights. The United States prevailed on this issue and Article 9(1) of TRIPS does not require states to enforce moral rights.

To highlight that TRIPS is not strictly a US document, the Europeans and Japanese prevailed on a number of issues of particular importance to them. Ultimately additional protection was extended to wines and spirits in the provisions on geographical indications and appellations of origin. Regarding the French video levies and Japanese music rental practices, the MPAA "lost" in so far as video levies were authorized in Article 3, and the music rental issue was resolved by a compromise that gave music companies the option to either permit *or* prohibit commercial rental.

EC and American differences over so-called "pipeline protection" for pharmaceutical products kept a pipeline protection provision out of the final TRIPS Agreement.[23] Article 70(1) explicitly denies pipeline protection. The European Community had been quite critical of the pipeline

[23] "Pipeline protection is the process of permitting the owner of a patent to obtain protection in another country when it becomes available for the duration of its term in the first country. Foreign patent protection traditionally must be sought when the invention

protection offered in NAFTA. The pipeline protection in NAFTA "enables pharmaceutical firms to acquire patent protection in third countries as soon as it become[s] available, notwithstanding that the product may no longer be 'new'" (Tancer, 1995: 156). The European pharmaceutical industry objected to the NAFTA provision arguing that it would limit its opportunities in Mexico by "creating a barrier that had not previously existed" (Tancer, 1995: 155–156).

Moreover, the TRIPS agreement includes some major concessions for developing countries. Articles 65 and 66 grant developing countries and least-developed countries five and ten-year grace periods respectively, before they are obligated by the terms of the agreement. Article 65 grants a further five-year grace period for pharmaceutical, agricultural, and chemical products, thereby offering longer grace periods for items of greater importance to developing and least-developed countries (Stewart, 1993: 2284). Furthermore, Article 27(2) stipulates that:

> members may exclude from patentability inventions, the prevention within their territory of the commercial exploitation of which is necessary to protect *ordre public* (emphasis added) or morality, including to protect human, animal or plant life or health or to avoid serious prejudice to the environment, provided that such exclusion is not made merely because the exploitation is prohibited by domestic law.
>
> (TRIPS, 1994: art. 27, para. 2)

Article 27(3)(a) exempts from patentability diagnostic, therapeutic, and surgical methods for the treatment of animals or humans; Article 27(3)(b) exempts plants, animals, and their biological processes from patentability, yet stipulates that any country excluding plants from patent protection must provide a *sui generis* system of protection. Some analysts argue that these provisions will allow developing countries to continue to pursue conscious policies of drug patent exemption (Kent, 1993: 176).[24] Additionally, agricultural chemicals may also fall under these exceptions, "provided the prevention of their commercial exploitation could be linked to a higher public order goal, such as the provision of an adequate food supply for the population" (Kent, 1993: 177). The "ordre public" criterion is open to a variety of interpretations, and enhances the role of state discretion in determining patentability.

---

is still new and unknown in the second country; yet obtaining patent protection abroad simultaneously with the grant of the original patent may be impossible because patent protection is simply not available" (Tancer, 1995: 166).

[24] For additional analysis of the scope and limits of this potential "loophole" see Weissman (1996: 1100–1101).

The final agreement on enforcement reflects a consensus among the United States, European Community, and Switzerland to include criminal procedures against IP violators. The enforcement provisions include criminal, civil, and administrative procedures and remedies. The Dispute Settlement Understanding (DSU) as elaborated in Article 64 of the TRIPS Agreement was based on the Swiss proposal (Stewart, 1993: 2312–2313), and instruments range from consultation and voluntary mediation to the suspension of trade concessions.

One of the chief aims of the US private sector in the Uruguay Round was to strengthen GATT dispute settlement procedures. This was a prominent feature of the IPC's agenda as well as the Trilateral group's proposals. The weakness of the GATT dispute settlement mechanism was an important factor motivating the US pursuit of aggressive unilateralism via Section 301. Under the old GATT system, losing defendants were able to veto decisions they found to be unacceptable. Furthermore, disputes could drag on for years and parties were free to engage in "forum shopping." The US private sector sought quicker and more binding decisions. In the WTO dispute settlement mechanism (DSM), the US private sector won an important victory. Negotiators agreed to the establishment of a Dispute Settlement Body (DSB) to oversee the dispute resolution process, effectively ending the forum shopping option. The WTO establishes strict timetables for processing disputes, and makes all the decisions binding unless the DSB votes unanimously to overrule them. This eliminates the ability of losers to block decisions. A new institution, WTO's Appellate Body, is charged with hearing appeals. Its decisions are binding unless the DSB unanimously votes to overrule it. Therefore, "the winning party may veto any attempt by other nations to reject a particular decision" (Shell, 1995: 850). Under the DSM cross-retaliation is now possible, so that, for example, infractions in intellectual property or services can lead to sanctions on goods. The WTO is empowered to monitor compliance to make sure that defendants carry out their obligations within a reasonable period of time. If the defendants fail to comply, the WTO will authorize the complainant to impose retaliatory trade sanctions if requested to do so. Thus, the new dispute settlement procedures represent significant improvement from the private sector perspective. Private sector actors lobbied for a new institution to help enforce the new rules, and the next chapter shows that they are quite willing to use it.

The TRIPS agreement notwithstanding, the United States has preserved its right to pursue both 301 and GSP actions against countries that fail to protect intellectual property. The Industry Functional Advisory Committee on Intellectual Property Rights for Trade Policy Matters takes the position that the United States can pursue these actions, but acknowledges that the extent to which the sanctions of domestic law can be invoked are more limited under the WTO (Shrader, 1994b: 13). Under TRIPS, the United States has to submit complaints to the Dispute Settlement Body (DSB) of WTO and abide by the WTO ruling. In its legislation on TRIPS, the US House of Representatives stated that, "Nothing in this Act shall be construed . . . to limit any authority conferred under any law of the United States, including Section 301 of the Trade Act of 1974, unless specifically provided for in this Act" (Morrison, 1994: 3). Section 301 and Special 301 remain live options for those practices that do not fall under WTO disciplines. In fact, in its implementing legislation the United States[25] strengthened Special 301 by clarifying that "adequate and effective" protection is not met merely by a country adhering to TRIPS and that the USTR must take into account the history of a country's appearance on Special 301 lists and its track record for subsequent policy amendment.[26] As will be demonstrated in the next chapter, the United States is using Special 301 to force TRIPS-plus commitments from developing countries. The WTO dispute settlement process is being used for TRIPS compliance issues.

This is important because many of the US industry representatives still are not fully satisfied with either the TRIPS or the NAFTA. Given the fact that they have been the most active in pressing for 301 action and GSP suspensions, one should expect this activism to continue. For example, even though industry associations praised NAFTA as the most comprehensive IP agreement ever negotiated, the Business Software Alliance (BSA) has complained that, "despite the NAFTA, Mexico has neither taken effective action against infringement of intellectual property rights, nor has it provided 'expeditious remedies' as effective deterrents to intellectual property violators" (Business Software Alliance, 1995: 4).[27] Another commentator warned high-technology businesses that NAFTA offered little protection. He stated that "the failings of the Mexican system of intellectual property enforcement are an inheritance

[25] Uruguay Round Agreement Act, tit. III, 315, Pub. L. No. 103–465, 108 Stat 4809 (1994) (also known as the URAA).
[26] Testimony of Eric Smith, president of the IIPA, US House of Representatives, Subcommittee on Trade of the Committee of Ways & Means, March 13, 1996. http://www/iIPa.com/html/pn_021897_press_release_html (downloaded 10/26/98).
[27] Business Software Alliance (BSA), "Fact Sheet: International Policies Governing the Software Industry" (May 5, 1995), Washington, DC, p. 4.

of past policies and a lack of understanding of the parameters of 'adequate' enforcement.... [Education and enforcement] efforts take far more time than simply changing the wording of laws" (Einstein, 1995: 29).

Industry representatives are even more dissatisfied with the TRIPS agreement, which is substantially weaker and less comprehensive than NAFTA. Industry associations have expressed dismay over the transitional period for developing countries, the lack of an obligation to protect against parallel imports (lawfully made goods which are not authorized for distribution in the country where importation is sought, also known as gray-market goods), the "public order" loophole, and weaker border enforcement of infringing articles than they desired.[28] Therefore, industry pressure to pursue 301 and GSP actions against infringing countries is unlikely to vanish.

This case illustrates the increasingly porous boundaries between public and private authority, domestic and international politics, and domestic regulation and international commerce. In the United States, corporate actors availed themselves of domestic institutional access to press their case and cultivated close working relationships with the legislative and Executive branches of government. In the TRIPS case, corporate actors mobilized their private sector counterparts both at home and abroad to press their governments and the GATT to support and produce an IP code.

While the US, European and Japanese private sector actors differed on some significant specifics, their concrete negotiating proposals reflected broad industry consensus on a multilateral IP agreement. The work of the trilateral group was a major breakthrough on the road to TRIPS and provided the IP negotiations with a momentum surpassing everyone's expectations. Chapter 6 explores life after TRIPS, and, in particular, the continued activism of the private sector as well as the emergence of opposition to TRIPS.

---

[28] On the issues of gray-market goods and border enforcement, see Shrader (1994a: 20).

# 6    Life after TRIPS – aggression and opposition

The TRIPS agreement is hardly the end of the story. In many ways, it is just the beginning. The machinery is now in place. Domestic and international institutions have been enlisted in the enforcement of TRIPS. The reach of private power has been extended far beyond its architects (Cutler, Haufler and Porter, 1999: 358). This new global regulation of intellectual property rights requires a "web of surveillance" (Braithwaite and Drahos, 2000: 87), particularly since the vast majority of countries signing on to TRIPS will be negatively affected (at least in the short term). Net importers of IP-based goods and services will pay higher costs. The web of surveillance operates on multiple levels. The private sector activists continue to play a central role in monitoring implementation and enforcement efforts. Domestic state institutions are responsible for adopting and enforcing TRIPS-compliant policies. The WTO provides an additional and crucial resource for the global regulation of intellectual property. This web of surveillance now becomes part of the structure. The process continues, and new areas of contestation have emerged. The first part of this chapter is devoted to the web of surveillance. The second half focuses on emerging areas of contestation, including active and increasingly mobilized opposition to TRIPS.

Since the adoption of TRIPS, its architects have remained vigilant in monitoring the implementation and compliance of TRIPS worldwide. They have continued to avail themselves of the US Section 301 apparatus to pressure developing countries to alter their domestic IP policies. They also have utilized the mechanisms of the WTO, through USTR, to file complaints over TRIPS. At the same time, as the impact of TRIPS has become more palpable, new pockets of resistance and social mobilization have emerged to challenge TRIPS. With the exception of initial developing country resistance to moving IP issues from WIPO to GATT, opposition to TRIPS emerged rather late – when the ink was dry. This implies that while TRIPS cannot be "undone" in any direct sense, the fight over loopholes, alternative interpretations of vague language, and perhaps, most importantly, effective resistance to further expansion of global IP rights are on the horizon.

## Industry strategies

In January 2000 an advocate for the IPC, Charles Levy, addressed the American Bar Association's Section of International Law and Practice and spelled out the IPC post-TRIPS strategy. Levy, a Washington lawyer and lobbyist who works closely with Jacques Gorlin, receives the IPC's lobbying dollars. For example, in 1998 the IPC paid Jacques Gorlin's "Gorlin Group" lobbying firm $160,000; its other listed lobbyist was Charles Levy of Wilmer, Cutler & Pickering who received $80,000 (Center for Responsive Politics, 1998a, b). Levy bemoaned the "significant non-compliance" with TRIPS and suggested that TRIPS supporters should use litigation "selectively, bringing, in the first instance, those cases they know they can win, and that present strategic issues that will develop the necessary body of precedent" (Levy, 2000: 789, 790). Further, he argued that members must display resolve by taking dispute settlement "as far as necessary" to ensure full compliance with TRIPS. The hope of this strategy is to turn high-profile dispute resolution decisions into a powerful example that other more lax countries will choose to follow. Levy also stressed the benefits of both intergovernmental and private sector diplomacy, emphasizing that the business community, and in particular "companies with a major presence in a country, can play a role in helping countries to understand the benefits of fully implementing the legal regime required by TRIPS" (Levy, 2000: 794).

Similarly, Eric Smith, president of the IIPA, emphasized a number of post-TRIPS strategies. At the multilateral level, besides urging use of the WTO dispute settlement machinery, Smith endorsed exploiting the opportunity provided by the TRIPS Council[1] practice of reviewing implementation and obligations to point out deficiencies in various countries' laws. The TRIPS Council is a committee of the whole consisting of all current WTO members. It is charged with overseeing TRIPS

[1] Formally known as the Council for Trade-Related Aspects of Intellectual Property Rights.

implementation. For the review process, states must notify the TRIPS Council of the steps they have taken to implement TRIPS, and then must respond to questions put to them by other TRIPS Council members. The IIPA, along with other interested parties, prepares questions and detailed enforcement information that it then submits to USTR for the TRIPS Council review process. In Smith's words "this is an important means to put pressure on countries that have not yet fully implemented their obligations to do so immediately or risk the commencement of a formal consultation and dispute settlement process" (Smith, 1996: 5). Indeed, in 1998 the USTR reported that it had been using the TRIPS Council meetings as "an opportunity to educate developing country members as to how these provisions must be implemented in their laws" (USTR, 1998b: 60). The USTR indicated that the Council meetings have been useful for keeping pressure on developing country members and have provided a valuable forum for confirming US interpretations of the TRIPS Agreement (USTR, 1998b: 60).

Predictably, given the IIPA's vigorous support of bilateral diplomacy to promote strong IP protection, Smith praised the fact that in its implementing legislation the United States expressly retained its prerogatives to suspend GSP benefits, and benefits under various regional initiatives. The United States sought to accelerate TRIPS compliance by developing countries prior to the negotiated deadlines, or transition periods. This reflected widespread industry dissatisfaction with the negotiated transition periods. Smith further underscored the continued importance of Special 301, "which has done more than any other provision of US trade law to improve the level of worldwide protection of US products embodying copyright" (Smith, 1996: 3). Special 301[2] is the US trade law requiring the identification of intellectual property rights priority countries. To the delight of IP activist industries, in its implementing legislation the United States strengthened Special 301 by requiring the USTR to take into account a country's prior status under Special 301, the history of US efforts under Special 301, and the country's response to such efforts. To the extent that this increases the information requirements for USTR it may make the USTR even more dependent on private sector groups for data and analysis. This amendment was designed to help highlight persistent recalcitrance in the face of Special 301 pressure. By agreeing to a higher multilateral standard for IP protection

---

[2] While widely known as "Special 301," this provision is Section 182 of the Trade Act of 1974, added by Section 1303 of the Omnibus Trade and Competitiveness Act of 1988.

many countries were hoping to make 301 pressure disappear. However, as Table 6.1 demonstrates, this pressure has hardly vanished. Furthermore, the European Union challenged the United States on its use of Section 301, but a WTO panel found that the United States had acted in accordance with its WTO obligations when invoking 301. The EU decided not to appeal and the panel report was adopted on January 27, 2000 (USTR, 2000b).[3]

Key private sector groups articulated three major post-TRIPS strategies for the United States: use of the WTO dispute settlement mechanism; the TRIPS Council process; and Special 301 of the Trade Act. Since private actors do not have standing at WTO, they must convey their wishes to the USTR and hope that the USTR will act on their behalf and take up their particular causes. Table 6.1 suggests that the USTR has been remarkably responsive to the expressed wishes of these key private sector actors. While the evidence does not demonstrate a causal relationship, it highlights a strong correlation between the expressed wishes of the IP activists and government monitoring and enforcement. Former general counsel and deputy general counsel for USTR, and now executive vice president of PhRMA, Judith H. Bello states that, "an administration's lawyers...rely upon and work closely with the directly affected private parties. The input provided by the latter serves as additional resources and thereby reduces the burden on an administration in WTO litigation" (Bello, 1997: 360–361).

In 1996 USTR established an Office of Monitoring and Enforcement, indicating its seriousness of purpose. This office oversees trade agreement implementation and pursues enforcement actions, "aggressively" litigating disputes to "compel compliance" with the WTO agreements, NAFTA, and other regional and bilateral agreements (USTR, 1998b: 235). This same office also addresses problems outside the framework of the multilateral and regional treaties by invoking Section 301 and Special 301 of the Trade Act. It is likely no coincidence that 1997 saw a 25 percent increase in the number of trading partners named under Special 301 in 1996 (USTR, 1998b: 244).

Table 6.1 presents data for five years, from 1996, when the WTO TRIPS Agreement became fully effective for developed countries and the United States brought its first IP case to the WTO, through 2000. Under Special 301, by April 30 each year, the USTR must announce the

---

[3] United States, Sections 301–310 of the Trade Act of 1974 (WT/DS152).

results of its review of foreign countries' IP practices. It must identify those countries that deny "adequate and effective" protection of IP rights or "fair and equitable" market access to IP-reliant US persons. Each February, interested private sector groups submit their requests to the USTR, highlighting problems with various countries, their suggested designations and loss estimates. These submissions include extensive information, analysis, and advocacy (Bello, 1997: 360). (The IIPA also adds its estimate of the copyright industries' contributions to the US economy in dollars, for example, $362.5 billion – or 5.69 percent of GDP in value added in 1996 (IIPA, 1996: 5).) In preparing this table I have used the February submissions of the IIPA to represent copyright interests, and the PhRMA to represent patent interests. The IPC member corporations participate in the IIPA and PhRMA process. Indeed, several pharmaceutical companies separately give Jacques Gorlin's "the Gorlin Group" their lobbying dollars (Center for Responsive Politics, 1998a, b).[4]

The far left column indicates USTR's April designations. "WTO/ TRIPS" filing indicates that the USTR has filed a WTO complaint over alleged TRIPS violations. "Section 306 Monitoring" indicates that USTR is monitoring the implementation of measures or agreements undertaken as the result of a previous Section 301 action (US House of Representatives, 1995) If USTR finds non-compliance, this is treated as a violation of a trade agreement subject to mandatory Section 301 actions. The United States may move directly to trade sanctions. The "Priority Foreign Country" designation is for those countries having the most onerous or egregious acts, policies, or practices and whose acts have the greatest adverse impact on the relevant US products. If a trading partner is identified as a Priority Foreign Country, the USTR must decide within thirty days whether to initiate an investigation. The "Priority Watch List" designation identifies countries whose practices and policies meet some, but not all, of the criteria for priority foreign country identification. Priority Watch List countries become the subject of increasing bilateral attention and require "active work for resolution and close monitoring." "Watch List" designations indicate that the named country has problematic practices or policies with respect to IP protection, enforcement or market access for IP-reliant persons.

---

[4] For example, in 1998 PhRMA paid the Gorlin Group $20,000; the IPC paid $160,000. In 1997 Bristol-Myers Squibb paid $60,000, Pfizer paid $100,000, and the IPC paid $140,000; 1997 data came from hyperlink (1997 DATA) at same site (Center for Responsive Politics, 1998a, b).

Table 6.1 *US Trade Representative monitoring and enforcement of intellectual property rights, 1996–2000*

| USTR Designation | Years | Private Sector Requests[a] | |
| --- | --- | --- | --- |
| | | IIPA[b] | PhRMA[c] |
| *WTO/TRIPS filing* | | | |
| Argentina | 99/00 | | yes |
| Brazil | 00 | | yes |
| Canada | 99 | | yes (*pwl*)[f] |
| Denmark | 97 | yes | |
| European Union | 99 | | yes |
| Ecuador | 97 | yes | yes |
| Greece | 98 | yes | |
| India | 96 | | yes |
| Indonesia | 96 | yes | |
| Ireland | 97 | yes | |
| Japan | 96 | yes | |
| Pakistan | 96 | | yes |
| Portugal | 96 | | yes |
| Sweden | 97 | yes | |
| Turkey | 96 | yes | |
| *Section 306 Monitoring* | | | |
| China | 97/98/99/00 | yes (98[h]) | yes (*wl*99/00; *pwl*97/98) |
| Paraguay | 99/00 | yes | |
| *Priority Foreign Country (pfc)* | | | |
| none | 97/99/00 | | |
| China | 96 | yes | yes (*pwl*) |
| Paraguay | 98 | yes | |
| *Priority Watch List (pwl)* | | | |
| Argentina | 1996/97/98/99/00 | yes (*wl*96) | yes (*pfc*) |
| Bulgaria | 1998 | yes (*pfc*) | |
| Dominican Republic | 1998/99/00 | yes (*gsp*)[d] | yes (*wl*98/99) |
| Ecuador | 1997/98 | yes (*wl*97) | yes (*wl*97) |
| Egypt | 1997/98/99/00 | yes (*wl*) | yes (*pfc*99[e]) |
| European Union | 1996/97/98/99/00 | | yes (*wl*96/97/98/99) |
| Greece | 1996/97/98/99/00 | yes (*pfc*97/98; *wl*00) | |
| Guatemala | 1999/00 | yes (*wl*99) | |
| India | 96/97/98/99/00 | yes (97[h]; *wl*) | yes (*pfc*) |
| Indonesia | 96/97/98/99 | yes (*wl*97/98/99) | yes[e] |
| Israel | 98/99/00 | yes (*pfc*; *pwl*98) | yes[e] |

Table 6.1 (*cont.*)

| | | Private Sector Requests[a] | |
|---|---|---|---|
| USTR Designation | Years | IIPA[b] | PhRMA[c] |
| Italy | 98/99/00 | yes | |
| Japan | 96 | | yes |
| Korea | 96/00 | yes | yes |
| Kuwait | 98/99 | yes | yes (*wl*) |
| Macau | 98/99 | yes | |
| Malaysia | 00 | yes (*wl*) | |
| Paraguay | 97 | yes (*pfc*) | |
| Peru | 99/00 | yes | yes[e] (*wl*00) |
| Poland | 00 | yes | yes (*wl*) |
| Russia | 97/98/99/00 | yes (*pfc*97) | yes (*wl*97/ 98/00) |
| Turkey | 96/97/98/99/00 | yes (*pfc*96; 98[h]; *gsp*00) | yes[e] (*pfc*96; *wl*00) |
| Ukraine | 99/00 | yes (*pfc*00) | |
| *Watch List (wl)* | | | |
| Armenia | 00 | yes (*gsp*) | |
| Australia | 96/97/98/99 | yes (96[h]; *pwl*98) | yes |
| Azerbaijan | 00 | yes | |
| Bahrain | 96/97/98 | yes | yes |
| Belarus | 00 | yes | |
| Bolivia | 97/99/00 | yes; (00[e]) | yes[e] (*pwl*99) |
| Brazil | 96/97/99/00 | yes (*pwl*) | yes (*pwl*96/00) |
| Bulgaria | 97 | yes (*pwl*) | |
| Canada | 96/97/98/99/00 | yes (96/98/99/00)[h] | yes[f] (96/97[h]; *pwl*99/00) |
| Chile | 96/97/98/99/00 | | yes |
| Colombia | 96/97/98/99/00 | yes (96 h; (*pwl*98) | yes[e] (*pwl*98)/99) |
| Costa Rica | 96/97/98/99/00 | yes (96/97/98)[h] | yes (96/97*pwl*) (99/00)[h] |
| Czech Republic | 98/99/00 | yes (*pwl*99/00) | yes (98[h]) |
| Denmark | 97/98/99/00 | yes[g] (97/98/00)[h] | |
| Dominican Republic | 97 | yes | yes (*pwl*) |
| Ecuador | 96/99/00 | | yes[e] (*pwl*99) |
| El Salvador | 96 | yes (*pwl*) | yes (*pwl*) |
| Egypt | 96 | | yes |
| Guatemala | 96/97/98 | yes (96[h]; *pwl*98) | yes (*pwl*96/97) |
| Honduras | 97/98 | | yes (*pwl*97) |
| Hong Kong | 97/98 | yes (*pwl*97) | |
| Hungary | 99/00 | yes | yes (*pwl*00) |

Table 6.1 (*cont.*)

| | | Private Sector Requests[a] | |
|---|---|---|---|
| USTR Designation | Years | IIPA[b] | PhRMA[c] |
| Indonesia | 00 | yes (*pwl*) | yes[e] |
| Ireland | 97/98/99/00 | yes (*pwl*99; 98/00)[h] | |
| Israel | 97 | yes | yes (*pwl*) |
| Italy | 96/97 | yes (*pwl*) | yes |
| Jamaica | 98/99/00 | | |
| Japan | 97/98/99 | | yes (97[h]) |
| Jordan | 97/98/99 | yes (*pwl*98) | yes (*pwl*98/99) |
| Kazakhstan | 98/00 | yes (98[h]; *gsp*00) | |
| Korea | 97/98/99 | yes (*pwl*97) | yes (*pwl*97/98; *pfc*99) |
| Kuwait | 96/97/00 | yes (96[h]; *pwl*97) | yes |
| Latvia | 00 | yes | |
| Lebanon | 99/00 | yes | yes |
| Lithuania | 00 | yes | yes |
| Luxembourg | 97 | | |
| Macau | 00 | yes (*pwl*) | |
| Mexico | 99 | yes (*pwl*) | yes |
| Moldova | 00 | yes (*gsp*) | |
| New Zealand | 99 | yes | yes[e] (*pwl*) |
| Oman | 96/97/98/99/00 | yes (96[h]) | yes |
| Pakistan | 96/97/98/99/00 | yes | yes[e] (*pwl*97/ 98/99/00) |
| Panama | 97 | yes | yes (*pwl*) |
| Peru | 96/97/98 | yes (*pwl*); (96/97[h]) | yes (*pwl*98) |
| Philippines | 96/97/98/99/00 | yes (*pwl*97/00) | yes (96[h]) |
| Poland | 96/97/98/99 | yes (*pwl*99) | yes |
| Qatar | 98/99/00 | yes (98[h]) | yes |
| Romania | 99/00 | yes | yes |
| Russian Federation | 96 | yes (*pfc*) | yes |
| San Marino | 97 | yes | |
| Saudi Arabia | 96/97/98/99/00 | yes (*pwl*96/ 97/00) | yes (96/97)[h] |
| Singapore | 96/97/98/99/00 | yes (97[h]; *pwl*98) | yes |
| South Africa | 98 | | yes (*pfc*) |
| Spain | 99/00 | | yes |
| Sweden | 97/98/99 | | |
| Taiwan | 99/00 | yes | yes[e] (*pwl*) |
| Tajikistan | 00 | yes | |
| Thailand | 96/97/98/99/00 | yes (*pwl*99) | yes[e] (*pwl*96/) 97/98/99 |
| Turkmenistan | 00 | yes | |

Table 6.1 (*cont.*)

| USTR Designation | Years | Private Sector Requests[a] | |
| | | IIPA[b] | PhRMA[c] |
| --- | --- | --- | --- |
| Ukraine | 98 | yes | |
| United Arab Emirates | 96/97/98/99 | yes (99[h]) | yes |
| Uruguay | 99/00 | yes | yes |
| Uzbekistan | 00 | yes (*gsp*) | |
| Venezuela | 96/97/98/99/00 | yes | yes[e] (*pwl*98/99) |
| Vietnam | 97/98/99/00 | yes (*pwl*97/98) | yes |

[a] = parentheses indicate the requested designation if different from USTR's
[b] = International Intellectual Property Alliance
[c] = Pharmaceutical Researchers and Manufacturers of America
[d] = generalized system of preferences
[e] = In 1999 PhRMA cites "TRIPS violations actionable in 2000"
[f] = In 1999 PhRMA cites "TRIPS violations currently actionable"
[g] = In 1999 IIPA recommends WTO filing
[h] = Indicates country did not appear on group's list that year or (years)
*Sources:* USTR, 1996; 1997; 1998a; 1999; 2000a; IIPA, 1996; 1997; 1998; 1999; 2000a; PhRMA, 1996; 1997a; 1997b; 1998a; 1998b; 1999; 2000.

## TRIPS cases – WTO

Not surprisingly, the United States has been the most aggressive country in the IP area. It has filed more WTO TRIPS complaints than all other member countries combined. True to the strategy advocated by Levy, all fourteen US TRIPS cases have been straightforward violation complaints where states simply failed to enact the TRIPS provisions (Samahon, 2000: 1059). Bello also predicted that the early IP cases would be easy wins that would help build support for the system (Bello, 1997).

The United States initiated the first six cases in 1996. The first TRIPS dispute settlement proceeding was against Japan in February 1996 for its failure to protect sound recordings created between 1946 and 1971. The Recording Industry Association of America, member of the IIPA, provided the USTR with loss estimates which the USTR cited in making its case. Several months after the United States and Japan held WTO consultations, Japan agreed to provide the retroactive protection required by TRIPS.

In May 1996 the United States brought a complaint against India, at the behest of PhRMA. This was the first IP case to be adjudicated under the WTO dispute settlement mechanism and the United States prevailed. The Appellate Body upheld the panel recommendation that the Dispute Settlement Body request India to bring its legislation into conformity with TRIPS. India had long been a target of PhRMA's efforts to get developing countries to ratchet up existing levels of patent protection. Indeed, according to PhRMA, "the Indian patent system was the most direct motivation for US efforts in the Uruguay Round negotiations relating to patents, and the negotiators of the TRIPS Agreement fully expected that India's implementation of its TRIPS obligations would produce the most dramatic level of reform" (PhRMA, 1999b).

The United States complained that India had failed to establish a so-called "mailbox" system for administering patent applications for pharmaceutical and agricultural chemicals. While developing countries were given additional transition periods for patenting these items under Article 65, Article 70(8) required that they establish a mechanism to preserve novelty and priority for product patents. This mechanism is referred to as the mailbox system, so that if a patent eventually is granted the patent term will be counted from the filing date. It effectively saves the prospective patentee his or her place in line for that day on which patents on such products become available. Article 70(9) requires that the state grant exclusive marketing rights for the product in question when the patent application has been received. The exclusive marketing rights are subject to three conditions: (1) marketing approval must be obtained in the country in question; (2) marketing approval must be obtained in another WTO country; and (3) a valid and current patent must exist in another WTO country (Evans, 1998: 87).

India's Patents Act did not include exclusive marketing rights and receipt of application provisions, but India provided a means for filing applications through a Presidential Ordinance. When the ordinance lapsed India instructed its patent offices to continue to receive and store patent applications in compliance with Article 70(8). India argued that it was free to choose an administrative, rather than legislative, method for complying with the provision. The WTO panel rejected India's submission. It affirmed India's right to choose how to implement the agreement but found that India had not established a means that adequately preserves novelty and priority, that India had not complied with respect to granting exclusive marketing rights, and had not complied with its obligations under paragraphs 1 and 2 of Article 63 to publish and notify such information. On Appeal the Appellate Body upheld the 70(8) and 70(9) rulings, but reversed the panel's findings with respect to Article 63 (Evans, 1998: 88).

The TRIPS Council process of reviewing legislation permitted the USTR to keep pressuring India and Pakistan to implement the mailbox system (USTR, 1998b: 60). In 1996 the USTR announced it would initiate formal consultations with Pakistan under WTO dispute settlement procedures over the mailbox system and exclusive marketing rights. After the United States requested the establishment of a WTO panel, Pakistan implemented the requirements under Articles 70(8) and 70(9). Thus, as in the Japanese case, the Pakistani case was resolved at the consultation stage.

Similarly the US-initiated case against Portugal was resolved a few short months after the United States initiated formal consultations under the WTO dispute settlement procedures. In PhRMA's February 1996 submission to USTR it highlighted Portuguese non-compliance with TRIPS Articles 70(2) and 33. It indicated that Portugal was in clear violation of TRIPS and thereby subject to the dispute settlement provisions of Article 64 (PhRMA, 1996: 76–77). The United States challenged Portugal's patent term. TRIPS mandates a twenty-year term to apply both to new and old patents. Portugal had interpreted the provision as applying only to patents granted after June 1, 1995. The United States requested consultations in April 1996, and by August 1996 Portugal had changed its law and satisfied US demands. In October the two governments notified WTO's Dispute Settlement Body that they had arrived at a mutually satisfactory resolution. The USTR used the TRIPS Council to confirm its interpretations of TRIPS and used the Portuguese case as an example. At the WTO Singapore ministerial meeting in 1996 the TRIPS Council commented on the case stating that, "the parties involved expressed their understanding that Article 70.2 in conjunction with Article 33 requires developed country parties to provide a patent term of not less than 20 years from the filing date for patents that were in force on 1 January 1996, or that result from applications pending on that date" (USTR, 1998b: 60).

The USTR pursued two other 1996 WTO cases at the behest of IIPA – one, a discriminatory box office tax in Turkey and the other, discriminatory trademark practices in Indonesia. The Turkish case reflected complaints by the MPAA, member of IIPA, that Turkish theaters charged a tax on movie tickets for foreign films. The Turkish case was resolved in December 1997 when Turkey issued regulations equalizing taxes on foreign and domestic films. Announcing the outcome, the USTR noted that "this action could save the US film industry millions of dollars in the coming year" (USTR, 1998a: 5). The Indonesian case involved trademarks for computer software, something near and dear to the BSA (largely funded by Microsoft),[5] also a member of the IIPA. In a press release accompanying the IIPA's February 1996 submission to the USTR it noted that "the US computer software industry has found Indonesia's enforcement regime to be among the worst in the world" (IIPA, 1996). In May 1997, Indonesia approved amendments bringing its copyright laws into compliance with TRIPS (USTR, 1998a: 28).

In April 1997 the USTR announced the initiation of WTO dispute settlement procedures against Denmark, Sweden, Ireland, and Ecuador. The software industry, represented by BSA, pressed for actions against Denmark and Sweden for their failure to provide for *ex parte* (unannounced) civil searches of suspected pirating facilities and organizations. TRIPS provides for the ability of courts to order unannounced raids to determine whether infringement is taking place, and to either seize the allegedly infringing products as evidence or order the cessation of allegedly infringing activities pending the outcome of a civil case. Sweden quickly committed to amend its law to bring it into conformity with TRIPS. Robert W. Holleyman, president and CEO of the BSA, commended USTR and the Swedish government and stated that the ability to obtain unannounced searches "is critical in the fight against software piracy, since evidence in software cases can often be erased at the touch of a button" (BSA, 1998). The Danish case was resolved in 2001 (USTR, 2001: 1, 9).

The IIPA identified Ireland as a problem country with regard to copyright. Irish law provided neither a rental right for sound recordings, nor an "anti-bootlegging" provision. Furthermore, its criminal penalties for copyright piracy were deemed too low to act as an effective deterrent. In July 1998 Ireland enacted legislation raising criminal penalties for copyright enforcement to the United States' satisfaction and the dispute was resolved in November 2000 (USTR, 2001: 8).

The case against Ecuador covered a broad spectrum of TRIPS violations covering patent, copyright, and trademark areas. The IIPA had been eager to persuade many developing countries to surrender their rights to the transition periods negotiated under Article 65 of TRIPS.

---

[5] The BSA was founded in 1988. For membership see: <http://www.bsa.org/>

Ecuador had been negotiating a bilateral IP treaty with the United States for several years. The two countries came close to an agreement on TRIPS-plus provisions, requiring a reduction in the grace period and stipulating that plant varieties be protected either by patents or a system comparable to the Union for the Protection of New Varieties of Plants (UPOV). In July 1996 an environmental non-governmental organization (NGO) blocked the ratification of the treaty and occupied the Congressional Chamber in Ecuador.[6] In its 1997 filing the IIPA expressed dismay over Ecuador's decision to renege "on its obligation to implement TRIPS obligations without transition" (IIPA, 1997). In its WTO filing, the USTR stated that Ecuador had acceded to the WTO committing to implement TRIPS within seven months of accession (USTR, 1997, April 30: 3). PhRMA complained in 1996 that Ecuador's Intellectual Property Directorship was paralyzed and had thus far failed to approve about 160 pharmaceutical patents that had been filed since 1994 (PhRMA, 1996: 44). PhRMA's USTR submission catalogued a complicated set of issues revolving around governance in the Andean Pact, of which Ecuador is a member (PhRMA, 1997a). Ecuador had agreed to implement TRIPS and TRIPS-plus obligations, including the establishment of pipeline protection for pharmaceuticals (a provision conspicuously absent in TRIPS).[7] However, according to PhRMA "Argentine, Chilean and Colombian multinational pirates operating in the Ecuadorian market" challenged Ecuador's pipeline provisions in the Ecuadorian courts. The Supreme Court of Ecuador upheld Ecuador's right to implement pipeline protection, despite the fact that the Andean Community's Decision 344 contained no such provision. In short, the Ecuadorian Supreme Court affirmed Ecuador's right to adopt Decision 344-plus provisions. In March 1996 the Junta del Acuerdo de Cartagena (JUNAC) presented a claim to the Andean Tribunal against Ecuador, emphasizing that pipeline protection had been rejected in the WTO. The Andean Tribunal filed against Ecuador, which subsequently derogated its regulatory decrees relating to pipeline protection.

PhRMA concluded that pharmaceutical "pirate" organizations had persuaded the Andean Tribunal to halt initiatives to increase levels of IP protection. In PhRMA's view the implications of the decision were

---

[6] This incident will be discussed further on pp. 143–144.
[7] By contrast, this type of protection is available in NAFTA, which is why PhRMA looks to NAFTA as the preferable standard.

broad, "as all potential efforts by other Andean countries to modern-ize their regimes will be stopped" (PhRMA, 1997a: 62). PhRMA also objected to "working" requirements for patents, compulsory licensing provisions, and the narrower scope of patentable items. The USTR's WTO case charged that Ecuador violated TRIPS by insisting upon local working requirements (TRIPS incorporated an explicit provision that importation satisfies working requirements), compulsory licenses, and exclusion of certain items from patentability. In copyright Ecuador failed to treat computer programs as literary works, as required by the TRIPS amendments to the Berne Convention, and denied national treatment in trademark policy (USTR, 1997, April 30: 3). In May 1998 the Ecuadorean Congress passed and the president signed a comprehensive law sub-stantially increasing protection for patents, copyrights, and trademarks (USTR, 1999, April 30: 27).

In 1998 the USTR initiated WTO dispute settlement procedures against Greece and the European Union over television piracy in Greece. The MPAA complained of Greece's extensive broadcast piracy of American films, and in 1997 the IIPA had recommended that Greece be designated a Priority Foreign Country over this issue. In its 1998 sub-mission to USTR the IIPA identified Greece as being in violation of its TRIPS obligations. The IIPA stated that despite years of complaints by the MPAA, "Greece has failed to reduce massive TV piracy, among the worst in the world. No TV pirate has ever paid one drachma in fines to the government. Overall, Greece's copyright enforcement regime is the black eye of Western Europe, adversely affecting all copyright indus-tries" (IIPA, 1998: 4). In September 1998 Greece passed a law to crack down on pirate stations, which US industry proceeded to test by filing lawsuits in Greece. The majority of these test cases were resolved to industry's satisfaction, and USTR noted a steep decline in TV piracy in 1999 (USTR, 2000b: 5). In March 2001 the two governments notified the WTO that their dispute was resolved (USTR, 2001: 8).

USTR targeted Canada, the European Union, and Argentina for WTO dispute settlement procedures in 1999. The Canadian case, inspired by PhRMA, was virtually identical to the earlier Portuguese case in which the United States prevailed regarding TRIPS patent terms. Canadian law provided the TRIPS twenty years from date of filing term only for patents filed on or after October 1, 1989. The earlier WTO decision had affirmed that Articles 33 and 70(2) of TRIPS require the twenty-year term to cover older patents as well. The United States prevailed in this case (USTR, 2001: 7). The European Union was challenged for allegedly denying national treatment in its procedures for registering geographical indications for agricultural products and foodstuffs; additionally, USTR stated that US trademarks were inadequately protected (USTR, 1999, April 30: 6). PhRMA had expressed concern about these alleged shortcomings in the European Union. As of May 2002, the case remained unresolved (USTR, 2002).

The case against Argentina was perhaps the most impassioned one for PhRMA, which had been wrangling with the Argentine government since 1985 over its patent regime. At PhRMA's behest, the USTR placed Argentina on the Special 301 list in 1989 and kept it there through 1993. The then president, Carlos Menem, pledged to strengthen Argentina's patent laws and successfully dodged US trade sanctions. However, due to the political power of Argentina's domestic pharmaceutical labs the Argentine Congress resisted Menem's efforts to ratchet up levels of pharmaceutical protection.[8] The Congress proposed weaker legislation, reflecting the interests of the domestic labs, but Menem vetoed Argentine legislation that did not meet US standards. "In April 1995, under intense pressure from the United States...Menem...issued a 'Regulatory Decree' which would protect pharmaceutical patents effective as of January 1, 1996 and give immediate retroactive pipeline protection" (Vicente, 1998: 1106–1107) (the latter provision clearly being "TRIPS-plus"). The Argentine Senate soon responded by overturning ten of the sixteen central provisions of Menem's PhRMA-friendly decree. The Argentine Congress passed Law 24,481 as revised by the Senate. The contest of wills continued as Menem submitted a "corrective law" "which reduced the transition period for implementing pharmaceutical protection from ten to five years" (Vicente, 1998: 1107). The Argentine Congress responded with a compromise bill, retaining the five-year transition period, but adding provisions for compulsory licensing. In March 1996 Menem finally signed the decree enacting this law.

In December 1996, the Argentine "Congress passed a surprising new non-patent provision which permits an innovator's competitors to use the innovator's test data when the competitor is seeking market approval" (Vicente, 1998: 1107). In the United States there is a five-year moratorium on the use of test data, after which time it may become available to potential competitors. PhRMA charged that the new Argentine test data provisions were a " 'thinly disguised attempt to invalidate

---

[8] The following summary is based on Vicente (1998).

the pharmaceutical patent protection which had just recently been approved' " (quoted in Vicente, 1998: 1107).

At the behest of PhRMA, the USTR in 1997 responded with the withdrawal of benefits for about 50 percent, or $260 million, of Argentine exports under the GSP program. The USTR "admitted that it had decided to enforce these patent law related sanctions based entirely on information and data supplied by PhRMA" (Vicente, 1998: 1108). These sanctions largely were based upon the test data exclusivity issue. TRIPS Article 39(3) mandates that such data be protected against unfair commercial use. The US drug industry interprets this strictly, whereas many developing countries favor a broader interpretation that gives them greater latitude. Argentina's Law 24,766, Articles 4 and 11 protect test data in cases of narrowly defined "dishonest commercial practices" and provides for no protection for data which has been published in scientific or academic circles (Vicente, 1998: 110–111). After the imposition of the trade sanctions Argentina threatened to avail itself of five additional years grace period for TRIPS compliance. PhRMA repeatedly declared Argentina the "worst expropriator of US pharmaceutical inventions in the Western Hemisphere" (PhRMA, 1998a: 3) and has tirelessly complained about the robust Argentine "pirate" pharmaceutical industry. The United States initiated consultations with Argentina via the WTO process in May 1999 for Argentina's failure to provide exclusive marketing rights and to try to prevent Argentina from watering down its existing levels of protection during the transition period. In May 2000 the USTR expanded its claims in this dispute to include the test data issue among other things (USTR, 2000b: 1).

The future of the Argentine case may be in doubt. Both the Argentine case and a Brazilian WTO case that the United States initiated in 2000 have attracted considerable attention. Whether or not these two involve straightforward TRIPS violations, they go to the heart of the "access to essential medicines" campaign. In 2000, in addition to expanding its claims against Argentina the United States initiated a new case against Brazil over a single patent law violation of TRIPS Article 27(1). Again, PhRMA inspired this action.[9] PhRMA had praised Brazil for its May 1996 industrial property law that reversed decades of lax protection; in fact PhRMA stated that as a testament to its renewed confidence in Brazil its member companies had committed about $2 billion

[9] This case was brought at the request of Merck in a dispute over the compulsory licensing of Stockrin, a drug Merck licensed from DuPont to sell in Brazil. E-mail from James Love, Tuesday, March 26, 2002 (on file with author).

in inward investment to Brazil by 2000 (PhRMA, 2000a). PhRMA pressed the USTR to object to Brazil's patent law provision that "local working" of the patent is required for the patent holder to enjoy patent rights in Brazil. TRIPS stipulates that importation of a patented item into a country satisfies the requirement that patents be "worked" in a given country. This provision had been very important to the pharmaceutical industry throughout the TRIPS negotiations. Brazil has retained a provision in its patent law that imposes a "local working" requirement as a condition for the enjoyment of patent rights. Brazil's provisions expressly state that only local production, and not importation, satisfies the "working" requirement. Unlike importation, local production is considered to hold better potential for technology transfer. Brazil's law permits it to issue compulsory licenses for goods that are not manufactured locally within three years of receiving patent protection; mere importation does not "count."

The Brazilian provision is seen as a threat in so far as it may inspire other developing countries to follow suit and insist upon an interpretation of Article 27(1) that limits rights enjoyed on the basis of importation (USTR, 2000a: 7). PhRMA expressed dismay at Brazil's stubbornness over this issue and noted that Brazil had "invited a WTO case to resolve the issue" (PhRMA, 2000a). Brazil has maintained that the threat of compulsory licensing has helped it negotiate reasonable drug prices with global pharmaceutical companies; it has used this threat effectively against Roche and Merck in its quest for affordable access to AIDS drugs. Activist citizen groups such as MSF have pointed out that Brazil's approach to this issue has permitted it to pursue stunningly successful policies to reduce AIDS deaths by making generic equivalents of lifesaving drugs and keeping prices down. On June 25, 2001, the USTR announced that it was officially withdrawing its WTO case against Brazil. USTR Robert Zoellick noted that "litigating this dispute before a WTO dispute panel has not been the most constructive way to address our differences, especially since Brazil has never actually used the provision at issue" (Yerkey and Pruzin, 2001). The United States withdrawal of this politically embarrassing case may portend reconsideration of the Argentine case as well. PhRMA continues to press it, citing Argentina as "the worst violator of intellectual property in our industry in the Western Hemisphere and one of the worst in the world" (PhRMA, 2001a: 179). In its submission to USTR for 2002, PhRMA claims that its industry loses $260 million annually because of Argentina's policies and that "only a decision by the WTO dispute settlement panel will induce change in Argentina" (PhRMA, 2001a: 181). In April 2002, the United States and Argentina agreed to notify the WTO that they had resolved some elements, such as the exclusive marketing rights regime, of their dispute (USTR, 2002). On the data protection issue the United States retained its right to pursue further WTO action. However, the United States may decide to leave it alone for the time being, due to the financial catastrophe that unraveled there in early 2002.

## Other actions under Section 301

Industry also has availed itself of other tools under Section 301. The IIPA and PhRMA lobbied actively in the 1980s to ensure additional forms of trade leverage by incorporating intellectual property protection as a condition for certain preferential benefits. The United States is free to suspend privileges under the GSP program and the Caribbean Basin Initiative (CBI) without abrogating its WTO obligations. The United States continues to use this form of bilateral leverage. For instance, in March 1998 USTR suspended a portion of Honduras' benefits under the GSP and the CBI because of pirated TV satellite signals. The Honduran case originated in 1992 when the MPAA filed a petition under the GSP program for "alleged widespread unauthorized broadcasting of pirated videos and re-broadcasting of US satellite-carried programming" (USTR, 1998c: 1). Argentina also lost GSP benefits on about $260 million worth of its exports in 1997. In February 2000, the IIPA petitioned the USTR's GSP Subcommittee for investigations of six countries' copyright policies (Armenia, Dominican Republic, Kazakhstan, Moldova, Ukraine, and Uzbekistan) (IIPA, 2000b). Most of these countries took steps to meet the US concerns, but in March 2001 the Ukraine was named as a Priority Foreign Country (the USTR's most serious designation) for its production and export of bootleg CDs and CD-ROMs (USTR 2001: 2). The USTR imposed $75 million worth of sanctions on Ukrainian products in January 2002. The Ukraine was renamed a Priority Foreign Country in 2002 and the sanctions remained in place (USTR, 2002).

Overall, industry strategies have been to press the USTR to invoke 301 and WTO dispute settlement measures, to use trade leverage and the TRIPS Council forum to achieve full-scale compliance with TRIPS. Industry has engaged in extensive monitoring of global IP protection. Charles Levy, the IPC lawyer, expressed his initial belief that the force of the concept "the rule of law" was "so infectious that it would necessarily spur voluntary compliance by developing countries to implement effective protection" (Levy, 2000: 790). Since TRIPS:

> the zeal with which the developed countries have thrown themselves into this monitoring...exercise has bred high expectations among rightsholders and their organized representatives...This euphoria stems...from the conviction that top-down pressures from governments in powerful developed countries, coupled with strategic litigation in defense of private rightsholders...will suffice to keep developing countries in line. (Reichman and Lange, 1998: 13–14)

They warn that this "euphoria" is misplaced in so far as there are many opportunities to "bargain around" TRIPS.

Despite the extensive monitoring efforts documented above, there is undoubtedly room for some foot dragging, some so-called passive aggression, slowness in implementation and the like (Sell, 1998). Numerous developing countries have requested extensions on the various negotiated grace periods, claiming among other things that their underfinanced administrations need more time to implement the complex agreement (Knapp, 2000: 191–192). Furthermore, a number of scholars have pointed out that vagueness, ambiguities, and loopholes abound in the TRIPS Agreement (Geller, 1994: 199, 216; Oddi, 1996: 415; Reichman, 1997b: 17–21; Sherwood, 1997: 491, 493). However, the next section focuses not on possible ways to get around the TRIPS strictures but rather on active and mobilized opposition to elements of the treaty.

## Opposition

The two most prominent threads of opposition to TRIPS concentrate on patents on life forms and patents on pharmaceuticals. Two major civil society action campaigns have gained momentum and have tempered some of the harsher edges of the agreement through their activity. While it is too late to "undo" TRIPS, these campaigns are a sign of things to come; efforts to obtain TRIPS-plus protection in the WTO now are likely to encounter active resistance. Furthermore, these groups have opened up the discussion that undoubtedly *should have* taken place before and during the negotiations themselves. As the United Nations Development Programme put it, the IP agreements were signed "before most governments and people understood the social and economic implications of patents on life. They were also negotiated with far too little participation from many developing countries now feeling the impact of their conditions" (UNDP, 1999: 66–76).

## Agriculture and plant varieties

The patenting of life forms raises a whole host of issues that have generated fevered debate. Participants in this debate claim that what is at stake here is no less than control over the world's food supply, not to mention the implications for scientific research and public access. The issue is shot through with economic, political, and philosophical significance. On one side of the debate are America's biotechnology, pharmaceutical, agricultural chemical, and seed industries. They champion patentability with no exceptions. On the other side are grassroots activists, farmers' groups, environmental groups, development groups, human rights groups, and consumer groups who are spearheading a global "no patents on life" campaign. While some of the issues in this debate are not new, what is new is the mobilization of these groups to oppose an increasingly aggressive approach to intellectual property by US corporations.

As early as 1993, when the TRIPS negotiations were still under way hundreds of thousands of Indian farmers demonstrated against TRIPS proposals claiming that their right to save, reproduce, and modify seeds could be jeopardized by the required implementing legislation (Sutherland, 1998: 293). Vandana Shiva, an Indian grassroots activist, has helped mobilize the campaign against "biopiracy"[10] (Shiva, 1997). Biopiracy is seen as a new form of Western imperialism in which global seed and pharmaceutical corporations[11] plunder the biodiversity and traditional knowledge of the developing world. Biopiracy is the unauthorized and uncompensated expropriation of genetic resources and traditional knowledge. According to this argument, corporations alter these "discoveries" with science, patent them, then resell the derived products or processes at exorbitant rates to the very people from whom they stole them in the first place. This turns the discourse of piracy, as bandied about in the TRIPS and 301 proceedings, upside down.

[10] Pat Mooney of the Canadian-based international NGO RAFI originally coined this term.

[11] In many instances, owing to extensive merger activity in the past decade, these corporations are one and the same. For example, when Sandoz and Ciba-Geigy completed their $63 billion merger in 1996 the new firm, Novartis, became "the world's number-one agrochemical corporation, second largest seed firm, third largest pharmaceutical firm, and fourth largest veterinary medicine company" (Shulman, 1999: 49).

A number of activists seek to demonstrate that, rhetoric to the contrary notwithstanding, America's global corporations are the biggest "pirates" on the planet.

Two Indian examples became particular lightning rods in the "biopiracy" campaign – the turmeric and neem tree cases. In 1995 the US Patent and Trademark Office granted two researchers at the University of Mississippi a patent on the use of turmeric as a healing agent. The New Delhi Council of Scientific and Industrial Research challenged the patent on the grounds that Indians had used turmeric in this capacity as a home remedy for generations. The researchers admitted in their patent application that it was a commonly used traditional remedy but they noted, "there are so many home remedies all over India, but are these scientifically valid or just gibberish? That's the point. We have used turmeric on patients. It has been clinically tested" (Hari Har Coyly quoted in Shulman, 1999: 144). By the US patent rules if a proposed invention has been mentioned in previously published material the patent will be denied. The Indian government ultimately prevailed in its challenge when it produced a 1953 article in the *Journal of the Indian Medical Association* documenting the healing properties of turmeric (Shulman, 1999: 145). Thus the patent was overturned. The turmeric case raised a larger question of the status of traditional methods and practices passed down orally, what is sometimes referred to as "folklore." Many so-called "scientific discoveries" are nothing more (or less) than folklore that researchers may stumble upon or seek out among indigenous peoples, farmers, shamans, and healers. Western patent systems have no protections for this type of innovation. They only recognize "individual innovations which were 'scientifically' achieved, the typically communal 'folk' knowledge of developing countries are excluded" (Marden, 1999: 292).

The infamous neem tree case began in the early 1990s. The neem tree is a culturally significant Indian resource with a broad variety of uses, including contraceptive, cosmetic, and agricultural applications, to name but a few. Farmers traditionally had used neem tree seed extracts as a natural pesticide for their crops. This traditional extract broke down quickly, however, and required repeated applications to be effective. In the early 1990s, researchers at W. R. Grace & Company, an agricultural chemical company, found a way to stabilize the active ingredient (azadirachtin) so that it could be stored and applied less frequently. In June 1992 the US Patent and Trademark Office (PTO) issued a patent to W. R. Grace for both the method of stabilizing the extract, and the resulting chemical solution. The Grace patent became a rallying point for activists against Western expropriation of developing countries' biological and knowledge resources. Farmers grew alarmed that they might be forced to pay huge royalties for using a resource they had relied upon for generations. In September 1995 a coalition of "225 agricultural, scientific, and trade groups as well as over 100,000 individual farmers, led by the Foundation on Economic Trends, filed a petition" with the PTO asking it to revoke the patent because it "lacked novelty, and in addition, was immoral" (Marden, 1999: 286). Jeremy Rifkin, an American lawyer and activist in the "no patents on life" campaign, participated in the neem tree petition and presented the stakes as follows: "the real battle is whether the genetic resources of the planet will be maintained as a shared commons or whether this common inheritance will be commercially enclosed and become the intellectual property of a few big corporations" (quoted in Marden, 1999: 292). While the neem tree issue remains unresolved, W.R. Grace & Company has gone ahead and established processing plants in India and is going forward with plans to increase its market share in neem-based products (May, 2000: 103).

In the agricultural sector, activists argue that patenting and *sui generis* plant variety protection have led to extensive economic concentration in the past decade. The vertical integration of plant breeding, agrochemical and food processing corporations has led to a situation in which "the top ten seed companies currently control 30 percent of the world's US$23 billion commercial seed market" (GAIA/GRAIN, 1998a: 13). Corporate plant breeders are obtaining broad patents that will have far reaching consequences. Breeders are patenting entire species (cotton), economic characteristics (oil quality), plant reproductive behavior (apomixis) and basic techniques of biotechnology (gene transfer tools) (GAIA/GRAIN, 1998a: 13). This combination of economic concentration with extensive and broad patenting means that a handful of global corporations are making huge inroads toward control of the world's food supply and are entangling farmers and indigenous peoples in an ever-more-complex web of licensing and royalty obligations.

Farmers traditionally have saved seeds and reused them. They traded seeds with each other, sold seeds to each other, and created and experimented with new hybrids. In these ways they have contributed to the planet's biodiversity. In the past, US law covering plant varieties incorporated the notion of farmers' rights in which farmers retained their freedom to engage in these important and traditional activities. However, in August 1994 the US Congress amended the Plant Variety Protection Act and removed the farmer's exemption so that now "it is expressly illegal for farmers to sell or save seeds from proprietary crop varieties without receiving permission from breeders and paying royalties" (Shulman, 1999: 90). Grassroots activists are convinced that American industries are seeking this same goal through TRIPS by pushing a particular interpretation of *sui generis* protection under Article 27.3(b).

TRIPS ultimately placed restrictions on such patenting (to the dismay of the American biotechnology industry). Article 27 permits the exclusion of plants and animals from patentability, but 27.3(b) requires that members provide protection for plant *varieties* either by patents or an "effective *sui generis*" system. However, there really is no consensus on what a *sui generis* system needs to include and, as Sutherland points out, the negotiating drafting history of Article 27 provides little guidance because the records are scant and there is no record on the meaning of *sui generis* (1998: 295). American IP industry activists have been pushing the Union for the Protection of New Varieties of Plants (UPOV) as the model *sui generis* system. UPOV, to which fifty (UPOV, 2002) mainly industrialized countries subscribe, was last amended in 1991. The 1978 version of the UPOV provided two limitations on the monopoly rights of plant breeders. First, other breeders could freely use UPOV-protected varieties for research purposes. Second, farmers could reuse the seed for the following year's sowing under certain conditions. The 1991 revision "narrowed down the exemption for competing breeders and it deleted the so-called farmer's privilege... [It] extends the breeders' monopoly right to the products of the farmer's harvest" (GRAIN, 1999d: 2). Therefore, the UPOV makes seed saving a crime. Any country wishing to join UPOV today must sign the 1991 treaty. It is very generous to the corporate plant breeder and the 1991 amendments sharply limited farmers' rights.

The USTR has pressed to incorporate TRIPS-plus provisions in its bilateral treaties. A case in point is the ultimately scuttled 1996 bilateral IPR treaty between the United States and Ecuador. The United States had convinced Ecuador to provide for either patenting or UPOV protection for plant varieties. TRIPS does *not* require UPOV protection; UPOV protection is not the only permissible approach to *sui generis* protection. Activists affiliated with a Canadian-based international NGO called the Rural Advancement Foundation International (RAFI) had been tracking US patent data bases for controversial ownership claims. They discovered that a US citizen had obtained a patent on a plant species that is the main ingredient of a sacred Amazonian hallucinogenic drink, ayahuasca

(Shulman, 1999: 127).[12] They passed the information on to the environmental NGO Accion Ecologica, which mobilized protests, occupied the Ecuadoran Congressional Chamber in July 1996, and blocked ratification of the IP treaty (Sutherland, 1998: 292). In the meantime, developing countries and NGOs have been pursuing alternative approaches to *sui generis* protection.

The principles enshrined in such alternatives are captured in the 1997 Thammasat Resolution.[13] In December 1997 the Thai Network on Community Rights and Biodiversity (BIOTHAI) and Genetic Resources Action International (GRAIN) assembled representatives of over forty NGOs from Africa, Asia, and Latin America to discuss strategies to combat the mounting pressure to patent life forms. This group issued the Thammasat Resolution enunciating its principles and strategies. The Resolution called for a revision of TRIPS to expressly permit countries to exclude life forms and biodiversity-related knowledge from IPR monopolies, the global mobilization of environmental, agricultural, consumer, health, food security, women's, human rights, and people's organizations, and asserted the primacy of the 1993 Convention on Biological Diversity (CBD) over TRIPS.

In 1985 Pat Mooney of RAFI developed the concept of farmers' rights as a counterweight to plant breeders' rights. RAFI introduced this principle in the United Nations Food and Agriculture deliberations over plant genetic resources in the so-called "seed wars" of the 1980s (Braithwaite and Drahos, 2000: 572; Fowler, 1994; Sutherland, 1998: 292). Farmers' rights were ultimately incorporated into the UN CBD, which has become an important metric for developing countries' approaches to TRIPS Article 27.3(b).

India was one of the first countries to advocate the primacy of the CBD over TRIPS 27.3(b). The CBD, unlike TRIPS, recognizes the rights of indigenous cultures to preserve their knowledge and resources (Article 8j). Article 8j of the CBD recognizes communal knowledge, which is clearly at odds with the individualistic conception embodied in TRIPS and the rejection of so-called "folklore" (*vs.* "science") protection in Western patent law. The Article calls for respect and preservation for "innovations . . . and practices of indigenous and local communities embodying

---

[12] Shulman attributes this action to the Indigenous Peoples' Biodiversity Network, but a researcher who has tracked these issues closely pointed out that this is a very small group that lacks the resources to do patent searches. Instead, the ayahuasca patent was discovered by someone working for RAFI. E-mail communication from Graham Dutfield, Feb. 15, 2002 (on file with the author).

[13] Reprinted in GRAIN (1997).

traditional lifestyles relevant for the conservation and sustainable use of biological diversity and to promote their wider application with the approval and involvement of the holders of such knowledge, innovations and utilization of such knowledge, innovations and practices" (UN Convention on Biological Diversity, 1992: 8j). Furthermore, the CBD stresses that biological resources are sovereign resources of states whereas TRIPS enforces private property rights over them. India argues that TRIPS needs to be amended to comply with the CBD (Tejera, 1999: 981). At the same time, numerous countries have joined the *sui generis* "rights movement" by proposing legislation that addresses the concerns raised by the anti-biopiracy activists. Countries such as Kenya, India, Nicaragua, Costa Rica, Zambia, Zimbabwe, Thailand, Bangladesh, Pakistan and the Organization for African Unity, have all been working on *sui generis* legislation that distances itself from the UPOV model and addresses the concerns raised above (GRAIN, 1999a; 1998b).

When the TRIPS Agreement was negotiated, participants agreed to revisit Article 27.3(b) four years after the date of entry into force (1999). In December 1998 the TRIPS Council met to discuss procedures for the upcoming review but fought over whether members were charged with reviewing "implementation" or actual "provisions." The United States was eager to confine discussions to implementation only, whereas India and the Association of Southeast Asian Nations (ASEAN) stressed that the mandate expressly covered provisions. Ultimately, the TRIPS Council members agreed that they were required to discuss substantive provisions. The US agenda included the deletion of exclusions to patents on life forms, and the incorporation of UPOV 91 into TRIPS. Given the building momentum over *sui generis* rights and the CBD–TRIPS conflicts, developing countries eagerly approached the review as an opportunity to follow through on the Thammasat pronouncements. Developing countries were prepared to resist the incorporation of UPOV 91 into TRIPS as the *sui generis* "alternative," request extensions for implementation, and insist upon the primacy of CBD over TRIPS in cases of conflict.

Throughout 1999, TRIPS Council deliberations in preparation for the December 1999 Seattle ministerial meeting dragged on with the Quad countries trying to restrict discussion to issues of implementation, and the developing countries pressing for more substantive discussions. In June 1999, GRAIN reported that the WTO, in conjunction with the UPOV, had been on an active campaign to push UPOV protection on developing countries (GRAIN, 1999d). With positions so far apart participants made no substantive progress towards clarifying or reformulating 27.3(b). The 1999 Seattle ministerial meeting yielded very little after the European Union and the United States deadlocked over agriculture, and huge protests organized by a broad array of international NGOs stymied deliberations.

While clearly disappointed in the lack of progress in the desired direction, the IPC lawyer Charles Levy noted the silver lining in the Seattle cloud. As Levy put it, "the good news is that members did not have a chance to tinker with TRIPS. Because there was no Ministerial Declaration, they did not have to deal with the cross-currents that were building on IP" (Levy, 2000: 794–795). It is hard to imagine that those "cross-currents" will disappear any time soon. Future efforts to negotiate multilateral TRIPS-plus provisions will meet with resistance. However, the proliferation of bilateral treaties codifying TRIPS-plus standards and requiring the adoption of UPOV-91 indicates that US and European pressure on developing countries to ratchet up their IP standards is alive and well (Drahos, 2001; GRAIN, 2001a, 2001b).

## Pharmaceutical patents

A related area of building opposition to TRIPS is pharmaceutical patents. A broad global campaign for access to essential medicines has emerged to protest US trade policy in intellectual property and the TRIPS tradeoff in favor of commercial interests over public health concerns. As the most successful campaign against TRIPS to date, it is worth examining in some detail. The so-called "rights talk" of the TRIPS deliberations obscured the fact that IP "rights" are actually grants of privileges (Weissman, 1996: 1087). "Grants talk" highlights the fact that what may be granted may be taken away when such grants conflict with other important goals. Public health is one such goal: "Had TRIPS been framed as a public health issue, the anxiety of mass publics in the US and other Western states might have become a factor in destabilizing the consensus that US business elites had built around TRIPS" (Braithwaite and Drahos, 2000: 576). Indeed, as this section reveals, public health activists have scored an important victory by achieving some retreat from the heretofore unqualified US government support for its global pharmaceutical companies.

American consumer activist Ralph Nader and his colleague James Love, director for the Consumer Project on Technology (CPT), have launched a post-TRIPS opposition campaign focused on health care issues and the high cost of pharmaceutical drugs. One of their strategies has been to reveal the government's (and taxpayers') contribution to the development of drugs. Escalating drug prices became a target of American protest in the early Clinton years when health care reform was high on the domestic agenda. In fact, in a clever and apparently defensive move, in 1994 the Pharmaceutical Manufacturers of America changed its name to the Pharmaceutical *Research* and Manufacturers of America to underscore its contributions to innovation. Curiously, despite the fact that the TRIPS deliberations focused on policies that affect virtually everyone on the planet, the GATT Secretariat received no complaints from consumer groups at the time of the negotiations.

In the wake of TRIPS an NGO campaign for access to essential medicines has gained momentum. In October 1995, Nader and Love wrote to then-USTR Mickey Kantor indicating that there were many different, legitimate views about health care, and that the USTR had been too narrowly focused on protecting the interests of US-based international pharmaceutical companies (Nader and Love, 1995). Their major concern was drug pricing. It seemed odd that taxpayer-funded drugs had become the very lucrative private property of global pharmaceutical firms. In 1995 and 1996, Nader and Love began to post their information, correspondence, and position papers on their internet newsletter "Pharm-policy." Another colleague published a law journal article criticizing the pharmaceutical industry's role in the construction of US trade policy (Weissman, 1996). Policymakers in India read this article and these postings, and in 1996 invited Nader to attend a major patent meeting in New Delhi, organized by B.K. Keayla and the Indian National Working Group on Patents.[14] Beginning with the Indians, other groups discovered Pharm-policy and it was (and continues to be, under its new name – IP-Health) an important vehicle for mobilizing interest in drug pricing and patent policy.

In 1996, Amsterdam-based Health Action International[15] (HAI) got involved in these issues; it was the first public health group to join the budding campaign. HAI's initial focus was exposing drug scams (e.g., placebos, bad drugs), but it increasingly became interested in the IP aspects of pharmaceuticals. HAI organized the first major NGO meeting on health care and TRIPS in October 1996 in Bielefeld, Germany. Love presented

[14] The organizers were mostly government officials and generic drug producers. E-mail correspondence from James Love, March 26, 2002 (on file with author).
[15] Health Action International is an informal network of over 150 consumer, health, development, and other public interest groups involved in health and pharmaceutical issues.

a paper on drug pricing and compulsory licensing (Love, 1996) which, according to Ellen 't Hoen of MSF, "was an eyeopener for everyone who was there."[16] That meeting brought together a number of people who would form the core of the early access to medicines campaign.[17] The CPT also became involved in the Free Trade Area of the Americas controversies in 1997. The FTAA treaty drafts proposed TRIPS-plus provisions for IP protection and provoked ardent dispute from Latin American health activists, including the Latin American HAI workers, and local pharmaceutical producers. CPT position papers were disseminated throughout the NGO community.[18]

Another important endeavor for the access campaign was its work on crafting a revised drug strategy for the World Health Organization's World Health Assembly (WHA) in January 1998. (The 2002 Doha Declaration owes much to this early effort.) The WHO Essential Drugs Policy concentrates on the supply and use of about 250 drugs that are considered to be most essential and important for public sector provision. Dr. Timothy Stamps, Zimbabwe's minister of health, asked Bas van der Heide of HAI to produce a draft resolution for a WHO "Revised Drug Strategy" on short notice.[19] HAI and CPT were already collaborating on comments for the FTAA negotiations (CPT and HAI, 1998) and incorporated language from the FTAA process advocating compulsory licensing and parallel importing, stressing the priority of health concerns over commercial interests. The WHO's Executive Board approved the resolution only because the United States was not on the Executive Board that year.[20] PhRMA was alarmed by the proposed Revised Drug Strategy, which provides guidance for developing countries, because it explicitly endorsed the very practices that PhRMA had been fighting through USTR.[21] The US and European governments acted to oppose the Revised Drug Strategy.[22]

[16] E-mail message from Ellen 't Hoen, March 22, 2002 (on file with author).
[17] In addition to Love and 't Hoen, Wilbert Bannenberg and Bas van der Heide of HAI participated. Bannenberg joined the WHO, working in South Africa. Ellen 't Hoen worked with HAI to lobby the World Health Assembly, and was later hired to work on the access campaign for MSF. E-mail message from James Love, March 26, 2002 (on file with author).
[18] Author's interview with James Love, Washington, DC, April 6, 2001.
[19] E-mail message from James Love, March 26, 2002 (on file with author).
[20] It is a rotating board; the United States is off every three years. Love (2001).
[21] PhRMA sharply reacted to a document written by two WHO employees, Pascale Boulet and German Velasquez (Velasquez and Boulet, 1999). Their document explicitly endorsed compulsory licensing to increase access to medicines. The controversy centered on the extent to which WHO would officially endorse compulsory licensing in its technical assistance to developing countries. Boulet later went to work for MSF.
[22] E-mail message from James Love, March 26, 2002 (on file with author).

A week prior to the May 1998 WHA meeting, HAI and CPT hosted a meeting for about seventy people to help equip NGO-friendly negotiators for the WHA deliberations (CPT, HAI *et al.*, 1998). When the WHA met in Geneva in May 1998 to discuss the Revised Drug Strategy, the United States sent *trade* negotiators to this public health forum. Dr. Olive Shisana, director-general of the South African Department of Health and key negotiator for the African countries at the meeting, presented extensive evidence of US compulsory licensing practices.[23] This tactic exposed the hypocrisy of the US stance, insinuating that the United States sought to deny others the right to do as the United States did. The USTR was caught off guard by this line of attack. Dr. Shisana was appointed executive director of Family and Health Services of the WHO in July 1998.

In the summer of 1998 Bernard Pecoul of MSF,[24] a highly regarded Paris-based humanitarian NGO, contacted CPT and HAI and expressed interest in joining the access campaign. The MSF became an important ally in the campaign. When it won the Nobel Prize in October 1999 for its humanitarian work, it donated its million dollar prize money to the access campaign. Along the way the campaign picked up the support of the United Nations Development Program (UNDP), the World Health Organization (WHO), and the World Bank (Vick, 1999: A18). In October 1998, negotiators reached a compromise on the Revised Drug Strategy, endorsing public health concerns. Developing country and NGO activists felt that this was a "near complete victory."[25] In December 1998 MSF, HAI, and CPT met in Geneva to plot out a strategy to move forward on the Revised Drug Strategy. They decided to host a meeting on compulsory licensing and Articles 30 and 31 of TRIPS. The three-day meeting was held in March to frame the "expected adoption" of the Revised Drug Strategy as a "referendum in support of compulsory licensing."[26]

In May 1999 the World Health Assembly unanimously enacted resolution WHA 52.19,[27] based on the October compromise, calling upon member states to ensure equitable access to essential drugs and review options under international agreements to safeguard access to these

[23] For examples see Love and Palmedo (2001).
[24] Also known as Doctors Without Borders.
[25] E-mail message from James Love, March 26, 2002 (on file with author).
[26] Ibid.
[27] World Health Assembly, Resolution 52.19, "Revised Drug Strategy" (May 24, 1999); available at: http://www.who.int/gb/EB_WHA/PDF/WHA52/e19.pdf (last visited 11/01/01).

medicines. In its open letter to WTO member states, the access campaign called upon governments to consider a number of measures in relation to TRIPS obligations to increase access to essential medicines. The campaign urged WTO member states to make public health their highest priority in implementing TRIPS obligations, explore the extension of grace periods for developing countries, and to encourage developing countries to actively invoke the public health and public interest considerations of TRIPS Articles 7 and 8.

The campaign also raised its objections to the test data exclusivity interpretations of Article 39 favored by the United States. This issue was raised in a number of PhRMA-inspired USTR actions. Article 39 of TRIPS requires member states to protect health registration data from unfair commercial use. The United States has interpreted this obligation to mean that generic drug companies may not even rely upon published scientific papers or foreign government regulatory approvals without permission from the owners of the data. Without data exclusivity generic products could be brought to market with simple bioequivalence tests instead of replicating the costly and time-consuming clinical trials for safety and efficacy. The flashpoint case for this issue is the drug Taxol (Paclitaxel), manufactured by Bristol-Myers Squibb. Taxol is used to treat a variety of cancers including Kaposi's Sarcoma (often afflicting HIV/AIDS patients). Taxol was invented by US government scientists working for the National Institutes of Health. Bristol-Myers Squibb acquired exclusive marketing rights to the drug, and has claimed marketing exclusivity under national laws protecting health registration data. "BMS received in excess of $1.2 billion annually for Taxol, and sponsored none of the clinical trials for which initial registration of the drug were based. The high prices charged by BMS for Taxol have led to serious access problems for patients suffering from malignant diseases" (MSF, HAI, CPT, 1999a: 6–7 at note III). The campaign strongly advocates generic drug competition. Pointing to another essential drug, Fluconazole, used to treat cryptococcal meningitis (afflicting many who suffer from HIV/AIDS), the campaign notes that this drug sells for $14–25 for a daily dose in markets where Pfizer has exclusivity but sells for $0.75 or less in those countries with generic competition. Clearly referring to the practices of the USTR, the Campaign urged WTO member states to prevent the use of trade sanctions against countries that do not implement TRIPS-plus obligations on policies concerning access to essential medicines.

## Reactions to trade pressure and the Gore campaign

While these early efforts were important, US trade pressure on both South Africa and Thailand really galvanized the criticism of TRIPS. Faced with debilitating HIV/AIDS crises, these two countries chose to avail themselves of provisions under TRIPS which provide for compulsory licensing in case of grave medical emergencies. Articles 30 and 31 permit compulsory licensing of patents under restricted conditions. These were two articles that the pharmaceutical industry "lost" on in the TRIPS negotiations. When a state grants a compulsory license, rights to produce a product are licensed to another party without the patent holder's permission. Compulsory licensing allows states to produce generic drugs which are more affordable. One of the conditions for compulsory licensing under Article 31 is that licenses must be used in domestic markets and not for export (Maskus, 2000: 178). Countries in the grip of the HIV/AIDS crisis also seek exceptions so that countries could export products produced under compulsory license, so countries with small domestic markets also could benefit from economies of scale.

The USTR also pressured Thailand on behalf of PhRMA in 1997 and 1998. After Thailand planned to produce a generic version of the AIDS drug ddI, US trade officials threatened sanctions on core Thai exports. Thailand subsequently dropped its compulsory licensing plans. Compulsory licensing, permitted under TRIPS, "was intended as a lifeline. But in practice, any country reaching for this lifeline has been handcuffed by US trade negotiators" (Vick, 1999: A1).

In December 1997, South African President Nelson Mandela signed the South African Medicines and Medical Devices Regulatory Authority Act (Medicines Act hereafter). The Medicines Act allowed the minister of health to revoke patents on medicines and to allow for broad-based compulsory licensing to manufacture generic versions of HIV/AIDS drugs. Article 15(c) permitted parallel importing so that South Africa could take advantage of discriminatory pricing policies and import the cheapest available patented medicines. PhRMA was outraged and wrote to USTR Charlene Barshefsky and Commerce Secretary William Daley denouncing the South African Act (Gellman, 2000). Subsequently thirty-nine members of the Pharmaceutical Manufacturers of South Africa (mainly local licensees of global PhRMA) filed a lawsuit challenging the Act's legality in Pretoria High Court.

At PhRMA's behest, the US government threw its full weight behind the South African case to press South Africa to revoke the offending provisions of its law. In its February 1998 submission to USTR, PhRMA recommended that South Africa be named a "Priority Foreign Country" and argued that South African law posed a direct challenge to the achievements of the Uruguay Round (PhRMA, 1998a: 10–11). PhRMA further pointed out that South Africa offered no protection for test data and had introduced price controls. In response, the USTR placed South Africa on the 301 "Watch List"and urged the South African government to repeal its law. Throughout 1998, US government pressure intensified. In June 1998 the White House announced a suspension of South Africa's GSP benefits (Bond, 1999: 771).

Despite USTR pressure, South Africa refused to repeal its law and gained some activist supporters in the process. In 1998 Greg Pappas, acting head of International Health in Donna Shalala's US Department of Health and Human Services, advised Love to get the AIDS advocacy group ACT UP involved in the medicines campaign.[28] Pappas made the connection and ACT UP Philadelphia invited Love to speak at its January 1999 meeting. Paul Davis and Asia Russell of ACT UP had been planning to take action to protest pharmaceutical companies' pricing policies. Initially their strategy was to shame pharmaceutical executives by ambushing them and throwing blood on them, like the anti-fur activists. Love convinced them that it was not just executives, but that the government was deeply involved in this and that the upcoming presidential primaries were a window of opportunity. Gore maintained a PhRMA-friendly stance in part because his main challenger for the Democratic presidential nomination was Senator Bill Bradley of New Jersey, home to many global pharmaceutical firms. Gore was eager to get PhRMA campaign dollars. Additionally, Gore was closely linked to PhRMA and its lobbyists, including his former chiefs of staff, chief domestic policy advisor, and Anthony Podesta (Gellman, 2000; Love, quoted in Bond, 1999: 782).

The US advocacy group ACT UP took up South Africa's cause. Group members repeatedly disrupted Vice President Al Gore's campaign appearances in the summer of 1999 with noisemakers and banners that said "Gore's Greed Kills." These had quite an impact on live television, and the results were nearly immediate. "The Clinton administration withdrew two years of objections to the new South African law in

[28] Author's interview with James Love, Washington, DC, April 6, 2001.

June, the same week that Gore declared his intent to run for president and AIDS activists began tormenting his campaign" (Gellman, 2000). Shortly thereafter, Gore met privately with South Africa's President Thabo Mbeki and on September 17, 1999 the US removed South Africa from the USTR watch list (Vick, 1999: A18). Nader, Love, and Weissman wrote a letter to USTR Charlene Barshefsky expressing pleasure with the decision to stop pressuring South Africa, and urging the USTR to extend its policy in the South African case to all developing countries (Nader, Love, and Weissman, October 6, 1999). Their letter urged the USTR to reconsider its position on Thailand's compulsory licensing efforts, parallel importing, and test data exclusivity.

## Seattle and the executive order

In late November 1999, on the eve of the Seattle WTO Ministerial Meeting, the access campaign held a conference in Amsterdam. The Conference's "Amsterdam Statement," addressed to WTO members, spelled out their agenda. It called for the WTO to establish a working group on access to medicines, endorse the use of compulsory licensing of patents under Article 31, allow exceptions to patent rights under Article 30 for production of medicines for exports markets when the medicine is exported to a country with a compulsory license. This latter exception would help countries with small domestic markets for whom local production is not feasible. The statement also called for the avoidance of overly restrictive interpretations of Article 39 regarding health registration data (MSF, HAI, CPT, 1999b). The Amsterdam Statement guided the work of the public health activists ('t Hoen, 2002: 35).

In Seattle, President Clinton signaled a major change in US policy by announcing that he supported African access to HIV/AIDS drugs and that the United States would alter its trade policy to promote access to essential drugs. USTR Charlene Barshefsky and Secretary of Health and Human Services Donna Shalala announced an institutional innovation mandating collaboration between the two agencies to include consideration of public health issues in the context of trade and intellectual property. Clinton announced that the United States would "henceforward implement its health care and trade policies in a manner that ensures that people in the poorest countries won't have to go without medicine they so desperately need" (MSF, 2000).

In May 2000, the Joint United Nations Program on AIDS (UNAIDS) program announced in conjunction with five global pharmaceutical companies (Boehringer Ingelheim, Bristol-Myers Squibb, Glaxo Well-come, Merck & Co., and F. Hoffman-La Roche) plans to slash prices of AIDS drugs for selected African countries. MSF instantly and harshly criticized the plan, characterizing it as a cynical attempt by corporations to prevent countries from availing themselves of compulsory licensing and parallel importing options. MSF suspected that this initiative was merely a way for corporations to prevent developing countries from seizing their patents. As Bernard Pecoul, director of the MSF Access to Essential Medicines Campaign, stated, "the fact that a serious discussion has begun among drug companies on dramatically reducing the price of AIDS drugs is a victory, but a small one, much like an elephant giving birth to a mouse... The agreement does nothing to stimulate countries' rights to produce or import inexpensive high-quality generic drugs, a key component to long-term sustainable solutions for improving access to essential medicines" (MSF, 2000: 1).

On May 10, the Clinton administration issued an executive order that incensed the pharmaceutical industry. His order was much bolder than the UNAIDS proposal. Clinton announced that he would prohibit the USTR from pressuring sub-Saharan African countries into forgoing legitimate strategies, such as compulsory licensing and parallel import-ing, aimed at increasing access to affordable HIV/AIDS drugs.[29] The Executive Order stated that "the United States shall not seek, through negotiation or otherwise, the revocation or revision of any intellectual property law or policy of a beneficiary sub-Saharan African country, as determined by the president, that regulates HIV/AIDS pharmaceuti-cals or medical technologies..."[30] This was a significant departure from past US policy in so far as it elevated public health into the framing of

[29] This Executive Order originated as a proposal by Representatives Jesse Jackson Jr. (D-IL) and Bernie Sanders (D-VT) in the HOPE for Africa bill (H.R. 772, avail-able at: <http://thomas.loc.gov/cgi-bin/query/D?c106:1:./temp/~c106fBtsPI:e74695:> accessed 4/18/02). Robert Weissman at CPT helped to draft language for the proposed bill emphasizing no "TRIPS-plus" for Africa. Section 601 of the HOPE for Africa bill covered "requirements relating to sub-Saharan Africa intellectual property and competition law." The bill did not survive deliberations in the House of Representatives. In the Senate, Di-anne Feinstein (D-CA) and Russell Feingold (D-WI) pushed a version of the bill (available at: http://thomas.loc.gov/cgi-bin/bdquerytr/z?d106:SN01636:@@@D&summ2 = m&> accessed 4/18/02). While the HOPE for Africa bill was superseded by the more con-servative African Growth and Opportunity Act, the IP provisions of HOPE for Africa reappeared in Clinton's Executive Order.
[30] Full text available at: "Text of the Africa/HIV/AIDS Executive Order 13155" [Pharm-policy] <http://lists.essential.org/pipermail/pharm-policy/2001-January/000613.html> accessed 11-01-01. Executive Order No. 13,155, 65 Federal Register 30,521 (2000).

trade issues, and this was the first time in many years that the executive acted against the expressed wishes of the non-generic pharmaceutical industry in the context of trade. The order endorsed no TRIPS-plus for AIDS in Africa. In February 2001, USTR Robert Zoellick of the Bush administration announced that it would uphold the Clinton order.

Predictably, Alan Holmer, president of PhRMA, expressed his organization's displeasure with Clinton's executive order. He stated that Clinton's approach to the issue set an "undesirable and inappropriate precedent, by adopting a discriminatory approach to intellectual property laws, and focusing exclusively on pharmaceuticals. This opens up opportunities to invoke exceptions to existing intellectual property protections. We recognize that AIDS is a major problem, but weakening intellectual property rights is not the solution" (PhRMA, 2000b).

In October 2000, Oxfam UK got involved in the access campaign and collaborated with MSF and CPT. Oxfam promoted civic activism and the campaign welcomed Oxfam on board.

## Pressure on prices

Companies increasingly have been forced to respond to the challenge posed by the HIV/AIDS crisis and the public health activists. Besides the UNAIDS program, in April 2000 Pfizer offered to provide Fluconazole tablets free to South Africa. Companies fear that cut-rate drugs provided for developing countries will begin to flood developed country markets and reduce profit margins, but public pressure in the face of what appears to be a treatable crisis demands a response. Participating companies hope that their counterparts will match their price reductions and that OECD governments will offer funds to help Africans buy the drugs. They also hope to preempt any compulsory licensing of their products.

During May 2000, CPT representatives spoke with Krisana Kraisintu, head of the Thai government's Pharmaceutical Organization's Research and Development Institute. Love asked what the best price for a three drug HIV/AIDS antiretroviral regime would be; Kraisintu estimated that it would be about $240 a year (as opposed to the $12,000–15,000 multinational pricing).[31] Love later met with William Haddad, an American generic drug manufacturer and advocate for the generic drug industry, to inquire about raw material prices for

[31] E-mail message from James Love, March 26, 2002 (on file with author).

HIV/AIDS drugs. The CPT was interested in acquiring the antiretro-viral d4T by compulsory license, and then selling it as cheaply as possible to developing countries. Haddad put Love in touch with Dr. Yusuf Hamied, CEO of Cipla, a generic pharmaceutical manufac-turer in India. (Haddad, 2001). Robert Weissman and Love met with Hamied, who presented data on the price per kilo of all the chemi-cals needed to make the three-drug HIV/AIDS cocktail. Market forces had dramatically reduced the cost of material to make the three drugs. In three years the price had dropped from $10,000 to $750 per kilo, largely due to Brazil's bulk purchases (Brazil had purchased $150–200 million worth of these raw materials). Dr. Hamied told Love that he could produce the pills for about $1 a day per dose. Love urged Hamied to make a dramatic offer as a humanitarian donation. Hamied agreed to sell it to MSF for $350 per year. A dollar a day had good symbolic value. MSF was immediately swamped by requests for the drugs. The February 7, 2001 announcement, featured on the front page of *The New York Times*, "shocked the world, and completely transformed the global debate on treatment for HIV in Africa. At this price it was clear that many would die needlessly, if steps were not taken to remove barriers to access to medicines."[32]

Mounting public pressure prompted a flurry of activity in 2001. Cipla asked the South African government for permission to sell generic ver-sions of eight of the fifteen anti-HIV drugs (Stolberg, 2001: A1). Cipla, in conjunction with MSF, "asked the South African government...to give it licenses to all antiretroviral drugs patented there by multinationals on the ground that they are not selling them at affordable prices" (McNeil, 2001: A3). Merck announced that it would offer to a number of countries its antiretroviral Sustiva and protease inhibitor Crixivan for $500 and $600 per year, respectively.

The access campaign scored another important victory in 2001 by pres-suring Yale University, which holds the patent on the antiretroviral AIDS d4T, and requesting that Yale permit South Africa to import generic ver-sions of d4T. Yale's patent contract with Bristol-Myers Squibb earns $40 million a year from the drug's licensing fees (McNeil, 2001: A3). Ini-tially, Yale refused the request claiming that Bristol-Myers Squibb had an exclusive license and that only the company could decide how to re-spond. A group of Yale law students organized campus protests, and one of the drug's developers, Yale pharmacology professor William Prusoff,

---

[32] Ibid.

supported the students. On March 14, 2001, Bristol-Myers Squibb announced that it would cut the cost of d4T to $0.15 for a daily dose (1.5 percent of the cost to an American patient). Dr. Prusoff wrote an editorial after the announcement, in which he cited the staggering numbers of HIV afflicted people in sub-Saharan Africa and stated, "the numbers seem too great to understand. But they are not. In a way, they are as easy to understand as 15 cents. I suppose this has now occurred to Bristol-Myers Squibb" (Prusoff, 2001: A19). He wrote, "I find it hard to see any pattern in all this, except perhaps that there is a moral urge among people that, however coincidentally, can sometimes bring results" (Prusoff, 2001: A19).

The PhRMA-led lawsuit against South Africa was scheduled to begin on March 5. The trial quickly became a high profile event marked by protesters, grim images of dying mothers and babies, street demonstrations, and extensive media coverage. The powerful imagery conjured up memories of apartheid, and presented a genuine public relations disaster for the pharmaceutical companies. Furthermore, during the trial it was revealed that Article 15(c) of the Medicines Act had been based on a WIPO Committee of Experts draft legal text ('t Hoen, 2002: 32). This weakened the companies' claims that the Medicines Act abrogated South Africa's international law commitments. Additionally, the South African activist group Treatment Access Campaign announced that it would provide evidence on the actual costs of developing HIV/AIDS drugs, which would be dramatically lower than the figures provided by the companies.[33] MSF initiated an internet petition drive asking the drug companies to drop the lawsuit; it received about 250,000 signatures, roughly the same number of persons who had died in South Africa of AIDS the previous year.[34] Amid intense public outcry the companies withdrew their lawsuit against South Africa. This was hailed as an important victory for developing countries and citizen group campaigns against the pharmaceutical industry.

The momentum generated by these developments accelerated into the summer. Developing countries increasingly had become mobilized and assertive on the access to medicines issue. The African group exercised leadership in pressing the issue further. In the spring of 2001, Ambassador Boniface Chidyausiku[35] of Zimbabwe requested a special TRIPS Council session on access to medicines. The Quaker United

[33] Ibid.    [34] Ibid.
[35] His full title is ambassador, permanent representative to the United Nations and WTO, Permanent Mission of the Republic of Zimbabwe.

Nations Office in Geneva provided support for developing country delegates[36] and a number of legal scholars, economists, and activists provided technical support.[37] The June TRIPS Council session, chaired by Chidyausiku, addressed the access to medicines issues. A building consensus emerged, which included the European Union, that TRIPS should not interfere with the protection of public health. Nonetheless, the United States continued to defend its global drug companies (Boseley and Capella, 2001). Developing countries sought official confirmation that measures to protect public health would not make them subject to dispute settlement procedures in the WTO. The TRIPS Council resolved to continue analyzing the degree of flexibility afforded by TRIPS in the context of public health, planned future meetings on the issue, and pledged to convene another special session on trade and pharmaceuticals in September 2001 (Capdevila, 2001). At the June meeting the Brazilian delegation highlighted Brazil's dramatically successful program of distributing HIV/AIDS medicines at very low or no cost to patients. Its access to medicines program has decreased AIDS-related deaths by half and reduced hospital admissions brought on by opportunistic infections by 80 percent. Brazil has become a beacon of hope for developing countries in their struggle against the HIV/AIDS pandemic. Brazil's policies received very prominent and positive press, most notably as the cover story in the Sunday magazine of *The New York Times* (Rosenberg, 2001).

Brazil's successful AIDS programs, widely touted upon the heels of the withdrawn South African lawsuit, made the United States' WTO case against Brazil look increasingly unsavory. The United States announced that it was officially withdrawing its case against Brazil on the first day of the first United Nations General Assembly Special Session devoted to a public health issue. The special session culminated in "The Declaration of Commitment" on HIV/AIDS on June 27, 2001. Applauded by the access to essential medicines campaigners such as MSF, the Declaration framed the issue as a "political, human rights, and economic threat" (Steinhauer, 2001: A1). The General Assembly endorsed the creation of a Global Fund; UN Secretary-General Kofi Annan called for a $7–10 billion annual goal. In April 2002 the Global Fund to Fight AIDS,

---

[36] For position papers and further information see <http://www.afsc.org/quno.htm> (accessed April 25, 2002).
[37] Argentine economist Carlos Correa, American legal scholars Frederick Abbott, Jerome Reichman, Australian legal scholar Peter Drahos, and activists James Love and Ellen 't Hoen were among those providing support.

Tuberculosis and Malaria announced its first grants worth $378 million to efforts to fight disease in thirty-one developing countries over two years. The Fund indicated that it would approve more grants worth an additional $238 million (*Washington Post*, 2002). Significantly, some of the projects are aimed at *treatment*, not just prevention, reflecting the goals of developing countries and the access campaign.

In September 2001 the TRIPS Council met and discussed the access issue. The African Group presented draft text for a ministerial declaration on TRIPS and public health emphasizing that "nothing in the TRIPS Agreement shall prevent Members from taking measures to protect public health" ('t Hoen, 2002: 41). As a consequence of these pre-Doha deliberations, Mike Moore, WTO director-general, announced at the outset of the Doha meeting in November that "the TRIPS and health issue could be a deal-breaker for a new trade round" ('t Hoen, 2002: 45).

## Doha and the Doha Declaration

In the run-up to the WTO's Doha Ministerial Meeting in November, 2001, PhRMA widely circulated two reports to demonstrate the irrelevance of patents to the access issue (Attaran and Gillespie-White, 2001). Both papers argued that patents were not a barrier to access, and that problems such as poverty and limited spending on health care were the most important barriers to access. Since the rise of the public health discourse on access to medicines, PhRMA has sought to deflect any culpability of strong patent protection. The CPT posted these papers on its internet newsletter, and they inspired impassioned debate.[38] In October, CPT, Essential Action, Oxfam, Treatment Access Campaign, and Health Gap issued a paper which carefully rebutted the authors' claims (CPT, *et al.* 2001). In the end, no one would deny that poverty and inadequate spending are important but the access advocates stressed that these problems should not deflect attention away from the contribution of patent protection to access problems. The activists' rebuttals diluted the potential impact of the papers and implied PhRMA sponsorship of the research, undermining its aura of scholarly objectivity. The fact that most of the policymakers involved in this issue subscribe to the CPT

---

[38] For examples of these debates see: IP-Health Digest, vol. 1, no. 662, Thursday, October 20, 2001, 8:59p.m. message 2 "Re: Attaran & Gillespie-White – JAMA paper is now published" (Richard Jeffreys); IP-Health Digest, vol. 1, no. 660, 2:31p.m., message 1, "MSF and Amir's paper" (Ellen 't Hoen); IP-Health Digest, vol. 1, no. 654, message 1 "Donnelly on Attaran/IIPI" (James Love).

newsletter meant that they were aware of the research, debate, and re-buttals before the Attaran/Gillespie-White study was published. Thus, its intended impact was less than PhRMA hoped it would be.

Another crucial event prior to the Doha meeting was the September 11 terrorist attack on the United States. Shortly after these attacks the United States was gripped by a bioterrorism scare as several postal and media workers handling anthrax-tainted mail contracted the dis-ease and died. Concerned over the availability of ciproflaxin (Cipro), an antibiotic effective in treating anthrax, Canada threatened to issue a compulsory license to override the patent and manufacture the drug generically. The United States also briefly considered compulsory licens-ing, promoted by Charles Schumer (D–NY) and Secretary of Health and Human Services Tommy Thompson. Ultimately neither Canada nor the United States followed through on the compulsory licensing threat, but they did negotiate deep price cuts with Bayer, the supplier of Cipro.[39]

This incident was important for two reasons. First, if the United States presumably was willing to engage in compulsory licensing to address a national emergency (in the wake of several deaths, but uncertain about the magnitude of the threat) how could it possibly deny that same pre-rogative to developing countries daily facing thousands of preventable deaths? Second, the dynamic of threatening compulsory licensing and then achieving deeply discounted drug prices was the exact strategy so successfully employed by Brazil in its HIV/AIDS program and a strat-egy for which the United States sought to prosecute Brazil in the WTO. This series of events caught the attention of the access campaign and de-veloping country negotiators and was on everybody's minds at Doha. As a Brazilian negotiator at Doha remarked, "It's not there in the [WTO] discussion... But everyone is conscious of it. It adds a lot of weight to our arguments" (quoted in Pruzin, 2001).

A group of eighty countries, led by the Africa Group, Brazil, and India, proposed the Declaration on the TRIPS Agreement and Public Health. The group sought a legally binding declaration that would affirm an interpretation of TRIPS that would permit them to pursue policies affording access to essential medicines without fear of retribu-tion from other WTO members. The United States and Switzerland, re-flecting the Attaran/Gillespie-White argument opposed the declaration

[39] William Haddad, CEO of a generic pharmaceutical firm, helped to negotiate the Cipro deal with Bayer as well as price cuts for Africa for HIV/AIDS drugs. For some of his reflections on the Cipro/Bayer deal see IP-Health Digest, vol. 1, no. 683, October 25, 2001, 12:38p.m., message 1 "Note from Bill Haddad" (James Love).

"on the grounds that patents are not a barrier preventing access to essential medicines" (Pruzin, 2001). In informal discussions prior to the full negotiations the United States floated a proposal that would provide an extension of transition periods for the least developed countries, and a moratorium on WTO disputes with sub-Saharan African countries involving HIV/AIDS policies. NGO groups and developing country delegations decried this proposal as a cynical attempt to undermine the solidarity of the developing country bloc and to isolate the middle-income developing countries such as India and Brazil that have the capacity to manufacture generic drugs for export.

The solidarity of the bloc remained intact, and in the end achieved notable success. The Declaration (WTO, 2001), adopted November 14, 2001, states: "we agree that the TRIPS Agreement does not and should not prevent members from taking measures to protect public health." Further:

> Each member has the right to grant compulsory licenses and the freedom to determine the grounds upon which such licenses are granted. Each member has the right to determine what constitutes a national emergency ... it being understood that public health crises, including those related to HIV/AIDS, tuberculosis, malaria and other epidemics can constitute a national emergency ...                    (WTO, 2001)

The Declaration affirms member countries' rights to protect public health and "to promote access to medicines for all" (WTO, 2001). In the end, developing countries failed to secure US support for a legally binding agreement. And crucially, paragraph 6 of the Declaration formally postponed resolving one of the access campaign's central issues – the ability of countries with little or no pharmaceutical manufacturing capability to make effective use of TRIPS compulsory licensing provisions (for a trenchant analysis see Abbott, 2002). The Africa Group and its supporters sought clarification that nothing in TRIPS should prevent countries from exporting generic drugs to poor countries. The Declaration instructs the TRIPS Council to resolve this issue by the end of 2002. Least developed countries have been granted an extension until 2016 to implement TRIPS.

The solidarity of the developing country bloc, the anthrax scare, and the access campaign all contributed to the triumph of Doha (Banta, 2001; 't Hoen, 2002: 45–46). However, the Declaration itself has had mixed reviews. Some argue that it did nothing but restate what was already in TRIPS. Others see it as an important, albeit incomplete, victory for the access campaign and public health advocates. Gillespie-White asserted that the activists' claims of victory were "naive and short-sighted" and summed up industry's position as follows:

> Wherever property rights are challenged, in a place where a market exists for the sale of a particular commodity . . . and the country which has taken steps to abrogate those rights is perceived to have used its discretion unwisely, the property right holder will challenge the decision made. This will happen with or without . . . [the Doha] Declaration . . . too much is at stake for the situation to be otherwise.
>
> (Gillespie-White, 2001)

Despite Gillespie-White's claims to the contrary, the NGO activists and developing countries have changed the politics of intellectual property. What is new is that public health issues have become linked to trade and intellectual property. There has been some movement away from the industry-sponsored IP orthodoxy that animated deliberations leading up to the TRIPS accord. To the extent that public health activists can succeed in persuading others of the merits of this framing they could have a significant impact indeed in redressing the imbalance between private and public interests in the context of intellectual property. While controversies remain, the access campaign has come a long way in a short time.

Overall, the post-TRIPS picture is mixed. TRIPS has energized industry to press further for TRIPS-plus policy changes in foreign countries (Drahos, 2001; GRAIN, 2001a, 2001b). TRIPS has galvanized an increasingly vociferous and mobilized civil society campaign to temper the previously unchecked industry dominance over the IP agenda. At the very least, the post-TRIPS trends have revealed new areas of contestation and portend a more difficult political environment for industry.

# 7    Conclusion – structured agency revisited

The emergence of TRIPS and the subsequent backlash against it demonstrate structured agency through one complete cycle of change and the beginnings of a second cycle. In the first cycle that led to TRIPS, structural change was a necessary but insufficient condition. Structural change delivered the TRIPS architects to the forefront of global business regulation, but it took agency to construct and achieve TRIPS. In the second cycle TRIPS confronted agents as a structure, crucially shaping the context for action. "Inevitably social processes generated to meet certain requirements represent impediments to other groups" (Archer, 1982: 476). TRIPS has divided agents into supporters and resisters and has animated new corporate agents to protest its effects. While agency has been important in this early phase of post-TRIPS resistance, particularly in the access to medicines campaign, the ultimate outcome of the contest over TRIPS will be conditioned by broader and deeper structural factors as well. This chapter further explores the concept of structured agency by comparing TRIPS with the other new issues in the WTO, examining issues of compliance and legitimacy, and discussing post-TRIPS constraints and opportunities. It goes on to discuss the implications of the argument for both theory and policy.

## The difference that agency makes: private power in comparative perspective

Viewed in isolation, TRIPS is a stunning triumph of the private sector in making global IP rules and in enlisting states and international organizations to enforce them. However, one must be careful not to generalize from one case. The TRIPS case reinforces the perspective of those who argue that private capital is ascendant in global governance. It fortifies a structural perspective that power begets power. While states have not withered away, the private sector is setting particular agendas. However, as the following comparisons suggest, structure alone does not determine outcomes.

The US private sector played a large role in the Uruguay Round. The US private sector actors were the driving forces behind TRIPS, the financial services agreement, the General Agreement on Trade in Services (GATS), and trade-related investment measures (TRIMS). Structural changes in the global political economy, changes in technology and markets, have empowered a new set of actors pushing for greater liberalization in investment and services, and stronger IP protection. These actors represent the most globally competitive industries and the strongest transnational corporate players. In services and IP protection, the US government responded to a sustained, decades-long effort of private sector actors to link these issues to trade. These actors succeeded in getting recognition for this linkage in amendments to US trade laws in the 1970s and 1980s, and the USTR pursued their goals by invoking Section 301, Super 301, and Special 301 and engaging in "aggressive unilateralism." The new agreements enshrined in the WTO were the culmination of decades-long efforts of these private sector actors to get states to classify these issues as trade-related, and assign them pride of place in multilateral negotiations. These agreements would not exist without the private sector efforts. However, despite these common origins, the outcomes of their multilateral quests were varied.

Agreements are authoritative if parties regard them as binding and the agreements alter outcomes for others (Strange, 1996: 184). Placing the new agreements – TRIPS, the agreement on financial services, GATS and TRIMS on a spectrum – the TRIPS and the financial services agreements are the most authoritative, the GATS is in the middle, and the TRIMS agreement is the least authoritative. Decisive factors leading to the TRIPS and financial services agreements were transnational private sector mobilization of an OECD consensus, along with the absence of sustained opposition. By contrast, in the weaker agreements, GATS and TRIMS, there was considerable transnational private sector mobilization but no OECD consensus, and sustained opposition. The TRIMS agreement was further stymied by two additional factors – substantial host country bargaining power and US government opposition to the private sector's goals on the grounds of national security.

## Intellectual property protection: TRIPS

Initially, acting primarily through industry associations in the 1970s and early 1980s, US firms urged the government to pressure foreign governments to adopt and enforce more stringent IP protection. They sought and won changes in US domestic laws – most notably Sections 301 and 337 of the US trade laws. A handful of US-based transnational corporations formed the IPC and spearheaded the effort to secure a multilateral instrument codifying their interest in stricter IP protection. They worked to build an OECD consensus for a multilateral trade-based instrument. The transnational leadership of the IPC was decisive in the achievement of TRIPS.

Initially, developing countries resisted the inclusion of intellectual property in the negotiations but by April 1989 had dropped their opposition. Having faced escalating US aggressive unilateralism, they hoped that cooperation on TRIPS would ease this pressure. Further, they were willing to go along with TRIPS in exchange for concessions on issues of greater short-to-medium-term salience, such as agriculture and the phasing out of the Multi-Fibre Arrangement. The transnational private sector mobilization of an OECD consensus and the collapse of developing countries' opposition were decisive factors in the TRIPS outcome.

## General agreement on trade in services

The spectacular growth of global trade in services and intensified competition in large markets has sharpened concerns over differences in domestic regulatory policy. Services trade is one of the most dynamic areas of the global economy, growing at an average annual rate of 8.3 percent (Hoekman, 1995: 329), faster than trade in goods. By 1993 global services trade amounted to US $930 billion, equaling 22 per cent of global trade (goods plus services) (Hoekman and Kostecki, 1995: 127). Activist private sector service providers sought expanded market access and the elimination of domestic regulations and practices that interfere with free trade. Unlike trade in goods, many services depend on the proximity of the provider and consumer; services trade often requires international direct investment to establish offices in host countries. Accounting for 60 percent of world consumption, services make up only 20 percent of world trade (Julius, 1994: 277); this discrepancy highlights the pervasiveness of domestic impediments facing foreign service providers.

US private sector actors sought significant liberalization of foreign services markets. Beginning in the 1970s, the financial services sector, including the insurance industry, lobbied for inclusion of services under the GATT umbrella to remove barriers to market access. Like the intellectual property lobby, private sector services activists convinced the US government to incorporate services in revisions to its trade laws, and the US pursued Section 301 actions against Europe and Japan for barriers to services trade. US private sector lobbyists found a receptive home government that was preoccupied with its burgeoning trade deficits in the mid-1980s. The services industries touted their surpluses as part of the solution to the trade problem. The US government, particularly the USTR and Treasury, came to champion their cause. Over time, this cross-industry group marshaled additional support from other services sectors and formed a Coalition of Service Industries to promote its concerns in the GATT deliberations. Its primary targets were the highly regulated Asian service markets. Initially, developing countries, led by India and Brazil, protested the inclusion of services in the Uruguay Round. However, negotiators reached a compromise to negotiate a separate services agreement.

To the extent that a GATS exists at all, the private sector won an important victory by obtaining recognition that services merit multilateral trade treatment. However, the private sector was disappointed with the results. First, the US private sector lobbyists favored, yet failed to achieve, an ambitiously liberalizing agreement, meeting with opposition from both developing countries and the Europeans. Second, the GATS agreement is weak, and codifies significant derogations from the GATT treatment of trade in goods. For example, GATS dilutes the twin pillars of non-discrimination – the GATT principles of most favored nation status (MFN) and national treatment. GATS signatories are free to include a list of sectors in an Annex, for which MFN will not apply (the "negative list" approach). Service providers in relatively open markets pressed for the MFN exemption out of concern that competitors based in sheltered markets would be able to free-ride on the agreements (Hoekman and Kostecki, 1995: 132). In a perfect world, US service providers preferred extensive market access; short of that, their fallback position was to reserve the right to deny insufficiently open countries MFN treatment. Since the GATS agreement failed to open foreign markets to their satisfaction, US private sector interests sought to maintain negotiating leverage by invoking sectoral (or mirror-image) reciprocity – withholding MFN privileges from those competitors in restricted markets. Third, the national treatment commitment was also watered down through a "positive list" approach in which national treatment applies only to those sectors listed in a Member's schedule of commitments (Hoekman and Kostecki, 1995: 131). As Low and Subramanian point out, "national treatment has been transformed from a principle into negotiating currency under GATS" (1995: 423). Thus, the GATS agreement only partly reflects the goals of the private sector; it is "second best," and is a substantially weaker agreement than the TRIPS. Rather than achieving substantial liberalization, the GATS essentially amounts to a standstill on existing restrictions in various services sectors – there was no significant rolling back of barriers to services trade. By binding themselves to general obligations in only services sectors they chose to list, states retained considerable discretion in regulatory policy governing services trade and investment. The USTR advisor to the US TRIMS Delegation concluded that the GATS is a "convoluted agreement with limited practical protection for globally active firms" (Price, 1996: 182).

## Financial services agreement

Throughout the course of the GATS negotiations, negotiators realized the financial services sector was proving to be exceptionally difficult and quite contentious. Therefore, participants agreed to negotiate this as a separate agreement after the conclusion of the Uruguay Round. Asian countries' reluctance to open their financial services markets became a major sticking point. Frustrated by the lack of progress at the end of 1995, the US delegation, prompted by its domestic industry, walked out. Two significant developments between 1995 and December 1997 turned the tide in favor of a strong multilateral agreement on financial services. First was the leadership of the EU and second, the Asian currency crisis.

In 1995 the EU "rallied other WTO members" and they negotiated an interim agreement without the United States.[1] Between 1995 and 1997 the European Union assumed leadership within the deliberations and worked hard to secure improvements in member states' commitments. While the United States had initially pushed hardest for a financial services agreement, by 1995 the European Union was eager for an agreement and worked hard to improve WTO members' offers and to get the United States back on board. The European Commission, national

---

[1] This discussion of the EU's role is based on Stephen Woolcock, "Liberalisation of Financial Services," *European Policy Forum*, London, October 1997.

governments and private sector sought to engage the US private sector in continuing the dialogue. In Davos, Switzerland in early 1996, transnational private sector mobilization began in earnest. US and European service providers discussed the prospects for a financial services agreement. After Davos, US, U.K., and European financial services industry representatives met at the office of British Invisibles and formed the "Financial Leaders Group" (FLG) to present a unified business view of objectives in the financial services deliberations. The FLG largely reflected U.K. and US views, but substantially broadened its base of support and made significant progress in identifying common ground.

Back in 1995 the United States was particularly frustrated with the lack of market access commitments from East and Southeast Asian countries. However, the currency crisis that erupted in Asia in July 1997 provided an unexpected boost to open Asian financial services markets that were recalcitrant targets of Uruguay Round talks. OECD governments and the International Monetary Fund urged affected countries to adopt market opening measures to inspire "investor confidence," and the crisis spurred a conclusion to the financial services negotiations. US negotiators were sufficiently satisfied with the improved market opening commitments and withdrew broad MFN exemptions based on reciprocity. American private sector representatives of Citicorp, Goldman Sachs, Merrill Lynch, and insurance industries set up command posts near the WTO and conferred with American negotiators throughout this last round of talks.[2] Negotiators reached an eleventh-hour agreement in Geneva on December 13, 1997. Vice Chairman of Salomon Brothers International said the agreement "will go some way to lock in a trend that was already in effect in the world toward liberalization...It's like an insurance policy for the structure of the world."[3]

## Trade-related investment measures

Foreign direct investment (FDI) has grown dramatically in recent years. Between 1985 and 1995 the annual global flow of FDI rose from $60 billion to $315 billion; in 1993 sales by foreign affiliates were estimated at $6 trillion, well above the total world trade in goods and services ($4.7 trillion) (Walter, 1997: 1). US private sector activists also spearheaded the

---

[2] "Accord is Reached to Lower Barriers in Global Finance," *The New York Times*, Saturday, December 13, 1997, A1 and B2.
[3] "Nations Reach Agreement on Financial Services Pact," *The Washington Post*, Saturday December 13, 1997, p. A17.

TRIMS effort, but in this instance were stymied by a complex array of factors: developing countries' opposition; host country market power; disagreements between OECD member states; and within the United States, disagreements between business and government. First, developing countries' opposition to the inclusion of investment issues led negotiators to address TRIMS on a separate track. Second, countries such as India and Brazil, with their large relatively protected markets, possess considerable negotiating leverage *vis-à-vis* foreign investors. Third, fundamental disagreements between OECD members meant that the ultimate provisions were likely to be weak. The negotiating committee was committed to producing an agreement to which all nations could unanimously subscribe, so that only the "most egregious of practices in clear violation of existing GATT articles" (Graham, 1996: 50) were ultimately included. And fourth, the US private sector activists found themselves at odds with the US government on security issues.

The US private sector lobbied on investment issues through the US Council for International Business (the American affiliate of the International Chamber of Commerce), the Coalition of Services Industries, and the Securities Industry Association (Walter, 1997: 17). TRIMS advocates sought non-discrimination, especially for rights of establishment, national treatment, and the elimination of trade distorting investment measures (e.g., requirements mandating local content, and export performance). They sought to open the Japanese, and East and Southeast Asian markets to foreign investment. European and Latin American markets already were comparatively liberal. At the outset of the negotiations, the United States produced an ambitious agenda to create a GATT for investment. Faced with stiff opposition from developing countries, "the United States conceded – for the sake of keeping TRIPS and services on the agenda – to a narrow mandate for the TRIMS negotiations" (Low and Subramanian, 1995: 416).

Furthermore, many OECD states were reluctant to lock in liberalizing reforms under a multilateral instrument on investment. As Low and Subramanian suggest, "doubts linger about how monopolistic MNE [multinational enterprise] behavior might become in some circumstances, and worries about sovereign control of resources also continue to cut political ice" (1995: 421). The TRIMS agreement protects only the "trade flows of investor-enterprises" (Price, 1996: 182) and affirms two GATT disciplines, national treatment and the prohibition of quantitative restrictions, for investment policies that directly affect trade flows. Signatories must notify the WTO Secretariat of performance requirements such as local content and trade-balancing policies that are in violation of these GATT disciplines. Members are then bound to eliminate such measures within the grace periods (ranging from two to seven years depending on the country's level of development). Rather than representing a strong instrument for investment liberalization, in legal terms the TRIMS is "retrograde, since it recognize[s] that countries were in violation of their GATT obligations, and then [gives] them time ... within which to establish conformity" (Low and Subramanian, 1995: 418). Significantly, the TRIMS agreement guarantees neither rights of establishment nor full national treatment for foreign investors. Additionally, much to the dismay of the private sector activists, export performance requirements were left untouched by the TRIMS agreement. Countries such as India have successfully reserved the right to require export performance of investors seeking entry into their large sheltered markets. Host country market power is an important factor militating against a strong investment agreement (Walter, 1997: 19).

The business community was deeply disappointed in the TRIMS negotiations; its initial enthusiasm waned as the process unfolded. It soon became apparent that the best it could hope for in the multilateral context was a "lowest common denominator"[4] approach, which is exactly what they got. Given the failure of the WTO effort, the private sector quickly shifted its attention to the OECD, and the OECD launched negotiations on a Multilateral Agreement on Investment (MAI) in September 1995. Investment enthusiasts hoped that a high standard OECD agreement would provide the eventual impetus for a meaningful multilateral agreement and inspire a "race to the top" among non-members trying to attract FDI. The US private sector sought, first and foremost, the right of establishment and an investor–state dispute settlement arrangement rather than the more limited WTO state–state dispute settlement mechanism.

However, like the TRIMS negotiations, the MAI negotiations revealed very deep and intractable differences even among allegedly "like-minded" states. While the United Kingdom, Germany, the Netherlands, and Japan were generally supportive of US aims, other OECD countries (France, Canada, Australia, New Zealand, and new members such as Mexico, South Korea, Poland, and the Czech Republic) were not. Furthermore, the US government opposed certain US business interests in the name of national security. The government defended its right to

---

[4] Based on Walter (1997: 28, 38).

Table 7.1 *Private power in comparative perspective*

| | Transnational private sector mobilization? | Sustained opposition (South)? | OECD consensus? | US firms/ US state consensus? | Authoritative outcome? |
|---|---|---|---|---|---|
| TRIPS | yes [IPC] | no | yes | yes | yes |
| Financial Svcs. | yes [FLG] | no | yes | yes | yes |
| GATS | yes [IAs][a] | yes | no | yes | mixed |
| TRIMS | yes [IAs] | yes | no | no | no |

[a] industry associations

uphold the Helms Burton Act prohibiting investment in Cuba, and the Iran–Libya Sanctions Act. Additionally, a transnational coalition of labor and environmental groups wrested control of the agenda from the business lobby. However, given the divergent interests of the OECD countries, the MAI likely was destined to fail irrespective of the NGO campaign. Negotiating countries consistently postponed the deadline for a final agreement because of fundamental disagreements. At the end of 1998 negotiators finally shelved the MAI effort.

## Summary of the cases

Table 7.1 summarizes the four cases. TRIPS and the financial services agreement provide the strongest evidence that private sector activists achieved their objectives. The GATS presents a mixed picture: the private sector achieved some of its aims, but the final agreement fell well short of its liberalizing intentions by reserving a broad scope for state discretion. The TRIMS agreement is the weakest; the private sector failed to achieve its objectives and the weakness of the agreement does little in terms of redefining options for others.

Private sector success in TRIPS was largely due to transnational private sector mobilization, led by the IPC, to produce an OECD consensus on specific negotiating proposals and the lack of persistent opposition among OECD states. The eventual collapse of developing countries' opposition to the inclusion of intellectual property further facilitated the IPC's goals. Developing countries were willing to accept the OECD IP agenda in exchange for concessions on agriculture and the Multi-fibre Arrangements. Similarly, in financial services, transnational

171

private sector mobilization – this time led by British and European service providers – and the Asian financial crisis, which prompted eleventh-hour improved market access commitments, led to private sector triumph. In both the TRIPS and Financial Services negotiations, streamlined groups, the IPC and the Financial Leaders' Group pursued transnational private sector mobilization. In the other cases the mobilization was pursued through more traditional channels, such as industry associations. Both the GATS and TRIMS deliberations revealed sharp differences among OECD countries in addition to differences between the OECD and developing countries. In the investment area, host country market power, and differences between the US private sector and the US government on national security issues further reduced the prospects that the private sector would achieve its goals.

Overall, these comparisons should inspire caution about structural determinism. Broad claims about globalization, whether derived from economic liberalism or variants of Marxism, appear to be somewhat suspect in light of these findings. The variation in these cases points to the difference that agency makes. In the IP and financial services agreements, the agents crafted a strong, united position. By contrast, the GATS advocates were a much more diverse group, representing insurance, banking, legal services, and the travel industry (among others). One can assume safely that the coordination problems of this group were much more daunting than those of the more streamlined advocacy groups.

Structure played an important part in the negotiations as well. For example, in the TRIMS case, within the United States, political debate reflected conflicting imperatives between the security structure on the one hand and the production and finance structure on the other. This reduced US government support for TRIMS. The most important structural feature in the TRIMS negotiations was the distribution of host country market power. Those resisting TRIMS had significant leverage. Agency must be analyzed in its structured context.

## Compliance, legitimacy, private power and public law

The process of public lawmaking reverberates far beyond the final agreement. Many scholars assume that states sign treaties because they are mutually beneficial. Some compliance scholars of international law emphasize this perspective (for a survey, see Raustiala, 2000: 387–440). Examining international agreements as "contracts" embodying reciprocal exchange implies that they leave "everyone better off," and suggests that such agreements are substantively valid and based upon consent (Gerhart, 2000: 371). The "contract" story of TRIPS implies that consent begets legitimacy. States may cooperate based on shared interests, reciprocal exchange, or coercion (Archer, 1995: 296). States also may cooperate because they see no better choice when powerful states have unilaterally altered the status quo (Gruber, 2001). Indeed, developing countries came to realize that their choice was not between WIPO and GATT (the old status quo), but rather between GATT and Super 301. In the TRIPS case, the OECD countries and the developing countries did not act on the basis of shared interests in extending IP protection. One finds elements of reciprocal exchange – IPRs in exchange for agriculture and textiles – in the WTO agreements. But it is important to understand how agreements were made. While negotiators linked issues and bargained for trade-offs, as emphasized in the "contract story," the TRIPS negotiations took place in a broader context of economic coercion and asymmetrical power. My analysis emphasizes the role of private power in making public international law. TRIPS largely reflected the wishes of the CEOs of twelve American companies.

The shaky foundations of this global regime raise important concerns about accountability and legitimacy. The process compromised the ultimate legitimacy of the agreement. If legitimacy and mutual benefits are the right yardsticks for public international law, the TRIPS process fails on both counts. Not only is there no compelling empirical evidence that TRIPS will make developing countries better off, there is also no evidence that developed countries are making good on their commitments to open their markets more widely to developing countries' agricultural and textile exports. The Doha Round of WTO negotiations is to take up this issue. Contrary to the pro-TRIPS rhetoric, however, there is plenty of evidence, particularly in the medicines issue, that TRIPS and aggressive TRIPS-plus enforcement are making developing countries much worse off.

## New constraints, opportunities, and the post-TRIPS backlash

This book explained how and why TRIPS came to be, and identified a second cycle in progress in which TRIPS is a structure that actors now either try to expand or resist. The endpoint of this cycle is difficult to predict, but the notion of structured agency highlights core features that will shape the outcome. So far, the most successful resisters of TRIPS are the members of the access to medicines campaign. In many respects their story reads like a vindication of liberal pluralism, agency, and faith in the marketplace of ideas. However, one must keep in mind that the campaign itself is embedded in broader and deeper structures. These structures militate against a thoroughgoing victory in favor of the public domain. Beginning with TRIPS ($T^4$ of the first cycle, $T^1$ of the second), the campaign addresses only one small part of a broad and complex agreement. In no way does the campaign challenge the agreement as a whole. My analysis is not meant to imply that every action changes the structure as a whole; one must "distinguish between changes of deep structural properties, that are important for the conditioning of the action, and changes of micro-structural properties, which have... a less significant impact on the framework of action" (Bieler and Morton, 2001: 10). Even if the campaign ultimately triumphs on the medicines issue, the rest of the agreement still locks in a commitment to intellectual property as a system to exclude and protect. The public-regarding side of the balance is vastly overshadowed by the private rights side of the ledger.

TRIPS itself is embedded in an even larger structure of multilateral and bilateral intellectual property agreements. The politics of intellectual property are shaped by power and resource disparities between advocates of high protectionist IP norms and the activists seeking a more public-regarding balance in IP protection. Manifestations of these imbalances include the private sector's tireless push to conclude bilateral, regional, and multilateral agreements that reflect TRIPS-plus standards. The TRIPS architects have embarked on an aggressive course to close any existing loopholes, to prosecute non-compliance, and to promote TRIPS-plus IP agreements outside the WTO in bilateral,[5] regional,[6] and multilateral agreements. WIPO's deliberations on the Substantive Patent Law Treaty reflect this trend (WIPO, 2002). This process envisions global

---

[5] See, e.g., "Agreement Between the United States of America and the Hashemite Kingdom of Jordan on the Establishment of a Free Trade Area," at <http://www.ustr.gov/regions/eu-med/middleeast/US-JordanFTA.shtml> (accessed 5/8/02).

[6] See, "Free Trade Area of the Americas, Draft Agreement, chapter on Intellectual Property Rights, FTAA. TNC/w/133/Rev.1 (July 3, 2001)," at : <http://www.ftaa-acla.org/ftaadraft/eng/ngip_e.doc>; see also The North American Free Trade Agreement at: <http://www.mac.doc.gov/naftach17.htm>, available at http://www.phrma.org (for a statement of PhRMA's goals and aspirations in these agreements).

harmonization of substantive patent law. WIPO receives 85 percent of its operating budget from the Patent Cooperation Treaty (Doern, 1999: 44). The PCT's biggest users are the global life sciences, pharmaceutical, agricultural, and financial services industries. The WIPO deliberations are bound to reflect these firms' preferences. Further, WIPO provides technical assistance to developing countries seeking to become TRIPS-compliant. Its advocacy undoubtedly is compromised by its heavy reliance on funds from advocates of high protectionist IP norms. WIPO will work hard to demonstrate its continued relevance to the private sector actors who promoted the initial forum shifting from WIPO to GATT/WTO.

Power and resource disparities are also evident in the terms of the various bilateral and regional agreements concluded with the United States. For example, the US–Jordan bilateral investment treaty includes protection of business method patents, which are controversial even in the United States. Many such agreements are TRIPS-plus, reflecting the US determination to ratchet up levels of protection. It is clear that while opponents see TRIPS as a ceiling, the United States sees it as a floor. Economic coercion remains a viable tool for US policymakers.

This broader IP regime is embedded in the deeper structures of global capitalism and American power. Until American commitments change or changes in global capitalism loosen the connections between the broader IP regime and the structurally powerful, opponents will face an uphill battle. However, in challenging these connections it bears noting that "social life is multifaceted and defined by many different types of activity, not all of which can be equated with capitalism *per se*" (Germain, 2000: 71). Germain distinguishes between global capitalism and the market economy, "the arena in which most products and services which people use on a daily basis are produced, exchanged, and purchased" (2000: 81). In resisting globalization, Germain advocates identifying "the boundaries of social organization over which globalization does not hold sway" and defending and supporting "dynamics and institutions which protect and promote the stable relationships of the market economy," to "counter and contain the more predatory aspects of globalization" (2000: 88). In many respects the various post-TRIPS backlash campaigns can be viewed in this light. For example, in the agricultural sector the contest can be construed as one between capitalism (e.g., Novartis and Monsanto) and market society (smaller-scale, sustainable, and/or traditional agriculture). Defending non-capitalist facets, such as public health, may help to check the predations of global capitalism or soften some of its harsher effects.

Analysts may focus on the form of cooperation (Koremenos *et al.*, 2000), rather than the substance of agreements. Exclusive focus on forms of cooperation renders politics antiseptic. I argue that it is the fights over substance, not merely the form, that matter. The substance of law embodies values, relationships, and processes (Finnemore and Toope, 2001: 749–751). Focusing on the substance of agreements helps us to understand developing countries' reportedly widespread non-compliance in the wake of TRIPS. Asymmetrical power relationships and non-consensual values are embedded in TRIPS. For example, "belief that intellectual property is 'western', that its acceptance was coerced, or that its goal is to make the wealthy wealthier (without any societal benefit) is likely to erode compliance" (Gerhart, 2000: 385). If developing countries saw TRIPS as a "win–win" contracting episode we should expect them to abide by TRIPS to the extent that their administrative capacities allow. Even if their compliance rate was perfect, given the power asymmetries, one cannot assume that developing countries view the norms as legitimate (Gerhart, 2000: 385).

By examining how TRIPS was made, my analysis suggests how it can be "unmade" or resisted. Seeing how public law is made, and by whom, those who object can be in a better position to challenge it (Bieler and Morton, 2001: 26; Bernard, 1997: 77; Cox, 1987: 393; Murphy and Nelson, 2001: 405). Public law is ultimately constructed. Law does not exist "out there" or come down from on high. Further, by "pigging out at the IP trough" (Merges, 2000: 2233) in the wake of TRIPS, the triumphant private sector activists spawned social and political backlash. The truly important resisters of the TRIPS regime are not "pirate" compact disc manufacturers or hawkers of bootlegged Disney videos, but those who see the grotesque nature of aspects of TRIPS and the heavy-handed TRIPS-plus demands of the United States "on the ground" in the HIV/AIDS pandemic and agriculture. For them, resisting these demands truly is a matter of life and death.

Two of the most effective activities of the access to medicines campaign so far have been recasting the debate and exposing hypocrisy. Opponents of TRIPS have promoted new ways of thinking about intellectual property. Skillfully exploiting political opportunities such as the HIV/AIDS pandemic, the Gore campaign, and the bioterror threat, TRIPS opponents have gained converts across groups, sectors, and states. In this context, "there is no reason to assume that the social groups most responsive to the new ideas with which they come into contact... are always the structurally subordinate ones" (Archer 1995: 317). A number of economically powerful US companies have launched a movement called "Business for Affordable Medicines" (BAM).[7] These companies have responded to the message of the access campaigners and redefined their interests. As large employers, these firms have had to deal with steeply rising costs of non-generic pharmaceutical drugs in their prescription benefit plans. BAM seeks changes in US laws to increase the availability of generic drugs. Remarkably, General Motors, an original member of the IPC, has been at the forefront of the BAM movement, directly confronting its old IPC partners over pharmaceutical patent protection. This suggests that the original "superimposition" of diverse sectors is breaking down. All structures are temporary and contingent. It appears increasingly evident that many pro-IP firms will be willing to support an exception for pharmaceuticals – recognizing that medicines *are* different – while at the same time continuing to support high protectionist IP norms for all other goods and services. Pro-IP firms do not want to be demonized along with PhRMA after the South African debacle and subsequent controversies. They will be willing to let PhRMA take the heat in the hopes of containing a broader and deeper critical dialogue about the (im)balance in IP protection.

Hypocrisy is rife in the politics of intellectual property. The access campaign has revealed important instances of this. The access campaign has carefully rebutted the "profits = research = cure" formula promoted by PhRMA. The CPT, in particular, has exposed the fact that PhRMA did *not* develop a number of important drugs – the US government did. Taxpayers footed much of the bill. CPT has exposed the fact that PhRMA has wildly inflated the estimated costs of developing particular drugs. Public Citizen has published data indicating that nearly 50 percent of PhRMA's profits do not go into research, but rather are spent on marketing, advertising, and administrative activities (2001). ACT-UP Paris came up with a succinct counter-framing, "Copy = Life." The Attaran/Gillespie-White paper addressed this frame, but again, the access campaign has engaged such arguments carefully and provided effective rebuttals. Particularly effective has been the documenting of compulsory licensing practices in the United States. This data proved to be quite compelling in the deliberations over the revised drug strategy at WHA. The access campaigners have acquired and deployed extensive

---

[7] <http://www.bamcoalition.org>

and detailed expertise, which is necessary for engaging in effective interaction with experts from the opposing side.

Historically, the United States has had lax IP policies; its commitment to very strong and extensive patent protection emerged only as recently as 1982. Throughout much of the twentieth century, US courts were concerned about abuses of monopoly power. It was only in the early to mid 1980s that the courts quit referring to patents as "monopolies." This historical perspective provides support for differential treatment for countries in the earlier stages of industrial development.

American reactions to the bioterror, anthrax, threat of autumn 2001 also provided an important opportunity to develop empathy for the victims of the HIV/AIDS pandemic, and the constraints posed by strict or narrow interpretations of TRIPS. The deaths of several postal and media workers became a national public health emergency raising the threat of compulsory licensing to ensure adequate supplies of Cipro. If compulsory licensing makes sense in light of several deaths it certainly should in light of tens of millions. Negotiators can exploit public outcry over the unintended consequences of stronger IP protection, that is, the prospect of lacking sufficient drug supplies because of limits on compulsory licensing, to minimize the damage of overly strong patent protection.

The IPC pursued a multilevel strategy and assembled a broad and powerful coalition. People like Jacques Gorlin synthesized various sectors' positions and tied them together in a coherent and compelling analytic framework. Despite inter-sectoral differences, the IPC members united behind the common cause of ratcheting up IP protection. Copyright interests began lobbying on behalf of patent interests and vice versa. The IPC connected a number of diverse and dispersed lobbying efforts.

The access campaign has begun to copy the strategies that worked for the TRIPS' architects; it has broadened, and gained the support of a number of influential NGOs and developing countries. There are resource constraints and undoubtedly genuine differences of opinion that must be reconciled or compromised. Even among access campaigners there is disagreement about whether TRIPS is acceptable if interpreted broadly, amendable, or whether it should be abolished altogether. But looking at the broader political landscape, a number of IP activist campaigns have scored victories in recasting the IP debate and injecting a more public-regarding conception back into the politics of intellectual property.

Like the access activists, fair use advocates have helped to keep the WIPO digital treaties from looking like TRIPS.[8] Napster, MP3, and the open source movement have brought the constraints of IP protection into public consciousness and raised important questions about the purpose and amounts of protection and the role of compensation. The very TRIPS-like 1998 Sony Bono Copyright Term Extension Act, promoted by the Walt Disney Corporation, has been sharply criticized as an egregious example of the overextension of property rights (Merges, 2000: 2233). Many of the same fair use advocates who participated in the WIPO digital treaties deliberations have led the charge against the 1998 law. The US Supreme Court finally has agreed to review this law (Greenhouse, 2002: C1). The civil society campaign against genetically modified foods has also raised important IP issues (Dutfield, 2003), and advocates for traditional knowledge and folklore are changing the debate over intellectual property. The Convention on Biodiversity and debates over *sui generis* forms of protection for agriculture have challenged high protectionist norms.

What all these campaigns have in common is a concern for preserving the public domain, and preventing the over-reach of IP protection. They all seek to retain a public balance in property rights. One can only imagine what might happen if activists, government agencies, and businesses working to prevent the overextension of property rights in agriculture, pharmaceuticals, and copyright got together in a unified protest. It would take creativity and hard work to coordinate their substantive positions, but it could lead to an alternative way of approaching property rights. The TRIPS advocates got as far as they did by banding together and taking advantage of unique and auspicious institutional and structural opportunities. By emulating this strategy, and highlighting multiple instances of the unintended, costly, and deleterious consequences of the over-extension of IP rights TRIPS opponents could make some important gains.

## Structures, agents, and institutions revisited

This book has provided an "analytic history of [the] emergence" of TRIPS (Archer, 1995: 327) and has identified the beginnings of a second cycle, focusing on structured agency. Structured agency recognizes

---

[8] In fact, James Love participated in the WIPO digital treaty deliberations and said that he learned a lot from the fair use proponents.

the way that structural factors condition agency, by examining the way that structure identifies and creates agents and distributes resources of "vested interests and bargaining power" (Archer, 1995: 327). Establishing these structural effects, the analysis went on to examine "social interaction" and the role of agency. This interaction may result in structural change, depending upon "how (or whether) bargaining power is converted into negotiating strength between corporate agents" (Archer, 1995: 327). Change or stasis arises from the social interaction phase of the cycle ($T^2$ to $T^3$), but is not reducible to it because all agency is structured (Archer, 1995: 295–296). The distribution of vested interests, produced by structure at the outset of a given cycle, confronts agents with different situational logics for their attainment; between $T^2$ and $T^3$, "exchange transactions and power relations" drive the process (Archer, 1995: 296).

Power alone does not determine outcomes. Structural power and agency are not logically dependent upon one another; their relationship is a contingent one (Archer, 1990: 81). According to Archer, "while systemic [or structural] factors can determine a given potential for transformation: 1) they may not be capitalized upon by those with the power to do so; 2) the exploitation of a given potential may not necessarily involve the use of power; 3) the deployment of considerable power may not actually produce transformation" (Archer, 1990: 81). While in the TRIPS case the "demanding state" happened to be hegemonic, one can imagine instances in which non-hegemonic states may demand and obtain rules and institutions that they seek. The Doha Declaration could be interpreted as an instance of this.

Returning to the WIPO digital treaties example from the introduction, power, agency, framing skills, and legal norms all played an important role. In many respects this process resembled the TRIPS story. However, in this instance, those advocating a TRIPS-style ratcheting up of copyright protection in the digital environment did not prevail. Instead they found themselves confronted by a powerful group of corporate actors and experts who offered an alternative way of framing the issues at stake. Representatives of economically significant companies such as Netscape and Sun Microsystems teamed up with public-regarding copyright NGOs. Employing the well-established legal norm of "fair use" this group was able to inject and preserve a public-regarding component in the digital treaties. Clearly, opposition groups who employ compelling alternative framing ideas complicate the success of the faction of global capital advocating high protectionist norms in intellectual property. While it is still too soon to tell, the battle over alternative framing of pharmaceutical patent "rights" versus public health in the context of the AIDS crisis is a good test case of advocacy without obvious economic (that is, structural) power.

Another factor that was different in the WIPO copyright treaty case, however, was that TRIPS pre-dated the WIPO copyright treaty process by two years. The very success of the pro-TRIPS activists has mobilized opposition. When I asked some public-regarding copyright activists "where they had been" during TRIPS, they told me they had been "sleeping" but that *because* of TRIPS they had "woken up."[9] The existence of TRIPS has animated new interests and altered stakeholders' political strategies. It has become a part of the structure.

Contingency and unintended consequences played a role in the two cycles of change analyzed here. For example, domestic institutional changes in the United States, adopted in response to the Watergate scandal, were designed to make policymaking more democratic and transparent. These had the unintended effect of facilitating unprecedented private sector access to the policymaking process, and ultimately led private power to become public law. In the post-TRIPS cycle, an unintended consequence of the TRIPS architects' success and vigorous prosecution of perceived wrongdoing was the hastening of the mobilization of opposition. The HIV/AIDS pandemic was a contingency that sped up the revelation of the negative consequences of TRIPS.

Structure, agency, and institutions all play an important role in my analysis. The structure of global capitalism helps to determine who the most important actors will be; representatives of leading economic sectors tend to enjoy enhanced political power. This power is compounded if they also happen to reside in the most powerful state. However, as the comparisons at the beginning of this chapter suggest, structure shapes but does not dictate outcomes. The elements of each component of the explanation, structures, institutions, and agents, can vary and with different consequences. For instance, the four structural elements of global capitalism that I identified are variable. Finance can be globalized or more localized. Production need not be internationalized. The structure may not be characterized by technologies that threaten core markets. The international regulatory context need not be "loose"[10] or liberal.

[9] Author's interview with members of the Digital Futures Coalition, December 1998, Washington, DC.

[10] As Vogel (1996) and Braithwaite and Drahos (2000) have pointed out, the current era is marked by considerable *re*-regulation (versus deregulation); however, in most instances the substantive outcome is the adoption of more liberal rules.

Similarly the international system also can vary considerably. One could examine these factors in different historical contexts to further understand the difference that structure makes.

After identifying agents and their interests, one must examine the skills that they bring to bear to achieve their goals (Fligstein, 1997). The state's dependence on private sector expertise and the arcane nature of the subject area made agents' expertise and information crucial in the TRIPS case. Timothy Sinclair has documented a similar degree of dependence on the technical knowledge of the private bond-rating agencies, Moody's and Standard & Poor's (Sinclair, 1999: 153–167). Certain kinds of knowledge are concentrated and exclusive, giving their purveyors additional power. When the required knowledge is accessible and disseminated, power is more widely dispersed – or at least not based upon privileged access to knowledge.

Beyond the nature of the relevant knowledge, the agents' framing skills are important. An agent who can frame an issue as being compatible with state goals and consistent with a public sense of legitimacy is more likely to be effective than one whose cognitive appeal is more elusive. Ideas that are seen as legitimate, appropriate, or correct have a better chance of prevailing. For instance, the IP activists' particular framing of the issues would have met with probable hostility in the mid-twentieth century when US courts viewed patents with suspicion. The legal environment may or may not be conducive to activists' advocacy. While legal norms may exist one also needs to look at the record of enforcement of such norms. This requires a focus on institutions. How salient are particular legal norms, and how well established are they? Are they enforced in institutions or are they contested? Do competing norms exist that are enforced? In the TRIPS case, the legal norm of property rights was well established, as was the propensity for free trade. These norms are an integral part of the United States' identity in the global political economy. In the immediate years prior to TRIPS, neither of these norms was effectively contested. Indeed, part of what made the IPC's framing of the issues so compelling was its synthesis of two such hallowed principles.

Agents who are not confronted with an alternative framing are more likely to succeed. In TRIPS the alternative framing initially came from developing countries; both power and expertise disparities reduced the significance of that challenge. In the 1996 WIPO copyright treaties, however, power was matched by power and expertise was matched by expertise. In the post-TRIPS context, alternative framing has begun to weaken the public sense of legitimacy about TRIPS achievements – especially in the HIV/AIDS context. Indeed, legitimacy was not a major issue until after the agreement was signed. Paradoxically, the TRIPS' architects got "95 percent" of what they wanted, yet created a structure that has empowered and altered the preferences of former allies (for example, GM and the BAM movement) and generated new opponents.

The organizational form of the agents can be important. The two Uruguay Round private sector efforts that met with the most unqualified success were those that were spearheaded by *ad hoc*, streamlined coalitions of the most well-connected corporate players with much at stake (Cutler, Haufler and Porter, 1999: 343). These efficient organizational forms might make a difference. The success of these "thoroughbred" groups may also be a function of their relationship to the larger, state-led trade regime (Cutler, Haufler and Porter, 1999: 350). Agents' institutional access is another potential resource; again, it can be extensive, denied, or perhaps irrelevant. This, in fact, may be an indicator of agents' relative power or importance in other realms. For example, in the TRIPS case the IPC members enjoyed excellent access by virtue of their economic might and importance to American competitiveness goals.

The state's view of the agents' goals can make a difference. The state may be neutral, or it may have strong negative or positive attitudes about the goals. The state also may have a positive view of the goals, yet not support them in any tangible sense. In the TRIPS case, the state's initial view was neutral but the state came to have strong positive views of the IP activists' goals. The state also became very supportive in a tangible sense as the process progressed. Also, degrees of dependence of the state on the agents can vary considerably. The state was very dependent on the IP activists for information and expertise. This clearly boosted the activists' power to influence policymakers. But the state could be moderately dependent or completely independent of the private sector in ways that could alter outcomes. Conversely, the agents can be highly dependent on the state, moderately dependent, or the state could be completely irrelevant to the achievement of the agents' goals. The TRIPS' architects were dependent on both the state and international organizations for the realization of their goals. As Cutler, Haufler, and Porter point out, "the greater the reach of private authority, the more formally organized are the institutions that are associated with it" (1999: 362). The global reach of the new IP regulations requires an elaborate state-sanctioned institutional architecture.

Looking to institutions, in the TRIPS case all branches of the US government were actively involved, and no branch of government stood opposed to any other. By contrast, in the TRIMS negotiations the US State Department and the Commerce Department did not see eye-to-eye and this hurt the private sector's quest for government endorsement of a fully liberalized global investment regime. It is easy to imagine instances in which the USTR declined to pressure a particular country for IP violations, despite private sector requests, due to security goals or other diplomatic aims, or sensitive moments in US diplomacy. USTR was not the only relevant institution in the TRIPS case. US history demonstrates the changing role of the courts, and changing judicial attitudes towards intellectual property. Additionally, international institutions were involved in the TRIPS case. Pre-TRIPS, WIPO was the most important international institution in this realm. By the outset of the Uruguay Round, GATT was fully involved, and after TRIPS both the WTO and WIPO are integral components of the new global IP regime.

## Conclusion

To say that structures, agents, and institutions are important is not to say that everything matters all the time. The morphogenetic perspective permits us to theorize about conditions under which freedom for action or stringency of constraints will predominate, and requires the identification of structures, the investigation of processes of interaction, and the specification of mechanisms linking the two (Archer, 1990: 82; 88).

This perspective underscores the fact that structure and ideas, like tectonic plates, can move in independent rhythms. They need not, but they can. Rather than positing some necessary relationship between the two, stressing the inherent predominance of one over the other, the morphogenetic perspective encourages analysts to examine, *not assume*, the relationship between material factors and ideas. Both neo-Gramscian marxists and constructivists in various ways seek to integrate the two. Invariably, the former emphasize the predominance of material factors (while acknowledging the centrality of ideas) (for example, Bieler and Morton, 2001: 24–25), or "the material structure of ideas" (Bieler, 2001: 94). The latter emphasize the importance of norms (while acknowledging the broader context) (for example, Klotz, 1995: 167–168). A neo-Gramscian account of TRIPS and the backlash would emphasize structural factors, the power of transnational capital in leading sectors. It would analyze the TRIPS opponents for their potential to be "organic intellectuals" to launch a counter-hegemonic movement. By contrast, the approach presented here incorporates agency and the difference it makes. Whether examining the variation in outcomes in the new issues in the WTO, the counterfactual in Chapter 2, or the WIPO digital treaties, it is clear that agency mattered. A constructivist account of these same events would emphasize the activities of "norm entrepreneurs," such as Jacques Gorlin, and James Love, and the skill of the agents in deploying norms and discourse to effect change. The constructivist assessment of the post-TRIPS backlash would focus on the transnational mobilization of NGOs and developing countries to bring moral pressure to bear on the United States to change its policies and practices (Keck and Sikkink, 1998). Constructivist accounts tend to leave out structural power and minimize the role of material, structural constraints. Skills of agents are embedded in broader and deeper structures; many constructivists do not address different layers of structure that are variably malleable. By overemphasizing voluntarism and efficacy, they miss the point that successful agents are those who take advantage of contingent *structural* constraints and opportunities.

The morphogenetic perspective is agnostic about the relative importance of structure and agency and expects their relationship to vary depending on the level, the problem, and the time period being addressed. Under conditions in which structure holds more explanatory weight than ideas, a morphogenetic perspective can be perfectly compatible with Gramscian political economy. Under conditions in which ideas hold more explanatory weight than structure, it can be consistent with a constructivist analysis. Archer outlines four possible configurations that alter the respective explanatory weight of these two factors. In cases of structural and ideational morphostasis, structure and ideas are completely reciprocal (Archer, 1995: 310). In instances of disjunction between ideational stasis and structural change, structure holds more explanatory weight. When ideas are changing but structure is static, ideational diversification will be more important (Archer, 1995: 316). Structure will slow down, not utterly repress, such differentiation. Finally, when both structure and ideas are changing simultaneously they are again mutually reinforcing (Archer 1995: 322). The challenge for analysts seeking to build upon these insights, just as is the case in applications of formal theory, is to be as transparent as possible in one's specification of a given case.

At the deepest level, TRIPS was embedded in a context of both structural and ideational change. The deep structural change was the globalization of capitalism, and the deep ideational change was the turn toward a radical free market agenda buttressing the structural changes. These deep changes became manifest at a shallower level, as technological change (a subset of deep structural change) challenged the merits of the pre-TRIPS IP regime. At this level, structural change encountered ideational stasis. Under this condition, structure (and material factors) will exert a stronger force than ideational factors; the disjunction between ideational stasis and structural change privileges the causal force of structure (Archer, 1995: 315).

Prior to TRIPS, IP rights at the ideational level were construed as monopoly rights. At the material level, technological and economic change increased the importance and value of these "suspect" privileges. The disjunction between the existing IP rules and technological and economic change obstructed the aims and diminished the potential fortunes of the IPC's firms. They had a structurally induced motive for acquiring ideas to challenge the existing thinking about intellectual property. Structure thus prompted the activities of agents; agents promoted new ideas about intellectual property to connect it to the deeper cultural shift toward a radical free market agenda. As Archer generalizes about this broader configuration, "the material interest group pounces on the contradictory items and brings about their counter-actualization. The fact that a single interest group can do *all* this is indicative of the stronger influence of structure on culture [ideas], *given this conjuncture* . . . [Its members are] embroiled in a situational logic of elimination" (1995: 314, emphasis in original). Private sector activists sought to eliminate the view of intellectual property as monopoly privileges, legitimate the importance of stronger IP protection in the new structure, and strengthen the enforcement of IP protection worldwide. In the 1870s IP protection was seen as antithetical to free trade (Machlup and Penrose, 1950); one hundred years later, in a different structural context, interested agents were able to redefine intellectual property as a central component of free trade. "Without the structural stimulus, rooted in the disjunction between" structure and ideas, this cycle of change "would never have got off the ground for agents with the power to promote it would have been lacking" (Archer, 1995: 315).

But this relationship, between structure and ideas, is not built to last. The new ideas that the material interest group promotes become targets of opportunity for those who come to resent and oppose the new structure. Post-TRIPS, its opponents have mobilized behind new ideas that shift the core issues from trade to public health, agriculture, equity, sustainable development, and human rights. "Ideational change stimulates social regrouping" (Archer, 1995: 318). The post-TRIPS developments are not reducible to neo-Gramscian forces of production; apart from the generic split between producers and consumers, one cannot make a convincing case that the access to medicines campaign was "generated by the sphere of production" (Bieler, 2001: 98–99). The campaign has pitted non-generic pharmaceutical producers against generic pharmaceutical producers, but these groups do not exhaust the membership of those engaged in this debate. Further, with the advent of Business for Affordable Medicines, structurally privileged factions of capital stand opposed to each other. Post-TRIPS, ideational forces seem ascendant in relation to structural factors, in so far as the access campaign is not connected to obvious economic power. The campaign has used political opportunities provided by the HIV/AIDS pandemic, the Gore campaign, and the bioterror threat to challenge TRIPS and press a broader agenda. In many respects this is consistent with a constructivist analysis. However, one must be careful not to overstate the possibilities and underestimate the obstacles to change; agency is *never* unstructured and must be examined in its structural context.

The "hardness" of TRIPS actually created new agents. These agents were constrained in new ways, and the harsh consequences of TRIPS almost immediately were apparent in the face of the HIV/AIDS pandemic. American economic coercion to keep South Africa and Thailand from producing generic medicines and the aggressiveness of global PhRMA created opportunities for skilled agents to re-frame IP discourse from trade to health. Structural changes, like downward pressure on the prices of raw materials to make antiretroviral drugs, also contributed to the campaign's momentum. It took skilled agents to turn the constraints presented by TRIPS into opportunities, but their agency was structured.

Politics lies at the heart of this analysis of international political economy. Who gets what, when, and why? Vested interests, exchange, and power are central features of the explanation. This empirical treatment of the way that structures and agents constitute each other (mutual constitution) incorporates structures, agents, and institutions, and has demonstrated that different factors mattered at different points in the process. This perspective holds promise for a more comprehensive understanding of the origins, evolution, and consequences of global business regulation. It isolates the permissive conditions and mechanisms linking structures, agents, and institutions that can be broadly applied to instances of foreign economic policymaking, the establishment of institutions, and institutional and structural change. Adding the dimension of time invites us to incorporate historical perspectives in the analysis of contemporary issues. Overall, the perspective presented here focuses on the process of change, while anchoring the inquiry in historical context and eschewing fixed notions of structure, agents, and institutions.

# References

Abbott, F. 2002. "Compulsory Licensing for Public Health Needs: The TRIPS Agenda at the WTO after the Doha Declaration on Public Health," Occasional Paper 9. February. Geneva: Quaker United Nations Office. Available at: <http://www.afsc.org/quno.htm> accessed 4/26/02.

Aley, J. 1995. "New lift for the U.S. export boom," *Forbes* November 13: 73–76.

Alford, W. 1994. "How theory does – and does not – matter: American approaches to intellectual property law in East Asia," *UCLA Pacific Basin Law Journal* 13: 8–24.

Amin, A. ed. 1994. *Post-Fordism: A Reader*, Oxford: Blackwell.

Amoore, L., R. Dodgson, R. Germain, B. Gills, P. Langley, and I. Watson. 2000. "Paths to a historicized international political economy," *Review of International Political Economy* 7, 1 (Spring): 53–71.

Aoki, K. 1996. "(Intellectual) Property and sovereignty: notes toward a cultural geography of authorship," *Stanford Law Review* 48, 5 (May): 1293–1356.

Archer, M. 1982. "Morphogenesis versus structuration: on combining structure and action," *British Journal of Sociology* 33, 4 (December): 455–483.

1990. "Human agency and social structure: a critique of Giddens," in J. Clark, C. Modgil, and S. Modgil (eds.), *Anthony Giddens: Consensus and Critique*, London: Falmer Press: 73–83.

1995. *Realist Social Theory: The Morphogenetic Approach*, Cambridge: Cambridge University Press.

Arup, C. 1998. "Competition over competition policy for international trade and intellectual property," *Prometheus* 16, 3: 367–381.

Ashman, K. 1989. "The Omnibus Trade and Competitiveness Act of 1988: the Section 301 amendments," *Boston University International Law Journal* 7 (Spring): 115–153.

Attaran, A. and L. Gillespie-White. 2001. "Do patents for antiretroviral drugs constrain access to AIDS treatment in Africa?" *Journal of the American Medical Association* 286, 15 (October 17): 1886–1906.

Augelli, E. and C. Murphy. 1993. "Gramsci and international relations: a general perspective with examples from recent US policy toward the third world," in S. Gill (ed.), *Gramsci, Historical Materialism and International Relations*, Cambridge: Cambridge University Press: 127–147.

Baik, C. 1993. *"Politics of Super 301: The domestic basis of U.S. foreign economic policy,"* Ph.D. diss., Department of Political Science, University of California at Berkeley, CA.

Baker, A. 2000. "Globalization and the British 'residual' state," in R. Stubbs, and G. Underhill (eds.), *Political Economy and the Changing Global Order*, 2nd. edn. Oxford: Oxford University Press: 362–372.

Band, J. and M. Katoh. 1995. *Interfaces on Trial: Intellectual Property and Interoperability in the Global Software Industry*. Boulder, CO: Westview Press.

Banta, D. 2001. "Public health triumphs at WTO Conference," *Journal of the American Medical Association* 286, 21 (December): 2655–2665.

Baumgartner, F. and B. Jones. 1993. *Agendas and Instability in American Politics*. Chicago: University of Chicago Press.

Bayard, T. 1990. "Comment on Alan Sykes' 'Mandatory retaliation for breach of trade agreements: some thoughts on the strategic design of Section 301,'" *Boston University International Law Journal* 8 (Fall): 325–331.

Bello, Judith H. 1997. "Some practical observations about WTO settlement of intellectual property disputes," *Virginia Journal of International Law* 37: 357–367.

Bello, J. and A. Holmer. 1988. "The heart of the 1988 trade act: a legislative history of the amendments to Section 301," *Stanford Journal of International Law* 25 (Fall): 1–44.

Bernard, M. 1994. "Post-fordism, transnational production, and the changing global political economy," in R. Stubbs and G. Underhill (eds.), *Political Economy and the Changing Global Order*. New York: St. Martin's Press: 216–229.

1997. "Ecology, political economy and the counter-movement: Karl Polanyi and the second great transformation," in S. Gill and J. Mittelman (eds.), *Innovation and Transformation in International Studies*. Cambridge: Cambridge University Press.

Bhagwati, J. 1989. "United States trade policy at a crossroads," *The World Economy* 12 (December): 439–479.

Bieler, A. 2000. *Globalisation and Enlargement of the European Union: Austrian and Swedish Social Forces in the Struggle Over Membership*. London: Routledge.

2001. "Questioning cognitivism and constructivism in IR theory: reflections on the material structure of ideas," *Politics* 21, 2: 93–100.

Bieler, A. and A. Morton, 2001. "The Gordian Knot of agency-structure in international relations: a neo-Gramscian perspective," *European Journal of International Relations* 7, 1: 5–35.

Biersteker, T. 1992. "The 'triumph' of neo-classical economics in the developing world: policy convergence and bases of governance in the international economic order," in J. Rosenau and O. Czempiel (eds.), *Governance Without*

*Government: Order and Change in World Politics.* New York: Cambridge University Press.

Bliss, J. 1989. "The amendments to Section 301: an overview and suggested strategies for foreign response," *Law and Policy in International Business* 20: 501–528.

Bond, P. 1999. "Globalization, pharmaceutical pricing, and South African health policy: managing confrontation with U.S. firms and politicians," *International Journal of Health Services* 29, 4: 765–792.

Borrus, M. 1993. "Global intellectual property rights in perspective: a concluding panel discussion," in M. Wallerstein, M. Mogee, and R. Schoen (eds.), *Global Dimensions of Intellectual Property Rights in Science and Technology.* Washington, DC: National Academy Press: 373–377.

Bosley, S. and P. Capella. 2001. "U.S. Defends drug companies," *The Guardian*, June 21 at: <http://www.commondreams.org/headlines01/0621-01.htm>

Boyle, J. 1992. "A theory of law and information: copyright, spleens, blackmail, and insider trading," *California Law Review* 80: 1415–1540.

1996. *Shamans, Software and Spleens: Law and the Construction of the Information Society.* Cambridge, MA: Harvard University Press.

Bradley, A. J. 1987. "Intellectual property rights, investment, and trade in services at the Uruguay round: laying the foundation," *Stanford Journal of International Law* 23 (Spring): 57–98.

Braithwaite, J. and P. Drahos. 2000, *Global Business Regulation.* Cambridge: Cambridge University Press.

Bridges, 2002. *Weekly Trade Digest*, no. 8 (March 5).

Burch, K. 1994. "The 'properties' of the state system and global capitalism," in S. Rosow, N. Inayatullah, and M. Rupert (eds.), *The Global Economy as Political Space.* Boulder, CO: Lynne Rienner Publishers: 37–59.

Business Software Alliance (BSA). 1995. "Fact sheet: international policies governing the software industry," Washington, DC: BSA (May 5).

1998. "BSA congratulates USTR and the government of Sweden," Dec. 3. available at: <http://www.bsa.org/pressbox/policy/912704816.html> accessed 7/19/00.

Capdevila, G. 2001. "WTO concedes developing world's plea for access to low-cost drugs," *Dawn: the Internet Edition*, June 24, at: <http://www.dawn.com/2001/06/24/intl1.htm>

Carlsnaes, W. 1992. "The agency–structure problem in foreign policy analysis," *International Studies Quarterly* 36, 3 (September): 245–270.

Center for Responsive Politics. 1998a. "Lobbying spending: intellectual property committee," available at <http://www.open.secrets.org> accessed 7/11/00.

1998b. "Lobbyists Profiles" available at: <http://www.open.secrets.org/lobbyists/98profiles/18808.htm> accessed 7/11/00. 1997 data available from hyperlink (1997 DATA) at same site.

*References*

Cerny, Philip. 1994. "The infrastructure of the infrastructure? Toward 'embedded financial orthodoxy' in the international political economy," in R. Palan and B. Gills (eds.), *Transcending the State-Global Divide: A Neo-Structuralist Agenda in International Relations*. Boulder: Lynne Rienner.

— 1995. "Globalization and the changing logic of collective action," *International Organization* 49: 4 (Autumn): 595–625.

Checkel, Jeffrey. 1998. "The constructivist turn in international relations theory," *World Politics* 50 (January): 324–348.

Chu, M. 1992. "An antitrust solution to the new wave of predatory patent infringement litigation," *William & Mary Law Review* 33 (Summer): 1341–1368.

Clapes, A. 1993. *Softwars: The Legal Battles for Control of the Global Software Industry*. Westport, CT: Quorum Books.

Cobb, R. and M. Ross. 1997. *Cultural Strategies of Agenda Denial*. Lawrence, KS: University Press of Kansas.

Coffield, S. 1981. "Using Section 301 of the Trade Act of 1974 as a response to foreign government trade actions: when, why and how," *North Carolina Journal of International Law and Commercial Regulation* 6 (Summer): 381–405.

Consumer Project on Technology and Health Action International, 1998. "Position Paper submitted to the Working Group on Technology and Intellectual Property Rights: Recommendations on Health Care and Intellectual Property," Free Trade Area of the Americas, Fourth Trade Ministerial and Americas Business Forum, San Jose, Costa Rica, submitted February 15, 1998, for meeting in March 1998. Available at: <http://www.cptech.org/pharm/ftaa-health98.html> accessed 4/24/02.

Consumer Project on Technology, Essential Action, Oxfam, Treatment Access Campaign, and Health Gap, 2001. "Comment on the Attaran/Gillespie-White and PhRMA surveys of patents on antiretroviral drugs in Africa," October 16th version 1, available at: <http://www.cptech.org/ip/health/africa/dopatentsmatterinafrica.html> accessed 2/28/02.

Consumer Project on Technology, Health Action International *et al.*, 1998. "Workshop on intellectual property, health care and international trade agreements," April 8. Available at: <http://www.cptech.org/may7-8/index.html>

Cornish, W. R. 1981. *Intellectual Property: Patents, Copyright, Trademarks and Allied Rights*. London: Sweet & Maxwell.

— 1993. "The international relations of intellectual property," *Cambridge Law Journal* 52, 1 (March): 46–63.

Correa, C. 1994. "TRIPS Agreement: copyright and related rights," *International Review of Industrial Property and Copyright Law* 4: 543–552.

Cox, R. 1987. *Production, Power, and World Order: Social Forces in the Making of History*. New York: Columbia University Press.

— 1993. "Structural issues of global governance: implications for Europe," in S. Gill (ed.), *Gramsci, Historical Materialism and International Relations*. Cambridge: Cambridge University Press: 259–289.

Cutler, A. Claire, Virginia Haufler, and Tony Porter (eds.). 1999. "The contours and significance of private authority in international affairs," in Cutler, Haufler, and Porter (eds.), *Private Authority and International Affairs*. Albany: State University of New York Press: 333–376.

D'Alessandro, J. 1987. "A trade-based response to intellectual property piracy: a comprehensive plan to aid the motion picture industry," *The Georgetown Law Journal* 76: 417–465.

Damschroder, M. 1988. "Intellectual property rights and the GATT: United States goals in the Uruguay Round," *Vanderbilt Journal of Transnational Law* 21.

David, P. 1993. "Intellectual property institutions and the Panda's Thumb: patents, copyrights, and trade secrets in economic theory and history," in Mitchel Wallerstein, Mary Ellen Mogee, and Roberta Schoen (eds.), *Global Dimensions of Intellectual Property Rights in Science and Technology*. Washington, DC: National Academy Press.

Deardorff, A. 1990. "Should patent protection be extended to all developing countries?" *World Economy* 13: 497–508.

Dessler, D. 1989. "What's at stake in the agent–structure debate?" *International Organization* 43, 3 (Summer): 441–473.

Destler, I. 1992. *American Trade Politics*. Washington, DC: Institute for International Economics.

Dhar, B. and C.N. Rao. 1995. "Trade relatedness of intellectual property rights," *Science Communication* 17, 3 (March): 304–325.

Doane, M. 1994. "TRIPS and international intellectual property protection in an age of advancing technology," *American University Journal of International Law and Policy* 9, 2 (Winter): 465–497.

Doern, G. 1999. *Global Change and Intellectual Property Agencies*. London: Pinter.

Doremus, P. 1995. "The externalization of domestic regulation: intellectual property rights reform in a global era," *Science Communication* 17, 2 (December): 137–162.

Drahos, P. 1995. "Global property rights in information: the story of TRIPs at the GATT," *Prometheus* 13, 1 (June): 6–19.

    1996. *A Philosophy of Intellectual Property*. Aldershot: Dartmouth Publishing Company.

    1997. "Thinking strategically about intellectual property rights," *Telecommunications Policy* 21, 3 (1997): 201–211.

    2001. "BITS and BIPS: bilateralism in intellectual property," *The Journal of World Intellectual Property Law* 4, 6 (November): 791–808.

    2002. "Developing countries and international intellectual property standard-setting," Commission on Intellectual Property Rights, Study Paper 8 (August 2), http://www.iprcommission.org/meetingsIndex.asp> accessed 2/20/02.

Dreyfuss, Rochelle. 1989. "The federal circuit: a case study in specialized courts," *New York University Law Review* 64, 1 (April): 1–77.

Dutfield, G. 2003. *Intellectual Property Rights and the Life Sciences Industries: A Twentieth Century History*. Aldershot: Dartmouth Publishing Company.

## References

Einstein, E. 1995. "NAFTA: Little protection for technology," *Les Nouvelles*, March 30.

Eisner, Marc. 1991. *Antitrust and the Triumph of Economics: Institutions, Expertise, and Policy Change*. Chapel Hill: University of North Carolina Press.

Emmert, Frank. 1990. "Intellectual property in the Uruguay Round – negotiating strategies of the western industrialized countries," *Michigan Journal of International Law* 11 (Summer): 1317–1399.

Engelberg, A. 1999. "Special patent provisions for pharmaceuticals: have they outlived their usefulness?: A political, legislative and legal history of U.S. law and observations for the future," *IDEA: The Journal of Law and Technology* 39: 389–428.

Enyart, J. 1990. "A GATT intellectual property code," *Les Nouvelles*, 25 (June): 53–56.

Evans, G. 1994. "Intellectual property as a trade issue – the making of the agreement on trade-related aspects of intellectual property rights," *World Competition: Law and Economics Review* 18, 2: 137–180.

1998. "Issues of legitimacy and the resolution of intellectual property disputes in the supercourt of the World Trade Organisation," *International Trade Law Reporter* 3: 81–98.

Feather, J. 1994. *Publishing, Piracy and Politics: An Historical Study of Copyright in Britain*. London: Mansell Publishing Limited.

Finnemore, M. 1996. "Norms, culture, and world politics: insights from sociology's institutionalism," *International Organization* 50, 2 (Spring): 325–347.

Finnemore, M. and S. Toope. 2001. "Comment on 'Legalization and World Politics'," *International Organization* 55, 3 (Summer): 743–758.

Fisher, B. and R. Steinhardt. 1982. "Section 301 of the Trade Act of 1974," *Law and Policy in International Business* 14: 569–603.

Fligstein, N. 1996. "Markets as politics: a political-cultural approach to market institutions," *American Sociological Review* 61 (August): 656–673.

1997. "Social skill and institutional theory," *American Behavioral Scientist* 40, 4 (February): 397–405.

Fligstein, N. and R. Feeland. 1995. "Theoretical and comparative perspectives on corporate organization," *American Review of Sociology* 21: 21–43.

Foray, D. 1995. "Knowledge distribution and the institutional infrastructure: the role of intellectual property rights," in Horst Albach and Stephanie Rosenkranz (eds.), *Intellectual Property Rights and Global Competition: Towards a New Synthesis*. Berlin: Ed Sigma: 77–117.

Fowler, C. 1994. *Unnatural Selection: Technology, Politics and Plant Evolution*. New York: Taylor and Francis.

Friedman, G. and H. Starr. 1997. *Agency, Structure, and International Politics*. London: Routledge.

Frischtak, C. 1993. "Harmonization versus differentiation in intellectual property right regimes," in Mitchel B. Wallerstein, Mary Ellen Mogee, and Roberta Schoen (eds.), *Global Dimensions of Intellectual Property Rights in Science and Technology*. Washington, DC: National Academy Press.

Gadbaw, M. 1989. "Intellectual property and international trade: merger or marriage of convenience?," *Vanderbilt Journal of Transnational Law* 22, 2: 223–242.

Gadbaw, M. and T. Richards. 1988. *Intellectual Property Rights: Global Consensus, Global Conflict?* Boulder, CO: Westview Press.

Gana, R. 1995. "Has creativity died in the Third World? Some implications of the internationalization of intellectual property," *Denver Journal of International Law & Policy* 24, 1: 109–144.

Geller, Paul Edward. 1994. "Legal transplants in international copyright: Some problems of method," *UCLA Pacific Basin Law Journal* 199, 216.

Gellman, B. 2000. "Gore in conflict for health and profit," *The Washington Post*, May 21. A1. Http://www.washingtonpost.c...rticle&nodecpntentID = A41297-2000May20.

Genetic Resources Action International (GRAIN). 1997. "Toward our sui generis rights," *Seedling* (December): 4–6. Available at: <http://www.grain.org/publications/dec97/dec971.htm> accessed 6/24/99.

The GAIA Foundation. Genetic Resources Action International (GRAIN). 1998a. "Intellectual property rights and biodiversity: the economic myths," *Global Trade and Biodiversity in Conflict*, 3: 1–20, available at: <http://www.grain.org/publications/gtbc/issue3.htm> accessed 7/25/00.

Genetic Resources Action International (GRAIN). 1998b. "The TRIPS Review takes off" (December): 7. Available at: <http://www.grain.org/publications/dec98/dec983.htm> accessed 6/24/99.

1999a. "Beyond UPOV: examples of developing countries preparing non-UPOV sui generis plant variety protection schemes for compliance with TRIPS," July. Available at: <http://www.grain.org/publications/reports/nonupov.htm> accessed 8/7/00.

1999b. "Intellectual property rights and biodiversity: the economic myths," *Global Trade and Biodiversity in Conflict* 3 (October). Available at: <http://www.grain.org/publications/gtbc/issue3.htm> accessed 8/7/00.

1999c. "Trips versus biodiversity," May. Available at: <http://www.grain.org/publications/reports/tripsmay99.htm>

1999d. "UPOV on the war path," *Seedling* (June). Available at: <http://www.grain.org/publications/jun99/jun991.htm> accessed 8/7/00.

Genetic Resources Action International, in cooperation with SANFEC, 2001a. " 'TRIPS-plus through the back door: how bilateral treaties impose much stronger rules for IPRS on life than the WTO," July. Available at: <http://www.grain.org> accessed 4/23/02.

2001b. " 'TRIPS-plus' Treaties Leave WTO in the Dust," GRAIN Press Release, July 27. Available at: <http://www.grain.org> accessed 4/24/02.

Gerhart, P. 2000. "Reflections: beyond compliance theory – TRIPS as a substantive issue," *Case Western Reserve Journal of International Law* 32, 3 (Summer): 357–385.

Germain, R. 1997. *The International Organization of Credit: States and Global Finance in the World-Economy.* Cambridge: Cambridge University Press.

*References*

2000. "Globalization in historical perspective," in R. Germain (ed.), *Globalization and its Critics*. London: Macmillan: 67–90.

Giddens, A. 1979. *Central Problems in Social Theory*. Berkeley: University of California Press.

1984. *The Constitution of Society: Outline of the Theory of Structuration*. Cambridge: Polity Press.

Gill, S. 2000. "Knowledge, politics, and neo-liberal political economy," in R. Stubbs and G. Underhill (eds.), *Political Economy and the Changing Global Order*, 2nd edn. Oxford: Oxford University Press: 48–59.

Gill, S. and D. Law. 1993. "Global hegemony and the structural power of capital," in S. Gill (ed.), *Gramsci, Historical Materialism and International Relations*. Cambridge: Cambridge University Press: 93–124.

Gillespie-White, L. 2001. "What did Doha accomplish?" November 19. International Intellectual Property Institute. Available at: <http://mail.iipi/org/db/views/detail.asp?itemID = 21> accessed 3/7/02.

Goodman, J. and L. Pauly. 2000. "The obsolescence of capital controls? Economic management in an age of global markets," in D. Lake and J. Frieden (eds.), *International Political Economy: Perspectives on Global Power and Wealth*, 4th edn. Boston: Bedford/St. Martin's: 280–297.

Goozner, M. 1999. "Third world battles for AIDS drugs," *Chicago Tribune*, April 28, A1.

Gorlin, J. 1985. "A trade-based approach for the international copyright protection for computer software," unpublished. On file with author.

1988. "The business community and the Uruguay Round," in Charls E. Walker and Mark A. Bloomfield (eds.), *Intellectual Property Rights and Capital Formation in the Next Decade*. Lanham, MD: University Press of America.

Graham, E. 1996. "Investment and the new multilateral context," in *Market Access after the Uruguay Round: Investment, competition, and technology perspectives*. Paris: OECD.

1997. "Should there be multilateral rules on FDI?", in J. Dunning (ed.), *Governments, Globalization, and International Business*. Oxford: Oxford University Press.

Granovetter, M. 1985. "Economic action and social structure: the problem of embeddedness," *American Journal of Sociology* 91, 3 (November): 481–510.

Greenhouse, L. 2002. "Justices to review copyright extension," *The New York Times* (Feb. 20), C1.

Greenwald, J. 1987. "Protectionism in U.S. economic policy," *Stanford Journal of International Law* (Spring): 233–261.

Grossman, G. and Helpman, E. 1991. *Innovation and Growth in the Global Economy*. Cambridge, MA: MIT Press.

Gruber, L. 2001. *Ruling the World: Power Politics and the Rise of Supranational Institutions*. Princeton: Princeton University Press.

Haddad, W. 2001. "Back to the future," Haddad Oslo Talk (Part I) WTO/WHO meeting on drug pricing and parallel trade, April 8, 2001, Hosjbor,

Norway. Available at: <http://wto.org/english/tratop_e/trips_e/hosbjor_presentations_ee/42haddad_e.pdf> accessed 4/24/02.

Hall, Stuart. 1988. "Brave New World," *Marxism Today* (October): 24–29.

Hayslett III, T. 1996. "1995 Antitrust guidelines for the licensing of intellectual property: harmonizing the commercial use of legal monopolies with the prohibitions of antitrust law," *Journal of Intellectual Property Law* 3 (Spring): 375–405.

Henriques, V. 1985. Testimony before U.S. Congress. House. Energy and Commerce Committee. H361-35.3, 26 July.

Hoekman, B. 1995. "Assessing the General Agreement on Trade in Services," in W. Martin and L. Winters (eds.), *The Uruguay Round and the Developing Economies*. Washington, DC: The World Bank.

Hoekman, Bernard and Michel Kostecki. 1995. *The Political Economy of the World Trading System: From GATT to WTO*. Oxford: Oxford University Press.

Hoff, P. 1986. *Inventions in the Marketplace: Patent Licensing and the U.S. Antitrust Laws*. Washington, DC: American Enterprise Institute.

Hollis, M. and S. Smith. 1991. "Beware of gurus: structure and action in international relations," *Review of International Studies* 17: 393–410.

1992. "Structure and action: further comment," *Review of International Studies* 18: 187–188.

1994. "Two stories about structure and agency," *Review of International Studies* 20: 241–251.

Hughes, D. 1991. "Opening up trade barriers with Section 301 – a critical assessment," *Wisconsin International Law Journal* 5: 176–206.

The Intellectual Property Committee, Keidanren, UNICE. 1988. *Basic Framework of GATT Provisions on Intellectual Property: Statement of Views of the European, Japanese and United States Business Communities* (June).

International Intellectual Property Alliance. 1985. *U.S. Government Trade Policy: Views of the Copyright Industry*. Submitted to the US Congress. House. Energy and Commerce Committee. H361–35.3. July 26: 80–81.

1986. *Piracy of U.S. Copyrighted Works in Ten Selected Countries: A report by the International Intellectual Property Alliance to the U.S. Trade Representative*. Submitted to the U.S. Congress. Senate. Senate Finance Committee. S361–88.4 14 May, 1986.

1996. "IIPA names 29 countries causing over $6 billion in trade losses due to copyright piracy in 1995," Feb. 20, available at: <http://www.iIPa.com/html/pn_specia;_301_pr_22096.html> accessed 7/18/00.

1997. "Letter to Joseph Papovich, Deputy Assistant USTR for intellectual property," February 24. available at: <http://www.iIPa.com/html/rbi_special_301_lttr_22497.html> accessed 10/26/98.

1998. "Letter to Joseph Papovich, Assistant USTR for services, investment and intellectual property," Feb. 23. available at: <http://www.iIPa.com/html/rbi_special_301_lttr_022098.html> accessed 10/26/98.

*References*

1999. "Copyright piracy in 62 countries causes at least $12.4 billion in trade losses in 1998," Feb. 16. Available at: <http://www.iIPa.com/html/pr_02161999.html> accessed 6/21/99.

2000a. "IIPA asks USTR to designate Israel and Ukraine as special 301 'priority foreign countries' in April 2000," Feb. 18. Available at: <http://www.iIPa.com> accessed 7/11/00.

2000b. "IIPA testifies at GSP hearings to urge six countries to comply with 'adequate and effective' standards of copyright protection and enforcement as required under U.S. trade program," May 12. Available at: <http://www.iIPa.com/homepage_index.html> accessed 7/12/00.

Jackson, J. 1989. "Remarks of Professor John Jackson," *Vanderbilt Journal of Transnational Law* 22, 2: 343–355.

Jones, B. 1994. *Reconceiving Decision-Making in Democratic Politics: Attention, Choice, and Public Policy.* Chicago: University of Chicago Press.

Julius, D. 1994. "International direct investment: strengthening the policy regime," in P. Kenen (ed.), *Managing the World Economy: Fifty Years After Bretton Woods.* Washington, DC: Institute for International Economics.

Kastriner, L. 1991. "The revival of confidence in the patent system," *Journal of the Patent and Trademark Office Society* 73, 1 (January): 5–23.

Katzenstein, P., R. Keohane, and S. Krasner (eds.). 1998. *International Organization at Fifty: Exploration and Contestation in the Study of World Politics* (special anniversary issue) 52: 4 (Autumn).

Kaye, H. and P. Plaia. 1981. "The filing and defending of Section 337 actions," *North Carolina Journal of International Law and Commercial Regulation* 6 (Summer): 463–483.

Keck, M. and K. Sikkink. 1998. *Activists Beyond Borders.* Ithaca: Cornell University Press.

Kent, C. 1993. "NAFTA, TRIPS affect ip," *Les Nouvelles* 28 (December): 176–181.

Klotz, A. 1995. *Norms in International Relations: The Struggle Against Apartheid.* Ithaca: Cornell University Press.

Knapp, Inti. 2000. "The software piracy battle in Latin America: should the United States pursue its aggressive bilateral trade policy despite the multilateral TRIPS enforcement framework?", *University of Pennsylvania Journal of International Economic Law* 21 (Spring): 173–210.

Kobak, Jr., J. 1995. "The misuse defense and intellectual property litigation," *Boston University Journal of Science and Technology Law* 1, 2: 1–43.

1998. "Intellectual property, competition law and hidden choices between original and sequential innovation," *Virginia Journal of Law and Technology* 3: 6.

Koremenos, B., C. Lipson, and D. Snidal. 2001. "The rational design of international institutions," *International Organization* 55, 4 (Autumn): 761–799.

Kosterlitz, J. 1993. "Rx: Higher prices," *National Journal*, 7 (February 13): 396–399.

Kowert, Paul and Jeffrey Legro. 1996. "Norms, identity, and their limits: a theoretical reprise," in Peter Katzenstein (ed.), *The Culture of National*

*Security: Norms and Identity in World Politics*. Ithaca: Cornell University Press: 451–497.

Krasner, S. 1985. *Structural Conflict: The Third World Against Global Liberalism*. Berkeley, CA: University of California Press.

1991. "Global communications and national power: life on the Pareto frontier," *World Politics* 43, 3 (April): 336–366.

Lande, S. and C. VanGrasstek. 1986. *The Trade and Tariff Act of 1984: Trade Policy in the Reagan Administration*. Lexington, MA: D.C. Heath and Company.

Lash, W. 1992. "In our stars: the failure of American trade policy," *North Carolina Journal of Law and Commercial Regulation* 18 (Fall): 7–57.

Lever, J. 1982. "The new Court of Appeals for the Federal Circuit (Part I)," *Journal of the Patent Office Society* 64, 3 (March): 178–208.

Levin, R. C. *et al.* 1987. "Appropriating the returns from industrial research and development," *Brookings Papers on Economic Activity* 3: 783–820.

Levy, C. S. 2000. "Implementing TRIPS – a test of political will," *Law and Policy in International Business* 31, 3: 789–795.

Levy, D. and D. Egan. 2000. "Corporate political action in the global polity: National and transnational strategies in the climate change negotiations," in R. Higgott, G. Underhill, and A. Bieler (eds.), *Non-State Actors and Authority in the Global System*. London: Routledge: 138–153.

Lindblom, C. 1977. *Politics and Markets*. New York: Basic Books.

1990. *Inquiry and Change: The Troubled Attempt to Understand and Shape Society*. New Haven, CT: Yale University Press.

Lipson, C. 1985. *Standing Guard: The Protection of Foreign Capital in the Nineteenth and Twentieth Centuries*. Berkeley: University of California Press.

Litfin, K. 1995. "Framing science: precautionary discourse and the Ozone Treaties," *Millennium: Journal of International Studies* (Summer) 24, 2: 251–277.

1999. "Constructing environmental security and ecological interdependence," *Global Governance* 5, 3 (July–Sept.): 359–377.

Litman, J. 1989. "Copyright legislation and technological change," *Oregon Law Review* 68, 2: 275–361.

Liu, P. 1994. "U.S. industry's influence on intellectual property negotiations and Special 301 Actions," *UCLA Pacific Basin Law Journal* 13: 87–117.

Love, J. 1996. "Comments on trade and pharmaceutical policies: a perspective from the U.S. consumer movement," presented at HAI Seminar: "World Trade Organization/GATT, Pharmaceutical Policies and Essential Drugs," October 4, Bielefeld, Germany. Available at: <http://www.cptech.org/pharm/bielefeld.html> accessed 4/24/02.

2001. Remarks presented at University of Florida Frederic G. Levin College of Law Symposium: Intellectual Property, Development and Human Rights. Gainesville, FL. March 24.

Love, J. and M. Palmedo. 2001. "Examples of compulsory licensing of intellectual property in the United States," CPTech Background paper 1, September 29.

*References*

Available at: <http://www.cptech.org/ip/health/cl/us-cl.html> accessed 4/24/02.

Low, P. and A. Subramanian. 1995. "TRIMs in the Uruguay Round: unfinished business?" in W. Martin and L. Winters (eds.), *The Uruguay Round and the Developing Economies*. Washington, DC: The World Bank.

Machlup, F. and E. Penrose. 1950. "The patent controversy in the nineteenth century," *Journal of Economic History* 10, 1 (May): 1–29.

Malott, R. 1989. "1990s issue: intellectual property rights," *Les Nouvelles*, 24 (December): 149–153.

Marden, Emily. 1999. "The Neem tree patent: international conflict over the commodification of life," *Boston College Environmental Affairs Law Review* 22 (Spring): 279–295.

Martin, W. and L. Winters (eds.). 1995. *The Uruguay Round and the Developing Countries*. Washington, DC: The World Bank.

Maskus, K. 1991. "Normative concerns in the international protection of intellectual property rights," *World Economy* 14: 403.

   2000. *Intellectual Property Rights in the Global Economy*. Washington, DC: Institute for International Economics.

Matsushita, M. 1992. "A Japanese perspective on intellectual property rights and the GATT," *Columbia Business Law Review* 1: 81–95.

Matthews, D. 2002. *Globalising Intellectual Property Rights: the TRIPS Agreement*. London, Routledge.

May, C. 2000. *A Global Political Economy of Intellectual Property Rights: The New Enclosures?* London: Routledge.

McNeil, D. 2000. "Companies to cut costs of AIDS drugs for poor nations," *New York Times*, May 11. Accessed through Lexis-Nexis Academic Universe, 11-01-01.

   2001. "Yale pressed to help cut drug costs in Africa," *The New York Times*, Mar. 12, A3.

Médecins Sans Frontières, HAI, CPT. 1999a. "An open letter to WTO member states," November 8. Available at: <http://msf.org/advocacy/accessmed/wto/reports/1999/letter> accessed 7/11/00.

   1999b. "Amsterdam Statement to WTO member states on access to medicine," November 25–26. Available at: <http://www.cptech.org/ip/health/amsterdamstatement/html> accessed 7/11/00; also available at: <http://www.accessmed.org/prod/publications.asp?scntid = 17122001173935&contenttype = PARA&

   2000. "MSF reaction to UNAIDS proposal," May 11. Available at: <http://www.msf.org/un/reports/2000/05/pr-unaids/> accessed 8/7/00.

Merges, R. 1990. "Battle of the lateralisms: intellectual property and trade," *Boston University International Law Journal* 8, 2 (Fall): 239–246.

   2000. "One hundred years of solicitude: intellectual property law, 1900–2000," *California Law Review* 88 (December): 2187–2240.

Mizruchi, M. 1992. *The Structure of Corporate Political Action*. Cambridge, MA: Harvard University Press.

Moravcsik, A. 1997. "Taking preferences seriously: a liberal theory of international politics," *International Organization* 51, 4 (Autumn): 513–553.

Morrison, S. 1994. "How will the Uruguay Round of GATT affect the U.S. computer industry?," *Congressional Research Service Report for Congress*, Report No. 94-840-E, Washington, DC: The Library of Congress (November 3).

Mossinghoff, G. 1984. "The importance of intellectual property in international trade," *Business America*, January 7, inside cover.

1985. Testimony of Gerald J. Mossinghoff, House Energy and Commerce Committee, H361–35.5, July 26, 189.

1991. "For better international protection," *Les Nouvelles*, 26 (June): 75–79.

Mowrey, D. 1993. "Global intellectual property rights issues in perspective: a concluding panel discussion," in M. Wallerstein, M. Mogee, and R. Schoen (eds.), *Global Dimensions of Intellectual Property Rights in Science and Technology*. Washington, DC: National Academy Press: 368–372.

Murphy, C. 1994. *International Organization and Industrial Change: Global Governance Since 1850*. New York: Oxford University Press.

1998. "Understanding IR: understanding Gramsci," *Review of International Studies* 24: 417–425.

Murphy, C. and D. Nelson. 2001. "International political economy: a tale of two heterodoxies," *British Journal of Politics and International Relations* 3, 3 (October): 393–412.

Nader, R. and J. Love. 1995. "Ralph Nader and James Love, letter to Michael Kantor on health care and IPR," October 9. Available at: <http://www.cptech.org/pharm/kantor.html> accessed 4/24/02.

Nader, Ralph, James Love, and Robert Weissman. 1999. "October 6, 1999 letter to Charlene Barshefsky regarding review of US trade policy as it relates to access to essential drugs," available at: <http://www.cptech.org/ip/health/country/cb-oct6-99.html> accessed 8/7/00.

Neuman, W. 1992. "IPR protection improves, but reforms not uniform," *Business Latin America* 20 (April): 127.

Newman, A. 1989. "The amendments to Section 337: increased protection for intellectual property rights," *Law and Policy in International Business* 20: 571–588.

Nicoson, W. 1962. "Misuse of the misuse doctrine in infringement suits," 9 *UCLA Law Review* 76.

North, D. 1981. *Structure and Change in Economic History*. New York: W. W. Norton & Company.

Novak, V. 1993. "How drug companies operate on the body politic," *Business and Society Review* 84 (Winter): 58–64.

O'Connor, D. 1995. "TRIPS: Licensing challenge," *Les Nouvelles* 30, 1.

Oddi, A. Samuel. 1987. "The international patent system and Third World development: reality or myth?" *Duke Law Journal* 87, 5 (November): 831–878.

1996. "TRIPS – Natural rights and a polite form of economic imperialism," *Vanderbilt Journal of Transnational Law* 29: 415.

*References*

Odell, J. and I. Destler. 1987. *Anti-protection: The Changing Face of U.S. Trade Politics.* Washington, DC: Institute of International Economics.

Onuf, N. 1997. "A constructivist manifesto," in K. Burch and R. Denemark (eds.), *Constituting International Political Economy.* Boulder, CO: Lynne Rienner Press: 7–17.

Ordover, J. 1991. "A patent system for both diffusion and exclusion," *Journal of Economic Perspectives* 5, 1 (Winter): 43–60.

Ostry, S. 1990. *Governments and Corporations in a Shrinking World.* New York: Council on Foreign Relations Press.

Palan, R. and J. Abbott, with P. Deans. 1996. *State Strategies in the Global Political Economy.* London: Pinter.

Patel, S. 1989. "Intellectual property rights in the Uruguay round: a disaster for the South?," *Economic and Political Weekly* (May 6).

Pharmaceutical Research and Manufacturers of America (PhRMA). 1996. "Submission of the Pharmaceutical Research and Manufacturers of America for the 'Special 301' report on intellectual property barriers," Feb. 20. Obtained from PhRMA, on file with author.

1997a. "Submission of the Pharmaceutical Research and Manufacturers of America for the 'Special 301' report on intellectual property barriers," Feb. 18. Obtained from PhRMA, on file with author.

1997b. "Trade barriers rob patients of new drugs says report," Dec. 19. Available at: <http://www.phrma.org/news/12-19-97b.html> accessed 7/18/00.

1998a. "Submission of the Pharmaceutical Research and Manufacturers of America for the 'Special 301' report on intellectual property barriers," Feb. 23. Obtained from PhRMA, on file with author.

1998b. "Trade barriers cost U.S. pharmaceutical industry $9 billion a year, PhRMA tells USTR," Dec. 4. Available at: <http://www.phrma.org/news/12-4-98.html> accessed 7/18/00.

1999a. "Submission of the Pharmaceutical Research and Manufacturers of America for the 'Special 301' report on intellectual property barriers," Feb. 16. Available at: <http://www.phrma.org/issues/nte/html> accessed 8/12/99.

1999b. "Submission of the Pharmaceutical Research and Manufacturers of America for the 'Special 301' report on intellectual property barriers: India," Feb. 16. Available at: <http://www.phrma.org/issues/nte/india.html> accessed 8/12/99.

2000a. "Submission of the Pharmaceutical Research and Manufacturers of America for the 'Special 301' report on intellectual property barriers," Feb. 18. Available at: <http://www.phrma.org/issues/nte.html> accessed 7/18/00.

2000b. Press release, "Alan Holmer, President, PhRMA ... statement in response to President Clinton's May 10, 2000 Executive Order on Access to HIV/AIDS Pharmaceuticals," May 10. Available at: <http://www.phrma.org/press/newsreleases//2000-05-10.12.phtml> accessed 8/7/00.

2001. "Submission of the Pharmaceutical Research and Manufacturers of America," *National Trade Estimate Report on Foreign Trade Barriers (NTE)* Dec. 17. Available at: <http://www.PhRMA.org> accessed 8/20/01.

Porter, Tony. 1999. "Hegemony and the private governance of international industries," in A. Cutler, V. Haufler, and T. Porter, *Private Authority and International Affairs*. Albany: State University of New York Press: 257–282.

Price, D. 1996. "Investment rules and high technology: towards a multilateral agreement on investment," in *Market Access after the Uruguay Round: Investment, Competition and Technology Perspectives*. Paris: OECD.

Price, R. 1998. "Reversing the gun sights: transnational civil society targets land mines," *International Organization* 52, 3 (Summer): 613–644.

Primo Braga, C. 1989. "The economics of intellectual property rights and the GATT: a view from the south," *Vanderbilt Journal of Transnational Law* 22, 2: 243–264.

Prusoff, W. 2001. "The scientist's story," *The New York Times*, Mar. 19: A19.

Pruzin, D. 2001. "WTO Talks on TRIPS, Public Health Declaration stall over compromise text," *International Trade Daily*, October 24. Bureau of National Affairs.

Public Citizen, Congress Watch. 2001. "Drug industry most profitable again," April 11. At: http://www.citizen.org/congress/reform/drug_industry/profits/articles.cfm?ID = 838, accessed 5/8/02.

Quaker United Nations Office, Geneva. 2001. "What did developing countries get at Doha? Some QUNO assessments of the WTO Ministerial Conference." Available at: <http://www.quno.org> accessed 4/26/02.

Raustiala, K. 2000. "Compliance and effectiveness in international regulatory cooperation," *Case Western Reserve Journal of International Law* 32, 3 (Summer): 387–440.

Reich, R. 1983. "Beyond free trade," *Foreign Affairs* 61 (Spring): 773–804.

Reich, R. and I. Magaziner. 1982. *Minding America's Business: The Decline and Rise of the American Economy*. New York: Harcourt Brace Jovanovich.

Reichman, J. H. 1993. "The TRIPS component of the GATT's Uruguay Round: competitive prospects for intellectual property owners in an integrated world market," *Fordham Intellectual Property, Media & Entertainment Law Journal* 4: 171–266.

1996. "Compliance with the TRIPS Agreement: introduction to a scholarly debate," *Vanderbilt Journal of Transnational Law* 29 (May): 363–390.

1997a. "Enforcing the enforcement procedures of the TRIPS Agreement," *Virginia Journal of International Law* 37 (Winter): 335–356.

1997b. "From free riders to fair followers: global competition under the TRIPS Agreement," *New York University Journal of International Law and Policy* 29: 17–21.

Reichman, J. H. and David Lange. 1998. "Bargaining around the TRIPS agreement: the case for ongoing public–private initiatives to facilitate worldwide intellectual property transactions," *Duke Journal of Comparative and International Law* 9 (Fall): 11–68.

*References*

Reiterer, M. 1994. "Trade-related intellectual property rights," in *The New World Trading System: Readings*. Paris: OECD.

Renouard, A.C. 1987. *Traité des Brevets d'invention*, 1844, reissued, Paris: CNAM.

Risse, T. 2000. "'Let's argue!': Communicative action in world politics," *International Organization* 54, 1 (Winter): 1–39.

Risse-Kappen, T. (ed.). 1995. *Bringing Transnational Relations Back In: Non-State Actors, Domestic Structures and International Institutions*. Cambridge: Cambridge University Press.

Rodrik, D. 1994. "Comments on Maskus and Eby-Konan," in A. Deardorff and R. Stern (eds.), *Analytic and Negotiating Issues in the Global Trading System*. Ann Arbor: University of Michigan Press.

Rosenberg, T. 2001. "Look at Brazil," *The New York Times*, Sunday, January 28 (Sunday magazine). http://www.nytimes.com/library/magazine/home/20010128mag.aids.html

Ryan, M. 1998a. "The function-specific and linkage-bargain diplomacy of international intellectual property lawmaking," *University of Pennsylvania Journal of International Economic Law* (Summer): 535–586.

1998b. *Knowledge Diplomacy: Global Competition and the Politics of Intellectual Property*. Washington, DC: The Brookings Institution.

Sally, R. 1994. "Multinational enterprises, political economy, and institutional theory: domestic embeddedness in the context of internationalization," *Review of International Political Economy* 1:1 (Spring).

Samahon, Tuan N. 2000. "TRIPS copyright dispute settlement after the transition and moratorium: nonviolation and situation complaints against developing countries," *Law and Policy in International Business* 31, 3: 1051–1075.

Samuelson, Pamela. 1997. "The U.S. digital agenda at WIPO," *Virginia Journal of International Law* 37 (Winter): 369–439.

Scotchmer, S. 1991. "Standing on the shoulders of giants: cumulative research and the patent law," *Journal of Economic Perspectives* 5, 1 (Winter): 29–41.

Sell, S. 1995. "The origins of a trade-based approach to intellectual property protection: the role of industry associations," *Science Communication* 17, 2 (December): 163–185.

1998. *Power and Ideas: The North–South Politics of Intellectual Property and Antitrust*. Albany: State University of New York Press.

1999. "Multinational corporations as agents of change: the globalization of intellectual property rights," in A. Cutler, V. Haufler, and T. Porter, *Private Authority and International Affairs*. Albany: State University of New York Press.

Sell, S. and C. May. 2001. "Moments in law: contestation and settlement in the history of intellectual property," *Review of International Political Economy* 8, 3: 467–500.

Shell, G. R. 1995. "Trade legalism and international relations theory: an analysis of the World Trade Organization," *Duke Law Journal* 44, 5 (March): 829–927.

Sherwood, Robert, 1997. "The TRIPS Agreement: implications for developing countries," *IDEA*, 491, 493.

Shillinger, K. 2000. "AIDS drug prices cut for Africa, pharmaceutical companies yield to pressure from the White House," *The Boston Globe*, May 12, 2000, 3rd edn. Accessed 11–0101, Lexis-Nexis Academic Universe.

Shiva, Vandana. 1997. *Biopiracy: The Plunder of Nature and Knowledge*. South End Press.

Shrader, D. 1994a. "Enforcement of intellectual property rights under the GATT 1994 TRIPS Agreement," *Congressional Research Service Report for Congress*, Report No. 94–228 A Washington, DC: Congressional Research Service (March 3).

____ 1994b. "Intellectual property provisions of the GATT 1994: The TRIPS Agreement," *Congressional Research Service Report for Congress*, Report No. 94-302-A. Washington, DC: Library of Congress (March 16).

Shulman, Seth. 1999. *Owning the Future*. New York: Houghton Mifflin Company.

Sikkink, K. 1991. *Ideas and Institutions*. Ithaca, NY: Cornell University Press.

Silverstein, D. 1991. "Patents, science and innovation: historical linkages and implications for global technological competitiveness," *Rutgers Computer & Technology Law Journal* 17, 2: 261–319.

____ 1994. "Intellectual property rights, trading patterns and practices, wealth distribution, development and standards of living: a north–south perspective on patent law harmonization," in George Stewart, Myra Tawfik, and Maureen Irish (eds.), *International Trade and Intellectual Property: The Search for a Balanced System*. Boulder, CO: Westview Press: 155–179.

Simon, E. 1986. "U.S. trade policy and intellectual property rights," *Albany Law Review* 50, 3 (Spring): 501–508.

Sinclair, T. 1999. "Bond-rating agencies and coordination in the global political economy," in A. Cutler, V. Haufler, and T. Porter (eds.), *Private Authority and International Affairs*. Albany: State University of New York Press: 153–167.

Smart, T. 1988. "Knights of the roundtable: tracking big business' agenda in Washington," *Business Week* (21 October): 39–44.

Smith, Eric H. 1996. Testimony of Eric H. Smith, President of the International Intellectual Property Alliance Representing the International Intellectual Property Alliance Before the Committee on Ways and Means, United States House of Representatives, March 13. Available at: <http://www.iIPa.com/html/rbi_trips_tstmn_31396.html> accessed 10/26/98: 1–10.

Stanback, W. 1989. "International intellectual property protection: an integrated solution to the inadequate protection problem," *Virginia Journal of International Law* 29 (Winter): 917–960.

Steinhauer, J. 2001. "U.N. redefines AIDS as political issue and peril to poor," *The New York Times*, June 28: A1.

Stewart, T. 1993. *The GATT Uruguay Round: A Negotiating History (1986–1992), Volume II: Commentary*. Deventer: Kluwer Law and Taxation Publishers.

Stolberg, S. 2001. "Africa's AIDS war," *The New York Times*, March 10: A1.

Strange, S. 1987. "The persistent myth of 'lost' hegemony," *International Organization* 41: 551–574.

## References

1988. *States and Markets: An Introduction to International Political Economy.* London: Pinter.

1991. "An eclectic approach," in C. Murphy and Roger Tooze (eds.), *The New International Political Economy.* Boulder, CO: Westview Press.

1996. *The Retreat of the State: The Diffusion of Power in the World Economy.* Cambridge: Cambridge University Press.

2000. "World order, non-state actors and the global casino: the retreat of the state?" in R. Stubbs and G. Underhill (eds.), *Political Economy and the Changing Global Order,* 2nd edn. Oxford: Oxford University Press: 82–90.

Sutherland, Johanna. 1998. "TRIPS, cultural politics and law reform," *Prometheus* 16:3: 291–303.

Tancer, R. 1995. "Trends in worldwide intellectual property protection: the case of the pharmaceutical patent," *The International Executive* 37, 2: 147–166.

Taylor, M. 1989. "Structure, culture and action in the explanation of social change," *Politics and Society* 17, 2: 115–162.

Tejera, Valentina. 1999. "Tripping over property rights: is it possible to reconcile the convention on biological diversity with Article 27 of the TRIPS Agreement?" *New England Law Review* 33 (Summer): 967–987.

'T Hoen, E. 2002. "TRIPS, pharmaceutical patents, and access to essential medicines: a long way from Seattle to Doha," *Chicago Journal of International Law* 3, 1: 27–50.

Thomas, G., J. Meyer, F. Ramirez, and J. Boli (eds.). 1987. *Institutional Structure: Constituting State, Society, and the Individual.* Newbury Park, CA: Sage Publications.

Thurow, L. 1985. *The Zero-Sum Solution: Building a World-Class American Economy.* New York: Simon and Schuster.

1997. "Needed: a new system of intellectual property rights," *Harvard Business Review* (September–October): 94–103.

Trebilcock, M. and R. Howse. 1995. *The Regulation of International Trade.* New York: Routledge.

Underhill, G. 2000a. "Global issues in historical perspective," in R. Stubbs and G. Underhill (eds.), *Political Economy and the Changing Global Order.* Don Mills, Ont.: Oxford University Press: 105–118.

2000b. "Global money and the decline of state power," in T. Lawton, J. Rosenau, and A. Verdun (eds.), *Strange Power: Shaping the Parameters of International Relations and International Political Economy.* Aldershot: Ashgate: 115–135.

Union for the Protection of New Varieties of Plants. 2002. "States party to the International Convention for the Protection of New Varieties of Plants." Available at: <http://www.upov.int/eng/ratif/pdf/ratifmem.pdf> accessed 5/2/02.

United Nations Development Programme. 1999. *Human Development Report 1999.* New York: Oxford University Press.

US Department of Commerce. 1984. *Roger D. Severance Trip Report on Consultations with Taiwan and Singapore on Commercial Counterfeiting.* International Trade Administration memorandum (June 6).

US Department of Justice. 1977. *Antitrust Guide for International Operations, reprinted in* [January–June] Antitrust & Trade Reg. Rep. (BNA) No. 799. (February 1).

1988. *Antitrust Guidelines for International Operations,* reprinted in 55 Antitrust & Trade Reg. Rep. (BNA) No. 1391 (November 17).

US House of Representatives. 1985. House Committee on Energy and Commerce. *Unfair Foreign Trade Practices: Hearings Before the House Energy and Commerce Committee,* 99th Congress, 1st session, 26 July.

Committee on Ways and Means. 1995. *Overview and Compilation of U.S. Trade Statutes.* 104th Congress, 1st Session: 104–106, August 4.

US International Trade Commission. 1988. *Foreign Protection of Intellectual Property Rights and the Effects on the U.S. Industry and Trade.* USTIC Pub. 2065, Inv. No. 332–245 (February).

US Senate. 1986a. Senate Finance Committee. *Intellectual Property Rights: Hearings Before the Subcommittee on International Trade of the Senate Finance Committee,* 99th Congress, 2nd session May 14.

1986b. Senate Finance Committee. *Possible New Round of Trade Negotiations: Hearings Before the Committee on Finance.* 99th Congress, 2nd session July 23.

US Trade Representative (USTR). 1985. Task force on intellectual property. Summary of phase I: Recommendations of the Task Force on Intellectual Property to the Advisory Committee for Trade Negotiations (October), unpublished report.

1986. Advisory Committee for Trade Negotiations' Task Force on Intellectual Property Rights. Summary of phase II: Recommendations of the Task Force (March), unpublished report.

1994. *The 1994 General Agreement on Tariffs and Trade* (27 August).

1996. "Fact Sheets: 'Special 301' on intellectual property rights and 1996 Title VII decisions," April 30. Available at: <http://www.ustr.gov/reports/special/factsheets.html> accessed 7/12/00.

1997. "USTR announces results of special 301 annual review," April 30. Available at: <http://www.ustr.gov> accessed 10/26/98.

1998a. "USTR announces results of special 301 annual review," May 1. Available at <http://www.ustr.gov> accessed 10/26/98.

1998b. "1998 trade policy agenda and 1997 annual report of the President of the United States on the trade agreements program." Available at: <http://www.ustr.gov> accessed 10/26/98.

1998c. "Report to Congress on section 301 developments required by section 309(a)(3) of the trade act of 1974." Available at: <http://www.ustr.gov/reports/301report/sec301.pdf> accessed 10/26/98.

1999. "USTR announces results of special 301 annual review," April 30. Available at: <http://www.ustr.gov/releases/1999/04/99-41.html> accessed 7/12/00.

*References*

2000a. "2000 Special Report," April 30. Available at: <http://www.ustr.gov/new/special.html> accessed 7/11/00.

2000b. "Highlights in U.S. international trade dispute settlement," June. Available at: <http://www.ustr.gov> accessed 7/18/00.

2001. "2001 Special 301 Report," April 30. Available at: <http://www.ustr.gov/enforcement/special.pdf> accessed 5/2/02.

2002. "2002 Special 301 Report," April 30. Available at: <http://www.ustr.gov/reports/2002/special301-pwl.htm> accessed 5/2/02.

Valenti, J. 1986. Statement of Jack Valenti to Subcommittee on International Trade, Senate Finance Committee, S361–88.4, May 14: 170–171.

van Wijk, J. and G. Junne. 1992. *Intellectual Property Protection of Advanced Technology: Changes in the Global Technology System: Implications and Options for Developing Countries*. Contract No. 91/026 (October). Maastricht: United Nations University, Institute for New Technologies.

Velasquez, G. and P. Boulet. 1999. *Globalization and Access to Drugs: Perspectives on the WTO/TRIPS Agreement*, 2nd edn. WHO/DAP/98.9 Revised. World Health Organization: Geneva.

Veliotes, N. 1986. Statement of Nicholas Veliotes to Subcommittee on International Trade, Senate Finance Committee, S361–88.4, May 14: 162–164.

Vicente, Wendy S. 1998. "Questionable victory for coerced Argentine pharmaceutical patent legislation," *University of Pennsylvania Journal of International Economic Law* 19: 1101–1140.

Vick, Karl. 1999. "African AIDS victims losers of a drug war," *Washington Post* (December 4: A1).

Vogel, S. 1996. *Freer Markets, More Rules: Regulatory Reform in Advanced Industrial Countries*. Ithaca: Cornell University Press.

Walker, C. and M. Bloomfield (eds.). 1988. *Intellectual Property Rights and Capital Formation in the Next Decade*. Lanham, MD: University Press of America.

Wallerstein, I. 1974. *The Modern World-System: Capitalist Agriculture and the Origins of the European World Economy in the Sixteenth Century*. New York: Academic Press.

Wallerstein, M., M. Mogee, and R. Schoen (eds.). 1993. *Global Dimensions of Intellectual Property Rights in Science and Technology*. Washington, DC: National Academy Press.

Walter, A. 1997. "Globalization and corporate power: who is setting the rules on international direct investment?" Paper prepared for conference on Non-State Actors and Authority in the Global System, 31 October–1 November, Warwick University, UK.

Waltz, K. 1979. *Theory of International Politics*. Reading, MA: Addison-Wesley Publishing Company.

*Washington Post*. 2002. "The AIDS fund gets going," editorial, *The Washington Post* (April 29): A20.

Webb, J. and L. Locke. 1991. "Recent development: intellectual property misuse: developments in the misuse doctrine," *Harvard Journal of Law and Technology* 4: 257.

Weissman, R. 1996. "A long, strange TRIPS: the pharmaceutical industry drive to harmonize global intellectual property rules, and the remaining WTO legal alternatives available to third world countries," *University of Pennsylvania Journal of International Economic Law* 17: 1069–1125.

Wendt, A. 1987. "The agent–structure problem in international relations theory," *International Organization* 41, 3 (Summer): 335–370.

    2001. "Driving with the rearview mirror: on the rational science of institutional design," *International Organization* 55, 4 (Autumn): 1019–1049.

Whalley, J. 1995. "Developing countries and system strengthening in the Uruguay Round," in W. Martin and L. Winters (eds.), *The Uruguay Round and Developing Economies*. Washington, DC: The World Bank.

Whipple, R. 1987. "A new era in licensing," *Les Nouvelles*, 22, 3: 109–110.

Wilks, S. 1996. "Comparative capitalism and the political power of business," in S. Strange (ed.), *Globalisation and Capitalist Diversity: Experiences on the Asian Mainland*. Florence: European University Institute: 31–63.

Woods, N. 1995. "Economic ideas and international relations: beyond rational neglect," *International Studies Quarterly* 39 (June): 161–180.

Woolcock, S. 1997. "Liberalisation of financial services," *European Policy Forum* (October), London.

World Intellectual Property Organization. 1988. *Background Reading Material on Intellectual Property*. WIPO Publication 40.

    2002. *Draft Substantive Patent Law Treaty*, Standing Committee on the Law of Patents, Seventh Session, Geneva, May 6 to 10, SCP/7/3 at: <http://wipo. org/scp/en/documents/session_7/pdf/scp7_3.pdf> (accessed 5/8/02).

World Trade Organization. 2001. "Declaration on the TRIPS Agreement and Public Health," WT/MIN(01)/DEC/2, 20 November. Available at: <http://www.wto.org/english/thewto_e/minist_e/min01_e/mindecl_ trips_e.htm> accessed 2/28/02.

WTO News. 1999. "The road FROM Seattle – latest edition: Post-Seattle Analysis" (December 14): 1–19. Available at: <http://www.newsbulletin. org/getcurrentbulletin.cfm?bulletin_id = 67 &sid = 38> accessed 7/17/00.

Yerkey, G. and D. Pruzin. 2001. "The United States drops WTO case against Brazil over HIV/AIDS patent," WTO Reporter, Bureau of National Affairs, June 26. Available at: <http://cptech.org/ip/health/c/brazil/ bna6262001.html>

Yoffie, D. 1987. "Corporate strategies for political action: a rational model," in A. Marcus *et al.* (eds.), *Business Strategy and Public Policy: Perspectives from Industry and Academia*. New York: Quorum Books.

Zalik, A. 1986. "Implementing the trade-tariff act," *Les Nouvelles*, 21 (December): 200–206.

Zysman, J. and S. Cohen. 1987. *Manufacturing Matters*. New York: Basic Books.

# Index

*Index*

CAMBRIDGE STUDIES IN INTERNATIONAL RELATIONS

5143989R0

Made in the USA
Lexington, KY
08 April 2010